Foodservice and Restaurant Marketing

Robert D. Reid

A CBI Book
Published by Van Nostrand Reinhold Company

To DCR, MLR, and RMR

Production Editor/Kathy Savago
Text Designer/Trisha Hanlon
Compositor/Pine Tree Composition
Cover Designer/Dick Hannus

A CBI Book
(CBI is an imprint of Van Nostrand Reinhold Company Inc.)

Library of Congress Catalog Number   82-12910

ISBN 0-8436-2263-6

Van Nostrand Reinhold Company Inc.
135 West 50th Street
New York, New York 10020

Van Nostrand Reinhold Company Limited
Molly Millars Lane
Wokingham, Berkshire RG11 2PY, England

Van Nostrand Reinhold
480 La Trobe Street
Melbourne, Victoria 3000, Australia

Macmillan of Canada
Division of Gage Publishing Limited
164 Commander Boulevard
Agincourt, Ontario M1S 3C7, Canada

16 15 14 13 12 11 10 9 8 7 6 5 4 3 2

Library of Congress Cataloging in Publication Data

Ried, Robert D.
  Foodservice and restaurant marketing.

  Bibliography: p.
  Includes index.
  1. Marketing. 2. Food service.
3. Restaurants, lunch rooms, etc. I. Title.
TX911.3.M3R44 1983 642′.068′8 82-12910
ISBN 0-8436-2263-6

Contents

Preface

The 1960s and 1970s brought tremendous change to the foodservice industry. New corporations were created, and many of these corporations are now industry leaders and models for others to follow. These two decades exhibited very rapid growth as indicated by the sales volumes of the vast majority of foodservice operations. Investors seeking better-than-average returns on their investments looked toward the foodservice industry, and generally speaking, they were rewarded.

As we move into the mid-1980s, however, the rapid growth and increasing customer counts seem to be in jeopardy of slowing down. As a country, we have taken a more conservative outlook, and our economic growth has slowed.

When corporations begin to slow the development of new units and individual investors are more careful about making investments, the role of marketing will increase in importance. It will become even more critical that foodservice owners and managers truly understand the functions of marketing and are able to implement these functions in a manner that will allow them to achieve the success they desire.

At one time, many foodservice managers believed that to achieve success, only one quality was needed—good food. If a restaurant could serve consistently good food, it was felt, then financial success would be the reward. If it were only that simple! Literally, thousands of restaurants have gone bankrupt despite their ability to serve good food. What then caused the failure of these operations? Numerous reasons can be cited, including poor cost control, employee theft, lack of adequate financial base, and lack of proper management practices. The failure of the management thoroughly to understand, appreciate, and practice sound marketing management is often, however, a direct contributing factor to business failure.

During the 1970s, the consumer who dined out became more sophisticated. The age of consumerism dawned, and individual consumers generally became more informed and better consumers. Foodservice managers need to acknowledge this change and develop new marketing thrusts designed to reach this new breed of consumer.

This book is designed to allow a foodservice manager of the 1980s to

- Develop an appreciation for the role of marketing in the management of a foodservice establishment
- Develop an understanding and working knowledge of the functions of foodservice marketing
- Design and implement a comprehensive foodservice marketing management program that will increase the likelihood of achieving financial success.

This book is organized into five major sections. The first section, encompassing Chapters 1 and 2, provides an overview of basic marketing terms and concepts. The section also includes a discussion concerning the marketing differences between services and products. Chapter 2 includes information concerning the marketing practices and trends within the foodservice industry.

The second section, Chapters 3 and 4, focuses on strategic planning and marketing information systems. Chapter 3 highlights planning, including types of planning as well as the advantages and disadvantages associated with planning. A systems approach to strategic marketing is also introduced. Chapter 4 focuses upon the vital area of marketing information systems and provides a discussion of the marketing information systems concept. In addition, use of marketing information systems is discussed along with sources of information, research methodology, and marketing audits.

The third section includes chapters 5 and 6 and addresses market segmentation, market positioning, and consumer behavior. Chapter 5 focuses on market segmentation and positioning. Market segmentation, segmentation methods, and criteria for effective segmentation are discussed. The discussion of positioning includes information relative to the use of market maps as well as the essential elements involved in establishing a position within the market. The measurement of market demand is also included in this section. Chapter 6 provides information concerning consumer behavior. Topics include consumer satisfaction, food and beverage consumption trends, consumer behavior models, and the role of the dining environment. A contemporary consumer behavior model is also presented.

The fourth section covers the area of menu planning and pricing. Chapter 7 focuses upon the important marketing functions of planning and designing the menu. Also included is a discussion of accuracy in menus. Chapter 8 is devoted to menu-pricing strategies and methods. In addition, several marketing factors affecting menu prices are also discussed.

The final section, Chapters 9, 10, and 11, is devoted solely to advertising and promotion, both vital marketing functions. Chapter 9 provides information concerning advertising terms, budgets, positioning, and strategy as well as advertising campaigns. Chapter 10 is focused on personal selling and internal promotion and provides a framework that management can use to improve performance in this area. Chapter 11 is devoted solely to external advertising media and includes information relative to working with an advertising agency as well as selecting and using all the major media.

Acknowledgments

I would like to thank all of the individuals who have provided assistance and encouragement during this project. In trying to list those who have helped, I am bound to omit someone, but I will attempt it nonetheless. I'd like to extend a special thank you to the following individuals:

Tom Phillips, for reading many of the early drafts;

Michael Olsen, Ryland Webb, and S. J. Ritchey, for their professional encouragement;

Phil Mason and Kathy Savago of CBI, for their fine work and patience; and

Roberta Reid, for her patience.

Chapter 1

Functions of Marketing

Chapter Outline

This chapter will introduce the subject of marketing and will define terms used by individuals engaged in the management of the marketing function. The chapter is divided into the following major sections:

Introduction
- brief review of major changes that have taken place within the foodservice industry

Marketing Defined
- traditional and contemporary definitions of marketing

Marketing Versus Selling
- how marketing differs from selling
- the marketing cycle

The Marketing Concept
- definition of the marketing concept
- uses and abuses of the marketing concept

Marketing as a Competitive Force
- the role of marketing in a healthy industry

The Role of Management in Marketing
- marketing planning
- marketing execution
- marketing evaluation

Marketing of Intangible Services and Tangible Products
- characteristics of intangibles and tangibles
- the foodservice mix of intangibles and tangibles
- successful marketing techniques for intangibles

The Foodservice Marketing Mix
- the traditional marketing mix
- contemporary foodservice marketing mix

Summary

Introduction

During the 1960s and 1970s a great many changes took place within the foodservice industry in the United States. Among the most notable of these changes were

- A decline in the percentage of independently owned foodservice operations, indicating the ever more powerful influence of large foodservice chains
- An increase in the percentage of the household food budget spent outside the home. The foodservice industry today receives 40 percent of all consumer expenditures for food, up from 33 percent in 1970[1]
- Numerous operational changes that have occurred as a result of the high rates of inflation for such basic necessities as labor, food, and energy
- New methods of food preparation and service that have also had an impact upon the industry. For example, Wendy's was successful in introducing a refined preparation and service system that had an immediate impact on the foodservice industry. New production technologies are currently being developed to allow prepared food products to be held in refrigeration for 30 days without deterioration. These too will affect the industry.
- Social and demographic changes have occurred in the United States as well. The sunbelt states have experienced tremendous growth, while the industrial Midwest and Northeast have declined both in population and in economic importance. In addition, the traditional roles of family members within households have changed, as evidenced by the number of dual-career families, single-parent families, and single-person households.
- The dietary habits of the American people have also changed, as many individuals are showing increased concern about the food they eat. The trend has been toward more "natural" and "healthy" foods. In support of this, the United States Department of Agriculture has published *Dietary Guidelines for Americans,* which outlines the dietary goals for the nation.

Along with these changes, the foodservice industry has experienced dramatic growth, and the future looks very positive, despite some very large obstacles looming on the horizon. In recent years, most of the growth in the foodservice industry has occurred in chain operations or in the industry's corporate segment. Independent foodservice operators have continued to prosper, but the marketplace is much more competitive today than it was even five short years ago. An increased level of competition has meant greater emphasis on marketing. No longer is it possible for an individual to open and operate a foodservice facility successfully on good food alone. To assure a steady flow of clientele, a foodservice manager must possess a thorough understanding of marketing. Without the marketing management skills the foodservice industry demands, a foodservice manager is less likely to achieve total success.

With this continual change and increased competition, what are the marketing functions that a successful foodservice manager must manage? This chapter introduces basic marketing concepts; the following chapters will explore specific areas of professional foodservice marketing management. Throughout this text, your overriding question should be, "What are the functions of marketing, and how can I apply these concepts?"

Marketing Defined

Marketing is a word used and often abused in the daily conversations of business people throughout the United States. It is used in business conversations, meetings, and professional publications. Some of the individuals who use the word have a clear understanding of it; others do not.

Think for a moment: What does marketing mean to you? Take a moment and jot down a definition. Managers use the term to discuss marketing strategies, marketing concepts, marketing tools, and marketing research. But what does the word *marketing* really mean?

The term *marketing* is indeed used to encompass many different activities. To confuse matters further, marketing has been defined in many different ways. The following paragraphs offer several of the major definitions of the term. Compare these definitions with your own.

During the mid 1960s the American Marketing Association defined marketing as "The business process by which products are matched with markets and through which transfers of ownership are affected."[2] At the time, this definition was certainly suitable, but since that time there has been tremendous growth in sales of intangibles known as services. Much of the economic growth in the United States in the last 15 years has been in the area of services. Part of this is the growth of the foodservice industry, which alone accounts for more than $137 billion in annual sales and represents a significant segment of the total value of services purchased each year.

A *service* is defined as an intangible product that is sold or purchased in the marketplace. A meal purchased at a fast-food restaurant or at any foodservice operation is considered a part of the service segment. Why? Simply stated, after the meal is consumed and paid for, the individual patron leaves the facility and does not have a tangible product in exchange for the money spent. This individual has consumed a service in the form of a restaurant meal. The foodservice industry is one of the largest *service industries.*

An allied industry, which is also part of the service industry segment, is the travel and tourism industry. Each year, millions of individuals spend billions of dollars vacationing and traveling for business and other reasons, yet when the trip is over, nothing tangible remains. On the other hand, if you purchase a new automobile or washing machine, the purchase is considered a tangible product and as such is not a part of the service industry segment.

In order to reflect the role of the foodservice industry and other service industries more clearly, the American Marketing Association revised the definition stating that, ''Marketing is the performance of business activities that direct the flow of goods and services from producer to consumer.''[3] Marketing might also be defined as the merging, integrating, and controlled supervision of all the company or organization's efforts that have a bearing on sales. In short, this definition holds that marketing is any activity that has an impact on sales. Finally, marketing has been defined as, ''Human activity directed at satisfying needs and wants (of consumers) through exchange processes.''[4]

These definitions are certainly adequate. The vast majority of foodservice establishments, however, are being operated to generate a satisfactory return on investment in the form of profits. These profits are used to pay dividends to stockholders and are reinvested by the organization to promote expansion and further development. Even nonprofit foodservice operations, such as selected hospitals, nursing homes, college or university foodservice operations, and governmental foodservice operations, must be concerned with marketing. Managers of nonprofit operations must still understand the needs and wants of their consumers and must strive to satisfy their consumers in order to succeed. A universal concern of all foodservice managers is the financial well-being of the organization. Whether a manager is trying to achieve a 20 percent return on investment before taxes or is instead aiming to break even on a very limited budget, the overriding concern is still financial. This overriding financial concern must be considered in the definition of the word *marketing* as it applies to the foodservice industry.

Another factor that any definition of marketing must include is the consumer, for the consumer should be the first priority of all foodservice operations. Unlike factories, which sell large quantities of manufactured products to distributors and other suppliers and may never have direct contact with the final consumer, a foodservice operation contacts each consumer individually and must deal with each consumer on an individual basis.

Therefore, a suitable definition of the word *marketing* must account for the financial concerns of management as well as the need to satisfy consumers on an individual basis. Foodservice marketing is therefore defined as

- Ascertaining the needs and wants of the consumer
- Creating the product-service mix that satisfies these needs and wants
- Promoting and selling the product-service mix in order to generate a level of income satisfactory to the management and stockholders of the foodservice operation.

This definition satisfies the objectives of the two major groups, the consumers and the stockholders and management.

The definition of marketing can be illustrated by the marketing cycle (Figure 1.1). In the marketing cycle, a foodservice manager engages in the

Figure 1.1. The Marketing Cycle.

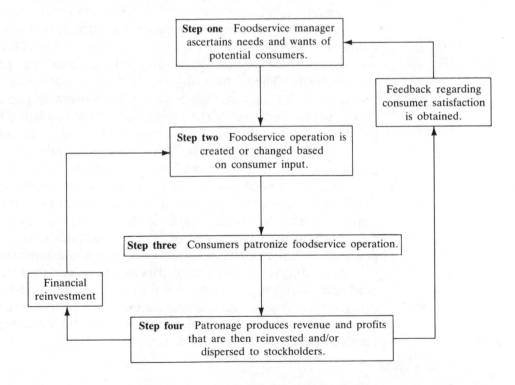

three components, or steps, which make up the definition of marketing, and also obtains feedback from the consumer regarding the degree of consumer satisfaction. Financial reinvestment must also occur if the foodservice operation is to remain a viable business, for without some portion of the profits reinvested in the operation, it will slowly decay and will eventually fail to meet the ever-changing needs and wants of the consuming public.

Marketing Versus Selling

Many foodservice managers engage in a series of activities that they incorrectly refer to as marketing. These activities include promotional functions, such as advertising in newspapers and on radio, internal promotions, such as posters and table tents, and personal selling, such as making a sales presentation for a prospective banquet client. While such activities are without question a part of the marketing function, alone and unsupported they cannot be referred to as marketing.

Managers engaged in activities of this type are merely attempting to sell their product-service mix. The *product-service mix* is composed of all of the tangible and intangible products and services that make up a foodservice operation. The product-service mix includes the food, beverages, atmosphere, table appointments, and personal attention by service personnel, as well as a host of other tangibles and intangibles. This type of activity, when practiced exclusively, is very "self-centered" or "product-service mix oriented." The focus is only on the foodservice operation's product-service mix, and the goal is to convince the consuming public to purchase and consume a portion of the product-service mix. Little consideration is given to the needs and wants of the consuming public; instead, the foodservice manager is hoping that a sufficient number of consumers will patronize the operation so that the operation might achieve its financial objectives.

The foodservice industry is filled with examples of operations that have failed because the owners created foodservice operations they liked or "always wanted to operate," yet the owners and managers failed to consider fully the needs and wants of the potential consumers. The results are predictable: low volume, poor sales revenue, and often bankruptcy.

Marketing is not the same activity as selling, and the two should not be confused. *Selling* is an activity that pushes the existing product-service mix on the consuming public; marketing seeks to satisfy the needs and wants of the consuming public. The following mini case study will illustrate the difference beween selling and marketing.

A Mini Case Study

A New Oriental Restaurant

This mini case study focuses on the foodservice market of a town with a population of 30,000. Several wealthy individuals who lived in this town frequently dined at an oriental restaurant in a large metropolitan area located some 40 miles from the town. These individuals noted that if oriental food and service were available in their home town, they would not have to drive the 80 miles to and from the city each time they desired oriental food and service.

After many hours of conversation over a two-month period of time, these individuals decided to combine their resources and build an oriental restaurant in the town in which they lived. They spared no expense in constructing and equipping the facility and in hiring and training a first-quality kitchen staff. In mid October, the investors along with the management personnel proudly welcomed the first guests.

Business was quite brisk for a period of eight weeks, averaging 275 covers per day for lunch and dinner combined. The investors and management were very proud indeed. None of the investors had ever operated a restaurant before, but all clearly thought they had built a "sure winner." In the weeks that followed, however, the number of lunch and dinner guests began to decline steadily to a point where the number of average daily covers had fallen below 100. In an at-

tempt to discover the problem, the owners and management pursued several avenues, but they found that the food, beverages, and service were of the same high quality as during the opening weeks of operation. Those customers who were patronizing the restaurant were very satisfied. What could be the problem?

After careful consideration, the investors and management launched an intensive promotional and advertising campaign using all available local media, and such internal promotional methods as tent cards and increased personal selling. After a four-week period, the results of the media blitz were disappointing. The average daily number of covers served hovered around 110 and showed no signs of increasing. Additionally, the level of banquet business activity exhibited further decline despite the promotional efforts.

The owners then hired a team of marketing consultants to conduct an in-depth study to determine the foodservice consumer trends in the town and surrounding areas. After several days of study, the consultants' final report concluded that the area lacked a sufficient number of people to support an oriental foodservice operation. The report also stated that the average daily number of covers was not likely to increase beyond 100 to 110. Simply stated, the consultants concluded that the potential market was too small to support a restaurant of this type successfully. Business had fallen off because of a lack of steadily returning clientele.

The consultants' report was carefully reviewed by both the owners and the management of the restaurant. They decided, however, that the restaurant should continue to operate in the same manner, with only minor menu changes made. The owners still believed very strongly in their original concept and felt that it could be successful. After an additional 30 days, the level of business remained the same, and at that time, the owners terminated the general manager and hired a new individual to fill the position.

The level of business increased slightly under the direction of the new manager, but not to the extent necessary for the restaurant to be a success. Debts continued to mount, and the restaurant was forced to settle all of its accounts on a cash-on-delivery (C.O.D.) basis only. None of the local purveyors would extend credit to the restaurant for fear of not receiving payment. The situation continued to deteriorate for another four months as losses mounted each week.

After being in business for a total of 10 months, the restaurant closed in mid August and was later sold to another group of investors. This second group remodeled the restaurant and operated a successful family steak house operation.

Questions for Discussion

1. Analyze the actions taken by the first group of investors.

2. What might the first group of investors have done differently? Why?

3. Why might the second group of investors have been successful, where the first group had failed?

This example clearly shows a group of rational business investors who let their personal feelings interfere with their critical evaluation of a business opportunity. Instead of investing in a restaurant that would appeal to a large group of potential consumers and therefore achieve success, they chose instead to build a facility that failed to attract a large enough percentage of repeat clientele to be successful.

The difference between selling and marketing is very simple. Selling focuses on the needs of the seller. These needs include the very basic need of having a product-service mix that must be sold to generate revenue necessary to remain in business. Clearly, the needs of the seller are very strong.

Marketing, however, focuses on the needs of the consumer. When a product or service is truly marketed, the needs of the consumer are considered from the very beginning of the process of product or service development, and the product or service is designed to meet the unsatisfied needs of the consuming public. When a product is marketed in the proper manner, very little selling is necessary because the consumer need already exists and the product or service is merely being produced to satisfy the need.

The Marketing Concept

If a foodservice organization is to market its product-service mix successfully, it is essential that the marketing concept not only be thoroughly understood but also fully implemented. Understanding the concept is not difficult, but implementing it may prove to be very challenging for management.

Simply stated, the marketing concept is a consumer-oriented philosophy that focuses all available organizational resources on the profitable satisfaction of the needs and wants of the consumer. As an old rhyme states,

> To sell Jane Smith
> What Jane Smith buys,
> You've got to see things
> Through Jane Smith's eyes.

Clearly, it is difficult to sell something to someone who has no need for it. If the organization adopts a consumer-oriented marketing philosophy, however, the product-service mix will be designed in direct response to unsatisfied consumer needs, and, as a result, very little actual selling will be necessary. In such instances, supply and demand are in balance, and both the consumer and the foodservice ownership are satisfied.

Table 1.1 illustrates the two different philosophies of the marketing concept that are often practiced in the foodservice industry. One shows the reactions of a foodservice manager using the marketing concept, while the other shows reactions that are not governed by the marketing concept.

Many foodservice organizations do use the marketing concept, yet many others do not. Does your organization use the marketing concept? Are consumers given priority, or is the operation run to suit the needs of the employees and management?

A manager of a foodservice operation has a difficult series of challenges to face each day. First, a manager is expected to successfully

Table 1.1. How the Marketing Concept is Used and Abused.

Decisions	When the Marketing Concept is used	When the Marketing Concept is not used
Menu Design	"Let's survey the current clientele to determine the desirability of adding new items to the menu."	"Let's add two more steaks to the menu; that's what I like."
Pricing	"What price will induce the largest number of consumers to purchase an appetizer and will yield the highest gross profit."	"Just aim for a 35% food cost and compute the price; that keeps everything simple."
Menu Substitutions	"Sure, we can substitute hash browns for a baked potato."	"We can't make any substitutions; that's too much trouble."
Reaction to Negative Consumer Comments	"That's a very good idea, and we'll try to use your idea in order to improve."	"That idea is impossible; we couldn't possibly change the way we do things."

satisfy the needs of the foodservice consumers. Second, the owners expect a manager to maintain the level of expenses within certain predetermined limits that are usually defined in absolute dollars or as a percentage of gross sales. Third, a manager is expected to generate a satisfactory return on investment for the owners. This return might be the breakeven point in a nonprofit operation or it might be a very high rate of return in a commercial operation.

The point is that a manager is faced with a series of difficult objectives to achieve, and these objectives often conflict with one another. Which of the three objectives defined in the preceding paragraph is the most important and should therefore receive priority? Managers often view profitability as the single most important objective of the firm, yet for the long-term financial well-being of the firm, profits may not be the most important objective. It is quite possible (and has often been done by short-sighted owners and managers) to achieve high levels of short-term profitability at the expense of long-term consumer satisfaction and long-term profits. After a period of time, consumers will perceive that they are not receiving a high level of value for their money, and the operation will develop a reputation for being overpriced and providing low value as a foodservice operation. As a result, the number of patrons is likely to decline, and so too will long-term profitability.

If the management establishes consumer satisfaction as the number-one objective, however, the consumers are more likely to be pleased. As a result, they will return more frequently to the foodservice operation, and this will have a positive influence on sales and profits. In addition, satisfied consumers are likely to induce others to patronize the establishment through word-of-mouth advertising. As volume (number of covers served) increases, profits should also increase, and the establishment of and adherence to managerial controls will hold expenses at projected levels.

When the marketing concept is established as a high priority, other objectives can also be achieved because the number of covers served and the revenues are likely to be high. Experience shows that when the marketing concept has been adopted by all members of the management and staff, substantial changes have often been made in the manner in which the establishment operates, and the financial results have often been improved significantly.

Marketing as a Competitive Force

Marketing and intensity of competition feed on each other in circular fashion. As the level or intensity of competition increases, an individual foodservice operation is forced to devote more time and attention to marketing in order to maintain its share of the market. Vast amounts of human energy are often devoted to marketing programs that allow the operation to gain a very slight advantage over other primary competitors.

Yet as more marketing efforts are undertaken, this fuels the competitive fires, increasing competition and thereby creating the need for still more marketing efforts. A foodservice manager might be tempted to say, "The heck with all of this; I'm not going to do any marketing." This is an extremely short-sighted view, one that, in the long run, is likely to result in reduced sales volume, greatly diminished levels of profitability, and perhaps even the failure of the business.

The competitive arena in marketing is due in large part to two factors. These are the increased tendency of the consumer to dine outside the home more frequently and the increased level of competition within and among all segments of the foodservice industry. In recent years, more and more families have undertaken dual careers, and the results have been very positive for the foodservice industry. More meals are being consumed away from home because, after long work days, the family members decide that no one wants to cook a meal and clean the kitchen. They dine out instead, and with both husband and wife working, more and more meals are eaten in a wide variety of foodservice operations. These two-income dual-career families allow greater independence and increased selection when dining away from home, and they represent a very large potential market.

Both independent and chain foodservice operators have seen and responded to this increased demand in a predictable manner. They simply built more units. Therefore, the intensity of competition has increased dramatically in the last several years, and many inferior foodservice operations have been the victims.

Some managers view competition as a productive force, one that is dynamic and growing. Competition tends to increase marketing efficiency, to keep price increases more modest, to promote innovation in new products and services. The result of all of this is a wider selection of foodservice operations from which the consumer may choose. Simply stated, competition forces managers to work harder to attract and satisfy foodservice consumers.

The Role of Management in Marketing

In large foodservice organizations, the marketing function is performed by marketing managers whose sole responsibility is the management of marketing activities. In most foodservice organizations, however, the marketing function is the responsibility of a manager who must be concerned with other functions as well. Because of the nature of these positions, the marketing function may be relegated to a position of secondary importance. When this occurs, the results are usually predictable; the foodservice operation suffers declining sales and sagging profits because competitive foodservice operations are actively marketing their product-service mix and, as a result, are winning consumers away from other operations.

The successful marketing of a foodservice operation is not something that can be accomplished overnight, nor is it something that can be successful with only a few hours of attention each week. The establishment and maintenance of a successful marketing program requires the management's time and effort.

The activities of management in marketing a foodservice operation can be divided into three major areas:

- Marketing planning
- Marketing execution
- Marketing evaluation.

A brief overview of the activities of marketing management for each of these areas follows:

Marketing Planning

- Develop marketing objectives.
- Develop marketing strategy.
- Develop short- and long-range plans.
- Develop the product-service mix.
- Forecast sales.

Marketing Execution

- Develop advertising and promotional materials.
- Establish communication within the organization.
- Train all sales personnel.

Marketing Evaluation

- Develop a marketing information system.
- Analyze organizational performance against forecasts.
- Analyze the effectiveness of advertising and promotional efforts.
- Review relative competitive position.

These points provide an overview of the major activities that a manager must perform to market a foodservice operation successfully. The three major functions—planning, execution, and evaluation—form a continuous marketing management cycle, as illustrated in Figure 1.2.

Marketing is not an on-off situation. It needs constant attention to be successful, and it must therefore be ongoing. Management must constantly obtain feedback and use it in developing revised strategic plans. Management's role in the marketing effort is critical, for without diligent effort, the results will be less than satisfactory.

Figure 1.2. Marketing Management Cycle.

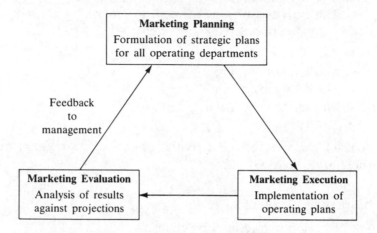

Marketing Intangible Services and Tangible Products

Marketing as practiced by other industries differs tremendously from foodservice marketing. In many other industries, marketing involves tangible manufactured products, such as automobiles, washing machines, and clothing. The product-service mix of a foodservice operation, however, is a mix of tangibles and intangibles. Consider the following as a partial listing of the product-service mix of a foodservice operation: service, convenience, hospitality, social contact, atmosphere, relaxation, entertainment, escape, and food and beverages.

The foodservice industry shares characteristics with other service industries, which in turn are vastly different from manufacturers. First, the product-service mix is more intangible than it is tangible. For example, in the preceding list, note that most of the items are intangible in nature. Services are "consumed," but are not "possessed" in the same manner as a tangible product, such as an automobile or a washing machine. Second, such services as foodservice are generally produced and consumed simultaneously, unlike product manufacturers, who produce, distribute, and then sell their products. In a foodservice operation, customers order meals; following placement of the order, the meals are produced, served, and consumed within a short time. In essence, production and consumption are simultaneous. Third, service marketing differs from product marketing in that services are less uniform than products. It is easy to standardize a product-manufacturing process simply by establishing an automated assembly line, but this method has limited applicability to the foodservice industry because the industry is people based rather than equipment based. Within the foodservice industry, the people become a major part of the product. For example, the waitress who serves the customer becomes a major part of the product-service mix that the customer consumes.

Given the relative intangibility of the product-service mix of foodservice operations, how can the product and service be successfully marketed? The management can adopt several strategies, but the following should be considered. First, because people become a major part of the product-service mix, personnel should be selected with great care and trained in a professional manner. Poorly trained personnel can sabotage in a few minutes what the marketing effort has sought to establish over a period of weeks or even months. Personnel should be considered an investment in much the same manner that manufacturers view equipment as an investment.

Second, people can be used to give the product-service mix more tangibility. Personnel can be featured in advertising and promotional efforts, thereby giving the product-service mix a tangible human quality. Perhaps the best example of this technique within the foodservice industry is Ronald McDonald. In the battle to win the children's market, McDonald's got off to a fast start with the Ronald McDonald character. This same personalization has been used successfully by many other foodservice and hospitality firms and by firms within other service industries as well.

Third, the service aspect of the product-service mix can be customized to the needs of the consumer. For many years Burger King used the slogan "Have it your way" in an effort to capitalize on custom-designed service. Wendy's has proudly promoted hamburgers with 256 possible topping combinations, thereby custom-designing the product-service mix.

Fourth, the environment in which the product-service mix is consumed is very important. Creation and maintenance of a specific type of environment is critical to the success of the operation. The environment includes many factors, including design, decor, personnel uniforms, lighting, and table appointments. For example, when McDonald's began in the 1950s, special attention was given to the environment. Cleanliness was seen as critical to the success of the fledgling fast-food operation, and cleanliness was correctly perceived as a means to gain a distinct competitive advantage. Control of the environment is even more important today. How do consumers perceive the environments of the foodservice operations in which they dine? The importance of the environmental aspects will be discussed further in Chapter 7.

Controlling the environment affords the foodservice marketing manager the opportunity to develop a tangible representation of a predominantly intangible product-service mix. This tangible representation is more easily perceived by the consumer and can favorably affect the success of the marketing effort.

The Foodservice Marketing Mix

In the 1960s Neil Borden first coined the term *marketing mix*. Since that time, the concept of the marketing mix has gained universal acceptance. It is an important concept to understand, both conceptually and strategically. This section outlines the major components of a contemporary marketing mix for the foodservice industry as well as the traditional marketing mix.

A successful foodservice organization is one that focuses on the needs and wants of the consumers and markets the product-service mix of the operation. The management of this type of operation is engaged in mixing or stirring these components into a form that the potential consumer will find attractive and will patronize time and time again. The results are obvious; the consumer is satisfied, and the operation achieves financial success through repeated patronage.

The Traditional Marketing Mix

The marketing mix, many believe, consists of four elements (sometimes called the four Ps):[5]

1. **Product.**   The unique combination of products and services.
2. **Place.**   The manner in which the products and services are sold, including channels of distribution.
3. **Promotion.**   The methods used to communicate with the tangible markets.
4. **Price.**   A pricing policy that stimulates sales and allows the firm to achieve its financial goals.

To achieve success in marketing a foodservice operation, a manager must closely examine all of the components of the foodservice marketing mix and must combine these components in the proper manner. There is no magical formula or recipe that, when followed, will guarantee success. If this were the case, no foodservice operation would ever fail and go out of business. Yet each year, many foodservice operations are not able to achieve the correct blend of these elements.

Even without a magical formula, however, there are guidelines and principles that, when followed and monitored closely, will greatly increase the chances for success. This book presents and discusses these guidelines and principles in the following chapters.

The Marketing Mix for Foodservice Operations

Just as researchers have demonstrated distinct differences between products and services, some researchers believe that the traditional four Ps approach to the marketing mix does not apply to the foodservice industry. Rather, a new marketing mix has been proposed. The new marketing mix for the foodservice industry is a product of three submixes:[6]

1. **Product-Service Mix.**   This is a combination of all the products and services offered by the foodservice operation, including both tangibles and intangibles.
2. **Presentation Mix.**   This includes those elements that the marketing manager uses to increase the tangibility of the product-service mix as perceived by the consumer. This submix includes the following: physical location, atmosphere (lighting, sound, and color), price, and personnel.
3. **Communications Mix.**   This involves all communication that takes place between the foodservice operation and the consumer. It includes advertising, marketing research, and consumer perception. The communications submix should be viewed as a two-way communications link, rather than a simple one-way link with the foodservice operation communicating to the consumer.

The marketing mix, whether designed in the traditional or a more contemporary format, is an important concept for managers of marketing functions. Initially, the marketing mix is used to formulate marketing strategy (see Chapter 3), but it pervades all aspects of marketing management.

As a manager attempts correctly to mix the components of the foodservice marketing mix, several external factors can reduce the effectiveness of the manager's marketing efforts. These factors, which either directly or indirectly influence the foodservice marketing mix, are consumer perceptions, attitudes and behavior, industry attitudes and trends, local competition, and government.

Consumer Perceptions, Attitudes, and Behavior. It is commonly accepted that people change their minds and that, as a result, their tastes also change. As tastes change, dining habits will also change, as evidenced by the development of new patterns of dining out and the decline of several old favorites in the last 10 years in different parts of the country. For example, many successful new restaurants have recently been established in the suburbs of most metropolitan areas. These restaurants have been able to compete successfully with well-established downtown restaurants and have achieved tremendous growth because the dining habits of the consuming public have changed significantly during the last 10 years.

Another example of ever-changing consumer tastes is the recent move toward lighter and more health-conscious foods. Examples of soup and salad foodservice operations abound in both the commercial and institutional segments of the industry. These new foodservice operations originated in direct response to changing consumer perceptions, attitudes, and behavior.

The point to remember is that no foodservice operation can afford to stand still and continue to offer the same menu items, beverage items, and dining experience indefinitely. Eventually, the consumer's perceptions of the operation will change, and the level of business will decline. The successful marketing manager must keep abreast of current trends and be willing to change and modify the operation in order to satisfy the ever-changing needs of the consumer.

Industry Attitudes and Trends.   Just as a manager must be aware of and responsive to the changing needs of potential consumers, so too must a manager be aware of changing attitudes and trends within the entire foodservice industry. Consider, for example, the growth of the fast-food segment of the industry in the 1970s. In the late 1960s, several experts felt that the fast-food segment of the industry had peaked and that the consumer demand for fast-food meals would level off. McDonald's and Burger King were the established leaders and seemed to be able successfully to withstand any new competition. Each of these foodservice giants had a well-established system to deliver their product-service mix, and both had achieved an admirable degree of success. To many, it appeared that the fast-food market was nearly saturated.

At about this same time, a small company began operating a fast-food chain of restaurants known as Wendy's. Wendy's offered a very simplified menu and a new type of production and delivery system. Slowly Wendy's achieved success and took a place in the top three corporations of the fast-food segment. Wendy's story shows that industry trends are important and that a manager must keep abreast of changes so that an operation does not decline in consumer popularity.

Local Competition. In addition to national competition and ever-changing trends, the successful manager must be very much aware of the efforts the local competition is engaged in to attract new and repeat clientele. The competition must be constantly checked to determine changes in the quality of products and services, types of products and services offered, pricing strategies employed, advertising and promotional activities used, design and decor changes, and personnel changes. A change in any one of these subfactors could dramatically affect the competitive relationship among foodservice operations in a local area.

Even traditionally noncompetitive and nonprofit foodservice operations need to be aware of this factor. For example, a hospital foodservice operation had been operated for several years as a nonprofit operation and had been subject to very little competition from local foodservice operations. As a result, the hospital achieved a very high level of employee and physician participation in cafeteria meal service. A new foodservice operation, however, was developed and located one-half block from the hospital. After the new foodservice opened, the level of employee and physician participation in the hospital cafeteria fell sharply, and it was obvious that these individuals were patronizing the new operation, despite the fact that the prices were much higher.

The foodservice manager and the hospital administration assumed that, after the newness of the commercial foodservice wore off, the staff would resume eating in the hospital cafeteria. Yet after six months, participation in the cafeteria continued to be greatly reduced, and the cafeteria was operating at a loss. Clearly, something had to be done to appeal successfully to the former clientele. Eventually the management decided that revised menus and prices should be offered to the staff. These changes would reflect the changes in tastes and needs of the staff and would compete directly with the commercial restaurant facility. Once these changes were thoroughly planned and implemented, the hospital was able to increase staff participation and was again able successfully to achieve a breakeven level of operation.

All foodservice operations, both commercial and institutional, for profit and nonprofit, need to be concerned with local competition. No foodservice establishment operates in a vacuum. All types of foodservices are immediately subject to competition and must engage in marketing efforts.

Government.   The government at the federal, state, and local levels exerts a major influence on the operation of all businesses including those of the foodservice industry. New and existing legislation, policies, and regulations seem to dictate every move that a manager wishes to make. Examples include wage and hour laws, tax laws, alcoholic beverage laws, local zoning ordinances, local sign ordinances, and truth-in-menu legislation. Clearly, today's foodservice manager must strive to keep abreast of proposed as well as new legislation. Professional associations, such as the National Restaurant Association (N.R.A.), can be a tremendous aid to a foodservice manager in this effort. Professional associations work very hard to see that governmental actions do not adversely affect the health and well-being of the foodservice industry.

These four factors—the consumer, industry attitudes, local competition, and government—all influence the formulation, adjustments, and readjustments that a foodservice manager must make in the marketing mix of an individual foodservice operation. A manager can exert only very limited control over these influential factors, but management must be prepared with contingency plans to deal with the changes that these four factors might easily bring.

Summary

This chapter has introduced and reviewed several key points. These will serve as the foundation for discussions in the future chapters. A major point is the definition of the word *marketing*. There are several definitions of marketing, but for this book, marketing is defined as

- Ascertaining the needs and wants of the consumer
- Creating the product-service mix that satisfies these needs and wants
- Promoting and selling the product-service mix in order to generate a level of income satisfactory to the management and stockholders of the foodservice operation.

Marketing is different from selling because marketing focuses on the needs of the consumer, while selling focuses on the needs of the seller. In addition, the marketing concept advances the philosophy that the needs of the consumer should be given priority over any financial goals that the firm may have. If the consumers' needs and wants are totally satisfied, the concept holds, then financial success will follow.

Marketing as a competitive force and the role of management in marketing suggest that the activities of the marketing manager focus on three major areas: planning, execution, and evaluation of marketing activities. The differences between marketing tangible products and intangible services are that services, as opposed to products, are more intangible than tangible, produced and consumed simultaneously, and less uniform in nature. Given these inherent differences, possible strategies for the successful marketing of service must include consideration of personnel, consumer needs, and environment.

Finally, a marketing mix must be specifically designed for a foodservice operation. The traditional marketing mix includes product, place, promotion, and price. A more contemporary marketing mix for the foodservice industry is a combination of three submixes: the product-service mix, the presentation mix, and the communication mix. Environmental factors can also affect the marketing mix.

Questions For Review and Discussion

1. Do you believe that marketing has assumed a position of increased importance in the management of foodservice operations? Why or why not?
2. Explain the difference between selling and marketing. How are the two similar? Different?
3. Discuss the components of both the traditional and the more contemporary foodservice marketing mix. What role does a manager play in establishing the mix? How is the marketing mix used?
4. What factors can affect the foodservice marketing mix? How do these factors affect the mix?
5. What is the marketing concept? How can it be successfully applied by a foodservice manager?
6. Explain and discuss the three major activities with which a marketing manager must be concerned.
7. Differentiate between tangible products and intangible services. What marketing strategies can be employed when marketing intangibles?

Notes

1. National Restaurant Association, *1981 Foodservice Industry Pocket Factbook* (Washington D.C., 1981).

2. E. W. Cundiff and R. R. Still, *Basic Marketing* (Englewood Cliffs, New Jersey: Prentice Hall, 1964).

3. Committee of Definitions (Ralph S. Alexander, Chairman), *Marketing Definitions: A Glossary of Marketing Terms* (Chicago: American Marketing Association, 1960).

4.   Department of Commerce, *U.S. Service Industries in World Markets* (Washington, D.C.), December, 1976.

5.   Philip Kotler, *Marketing Management,* 4th ed. (Englewood Cliffs, New Jersey: Prentice-Hall, 1980).

6.   Leo M. Renaghan, "A New Marketing Mix for the Hospitality Service Industries," presented at the CHRIE Annual Conference, August 13–16, 1980.

Chapter 2

Overview of Marketing Within the Foodservice Industry

Chapter Outline

This chapter will focus on the management function of marketing as it applies to the foodservice industry. The chapter is divided into the following major sections:

Introduction
- marketing as one of the six management functions

The Product Life Cycle
- the product life cycle concept
- pros and cons of the product life cycle concept
- management strategies for the product life cycle

Current Foodservice Marketing Thrusts
- a brief review of marketing trends
- the corporate mating game

Managing Personnel for Improved Marketing
- management's role in personnel development

Summary

Introduction

Marketing as practiced today differs tremendously from the techniques used several years ago. Foodservice marketing is in a constant state of flux, as corporations implement new marketing strategies. General practices and techniques should be analyzed and used as guidelines, but it is necessary for each individual foodservice organization to adjust and modify these general guidelines and techniques, as they are dictated by the competitive environment. The one constant within the foodservice industry is change, and this serves to attract management personnel who want to be stimulated by the ever-changing competitive environment.

It is also important to remember that marketing is but one of the functions with which management must be concerned. Within large foodservice organizations, specialists are hired to staff positions for each of the functional areas. In small organizations, however, management must wear many hats and successfully perform all of the managerial functions. The following discussion of the functions places marketing in its proper place as a major part of the successful management of any foodservice organization. To fulfill an organization's potential, management must place function in perspective and manage each successfully. The functions are interdependent and must support each other, thereby increasing the overall strength of the organization.

The major management functions include

- **Operations.** Management is responsible for the day-to-day operation of the foodservice facility. This includes such diverse activities as purchasing, receiving, inventory control, production, service, and sanitation. Without a strong focus on operations, the quality of the product-service mix is likely to be poor and/or inconsistent. The results of this are fully predictable, declining customer counts and possible business failure.
- **Finance.** An overriding goal of all commercial foodservice operations is to increase the wealth of the owners or stockholders. In periods of economic uncertainty, high rates of inflation, and high interest rates, the management of the financial function often becomes more critical to the success of the foodservice organization. All foodservice organizations need to focus considerable attention on this function to manage the organization's assets and financial affairs successfully.
- **Administration.** This function is very much a behind-the-scenes function and is often neglected. Administration includes such activities as accounts receivable, accounts payable, and payroll.
- **Human resource management.** The foodservice industry is a people business. As discussed in Chapter 1, people assume a major role in the

product-service mix. The major activities of this function include recruitment, selection, orientation, training, professional development, and personnel relations. Historically, the turnover rate in the foodservice industry has been much higher than in other industries. High rates of turnover for all positions, but especially among key positions, adversely affect the entire organization. The human resources of a foodservice organization are just what the name implies, a valuable resource that should be developed. Many foodservice firms expend very little effort in professional development, much to the detriment of the organization.

– **Research and development.**   In order to compete successfully in the years ahead, foodservice firms must invest time and money for research and development. These efforts typically focus on developing new market segments and new elements of the product-service mix. Because it is unlikely that a single foodservice concept will be successful indefinitely, management must be future oriented and anticipate necessary changes.

– **Marketing.**   The final area for which management is responsible is marketing. Successful marketing calls for the professional management of the marketing mix and the three submixes discussed in Chapter 1. Management must always be ready to adapt the elements of the marketing mix in order to gain a competitive advantage in the ever-changing market conditions.

The Product Life Cycle

A major goal of operating a commercial foodservice operation is to maximize the wealth of the owners. In the case of noncommercial foodservices, a similar goal would be to achieve a breakeven point based upon a very limited operating budget. To reach this goal, foodservice organizations have adopted numerous strategies. One of the most popular strategies throughout the 1960s and 1970s has been the *rapid growth strategy*. It was believed by many foodservice firms that the best strategy to employ would be one that led to rapid expansion in number of units. The anticipated results would, of course, be increased sales and profits. This strategy was employed very successfully by numerous corporations including most of the giants in the fast-food segment of the industry.

As a result of the rapid growth strategy's success, many leading management experts began to study the phenomenon. The experts have now identified what is known as the product life cycle of an organization. The product life cycle of a foodservice organization can be divided into five separate and unique stages, as illustrated in Figure 2.1.

Stage I of the life cycle is called the introduction stage. Here the organization is in its infancy, having just been created by a single entre-

Figure 2.1.   The Life Cycle of Foodservice Organizations.

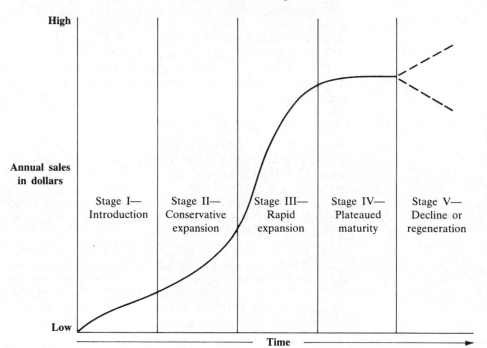

preneur or a group of investors. During this stage, the operation is seeking to establish itself firmly in the marketplace and is seeking to build a firm clientele base. If the organization succeeds in establishing itself, business soon begins to increase, and the owners may be faced with a decision regarding expansion.

Stage II, or conservative expansion, is a period of slow and steady growth, usually in the form of an increase in the number of units. New units are constructed using the original unit as a model. The owners' rationalization is that, if the original unit is successful, then so too will additional units be successful. This thinking often is the downfall of owners, for in expanding, they fail to consider the market structure in which new units are located and therefore fail to achieve the level of profitability they desire. Many companies, however, do achieve success when expanding from a single unit to perhaps as many as 10. At this stage, economies of scale may begin to play a more important role in the management of the organization. These economies of scale apply to the marketing function as well, particularly in the areas of advertising and promotion.

Assuming that the organization is able to overcome the problems that may arise during the conservative expansion stage, the firm then advances to stage III, the rapid expansion phase. It is during this stage that the organization commits itself to expand as rapidly as possible, either through franchising or through financing obtained through other sources and managed directly by the organization. During the rapid expansion stage, the organization expands with many new units in a process known as *cookie cutting*. Cookie cutting involves the establishment of new units, which are modeled on existing ones and are merely located in new locations. These units are often located in clusters within geographic regions. During stage III, the product-service mix is standardized, and the role of marketing is heavily oriented towards site selection. This is an area in which many regional chains make fatal errors. Instead of concentrating their efforts on both expansion and product-service mix research and development, they place too much emphasis on expansion, and research and development of new products and services suffers.

Assuming that the organization is able to achieve the desired success in the rapid expansion stage, it will then enter stage IV, the plateaued maturity stage. At this point, the organization has expanded as much as the market will allow, and volume, as measured in annual gross sales, will level off. This mature life cycle may remain stable for some time, perhaps many years, but eventually this stage too will end. The organization then enters into stage V, which is a real turning point. Rarely will the plateaued maturity stage continue indefinitely. Instead, the organization will slowly decline, or sales will again increase and the process may begin anew. Stage V is called decline or regeneration.

The McDonald's Corporation serves as an excellent illustration of the way a corporation progresses through the organizational life cycle. McDonald's Corporation, under the direction of Ray Kroc, began with a few units in the middle 1950s. The corporation quickly achieved a sound financial base and rapidly moved into stages II and III of the life cycle. New units were continually under construction, and soon the familiar red and white buildings with the golden arches could be found throughout the country. As McDonald's reached stage IV of the life cycle, however, an important decision was made.

The upper-level management felt that the red and white buildings with the golden arches had lived their useful life and that a new image was needed. With this in mind, the entire corporation began to rethink the design and decor of all new units as well as the vast majority of existing units. They determined that a more subdued appeal was needed in order to attract a broader target market. The words *fast-food* were not used in any promotional or corporate literature. Instead, emphasis was placed on the image of McDonald's as a restaurant. Instead of leveling off sales, McDonald's was able to inject new life into their concept and therefore continued to expand and increase the number of units, total sales, and bottom-line profits.

While this section has focused upon the product life cycle as it pertains to foodservice organizations, the product life cycle is also frequently applied to such elements of the product-service mix as individual menu items and design and decor treatments.

Pros and Cons of the Product Life Cycle

As you might expect with most concepts or theories, the product life cycle concept has its supporters and its opponents. Those who support the concept argue that those firms that use the concept successfully are able to identify the stage in which the organization or an individual product finds itself and then use this knowledge in formulating better marketing plans. Experts believe that these firms are able to find out where each of their products and services are positioned within the life cycle, determine the correct mix of products and services to improve the performance of the entire organization, and analyze trends in the product-service mix as well as the impact this mix will have on short- and long-term financial performance.

Those supporting the product life cycle concept indicate that specific strategies can be adopted for each stage in the life cycle. When implemented properly, these strategies can have a positive impact on the financial performance of the organization. In effect, proponents claim that the product life cycle is not merely charted; instead, the organization's marketing managers seek to shape the life cycle by prolonging its positive aspects and improving profitability.

The opponents of the product life cycle concept state their case with equal vigor. They contend that few products or services actually conform to the life cycle curve illustrated in Fig. 2.1. Rather, the curve may rise and fall in any number of patterns, each unique to the product or service itself. If managers believe that a product follows the normal life cycle curve when a decline (stage V) begins, they may choose to discontinue the product. Those who do not support the product life cycle concept contend that this "death" may be inappropriate and that the product may instead be experiencing a temporary plateau or slight decline prior to a growth period. This premature death could result in reduced profitability. Furthermore, some products may remain in the plateaued maturity stage (stage IV) indefinitely. Within the foodservice industry, certain types and brands of liquors exhibited this type of plateau.

Opponents of the concept also claim that it is often difficult to determine the exact stage in which a product lies. There are clearly no indicators to mark the transition from one stage to another. Similarly, if a product experiences a slowdown in growth following a period of rapid growth does this mean that stage IV, plateaued maturity, has begun? Or is this simply a slight slowdown in growth prior to continued expansion?

Finally, opponents of the product life cycle concept indicate that some marketing managers place too much faith in it. It is as if they were wearing blinders like the blinders used on race horses. These individuals focus too much attention on the product life cycle and forget about all the other environmental factors that can influence the success of a product or service.

Developing Strategies for the Product Life Cycle

A wide variety of strategies has been used for the various stages in the product life cycle. To develop strategies, however, management must first analyze the life cycle. This can be done in a six-step process, as follows:

1. **Compiling historical data.**   It is imperative that a foodservice firm begin to compile as much historical sales data as possible. Ideally, these data should be available for the entire history of the organization. The specific types of data needed include unit and dollar sales, profit margins, total profit contributions, return on investment, and prices.
2. **Identifying competitive trends.**   Recent activities of major competitors should be monitored closely to determine changes in market share and position, as well as changes in quality of the product-service mix. Additionally, all elements of the marketing mix (as discussed in Chapter 1) should be monitored for significant changes.
3. **Determining changes in product-service mix.**   The marketplace must be monitored in order to learn about new products and services that other foodservice operations are introducing. What are the potential effects of their changes on your foodservice operation?
4. **Studying other product life cycles.**   It is helpful to study the product life cycle of similar products or services to determine whether a pattern exists. Rarely is a product or service so new and unique that it is not possible to compare it with a previous one.
5. **Projecting sales.**   Based on the data collected, sales for a three- to five-year period should be projected. Computer applications are par-

ticularly useful at this stage, as recently developed forecasting models can improve the accuracy of these forecasts. In addition to projecting sales, management should also measure other indicators of financial success, including profits, returns on investment, and debt-to-equity ratios.

6. **Locating current position on the life cycle.**   Based on the historical data, as well as the projections, it should now be possible to locate the position on the product life cycle. Once this is done, strategy formulation begins.

Table 2.1 illustrates the characteristics and strategies that apply to different stages in the product life cycle. These strategies should not be viewed as absolute, but they do represent the most widely accepted ideas in the marketing community.

Current Foodservice Marketing Thrusts

One of the major reasons for McDonald's Corporation's tremendous success over the last 25 years is the success of its marketing efforts. Constant research and development related to the product-service mix and the entire marketing mix has allowed McDonald's to establish and maintain a leadership position in the fast-food segment of the foodservice industry. Consider that McDonald's was the first of the major fast-food chains to expand the limited hamburger menu to appeal to more adults, with the Big Mac™ and the Quarter Pounder™. Since then, McDonald's has added many other menu items, including desserts, and a very successful breakfast program. In addition, drive-through windows have expanded markets. For McDonald's, the research and development process continues to produce winners.

The point to all this is that McDonald's has continued to expand beyond the plateaued maturity stage of the product life cycle (stage IV) because its management has been innovative and has invested time and money in the development of new products and services to appeal to ever-expanding markets. The money invested in research and development is extremely important if McDonald's or any other foodservice firm is to achieve increased rather than decreased sales in stage V of the life cycle.

The Corporate Mating Game

Many corporations have looked to the foodservice industry with expansion in mind. This expansion of large corporate enterprises into the foodservice industry has been one of the major marketing thrusts of recent years, and

Table 2.1. Characteristics and Strategies for the Stages of the Product Life Cycle

	Stage I—Introduction	Stage II to Stage III—Conservative Expansion and Rapid Expansion	Stage IV—Plateaued Maturity	Stage V—Decline or Regeneration
		CHARACTERISTICS		
Sales	Low	Fast increases	Little or no growth	Declining
Profits	Negligible	Peak levels	Declining	Very low or zero
Cash flow	Negligible	Moderate	High	Low
Customers	Risk takers/innovators	Mass market	Mass market	Small segment of late adaptors
Competitors	Few	Increasing in number and strength	Highly competitive	Declining in number and strength
		STRATEGIES		
Strategic focus	Expanded market	Market penetration to capture mass market	Maintaining competitive position and market share	Prepare to remove from market; milk of all possible benefits
Marketing expenditures	High	Continued high but declining as percentage of total sales	Declining	Very low
Marketing emphasis	Awareness of products and services	Building repeat patronage and word-of-mouth advertising	Maintaining repeat patronage	Selective patronage
Price	High to cover initial costs	High due to high demand	Declining to retain competitive advantage	Declining to increase volume
Advertising strategy	Aimed at needs and wants of innovators	Make mass market aware of products and services	Used to differentiate among major competitors	Emphasize low price to increase volume

the trend is likely to continue. According to *Restaurants & Institutions,* the 400 largest foodservice firms now hold a 48 percent market share (they account for 48 percent of all foodservice sales), and this figure continues to increase. Even more remarkable, the top 10 foodservice firms hold a 17.2 percent market share.[1] Table 2.2 summarizes a recent fiscal year for the 10 largest foodservice organizations in the United States.

Within the structure of corporate ownership of foodservice operations lies a maze of subsidiaries that are owned and/or operated by parent companies. The parent companies are often well-established companies with vast experience in the food industry. As an avenue of growth, many of these companies have expanded into the foodservice industry, seeking to build on their expertise in food and establish a positive combined operation with a foodservice firm. Several examples of the interrelationships of the corporate mating game are illustrated in Table 2.3 (see p. 34).

The large corporations that dominate the foodservice industry have been the major marketing thrusts of the late 1970s and the early 1980s. What does all this mean for the industry? Clearly it means only one thing: that the independent owner will be faced with an ever-increasing challenge in confronting the corporate giants. Many independent owners will fail to meet this challenge, and those that survive will be changed in many ways. The influx of major corporations into the foodservice industry will dramatically alter the structures of the marketing programs developed in the years to come.

Changing consumer tastes and dining patterns will also force foodservice managers to change their marketing efforts in the years ahead. Consumer behavior is discussed in greater depth in Chapter 7, but a few changes in consumer behavior are noteworthy here.

First, consumers have become more concerned with the nutritional value of the food they eat. No longer are only a few consumers concerned with nutrition; now millions of consumers are paying closer attention to diet. Examples of some of these dietary concerns include sugar intake, the amount of fat in the diet, and total caloric intake. A foodservice manager would do well to note changing consumer tastes and do everything possible to modify the product-service mix in order to make it more appealing.

Second, the growth in the sale of wine has shown continued expansion, a trend that is likely to continue. While Americans lag far behind Europeans in wine consumption per capita, the growth in sales is a very positive sign. Yet despite this growth in sales, many foodservice operations fail to market wines properly. Often, the wine list is unavailable or may be out of date or badly soiled. Wine is filled with romance; it should receive special personal marketing and merchandising attention. Wine can be extremely profitable for many types of foodservices.

Table 2.2. The 10 Largest Foodservice Organizations in the United States.
Source: Restaurants & Institutions vol. 90, no. 1, July 1, 1981.

Foodservice Rank 1981	1980	Organization	Foodservice Volume (in millions of dollars) 1980	1979	Foodservice Units 1980	1979
1	1	McDonald's Corporation, Oakbrook, Illinois	6,226	5,384	6,263	5,747
2	3	The Pillsbury Company, Minneapolis, Minnesota	2,737	2,218	3,097	2,981
3	4	United States Department of Agriculture and Nutrition Service, Washington, D.C.	2,479	2,065	92,552	95,612
4	2	Kentucky Fried Chicken Corporation, Louisville, Kentucky	2,298	2,242	5,868	6,353
5	5	Marriott Corp., Washington, D.C.	1,798	1,601	1,583	1,513
6	6	Holiday Inns, Inc., Memphis, Tennessee	1,614	1,540	2,900	2,864
7	8	ARA Services, Inc., Philadelphia, Pennsylvania	1,409	1,138	2,656	2,156
8	7	PepsiCo., Inc., Purchase, New York	1,376	1,200	5,255	5,044
9	9	Wendy's International, Inc., Dublin, Ohio	1,201	1,002	2,034	1,818
10	10	International Dairy Queen, Inc., Minneapolis, Minnesota	1,020	926	4,833	4,860

Third, the rapid escalation of the operational costs for foodservice organizations will change the service and delivery system employed in the coming years. Rapid increases in the costs of labor and energy will force many operations to adopt more self-service delivery systems. The question remains: How will this be implemented without undue negative consumer

Parent Corporation	Foodservice Chain(s)
The Pillsbury Company	Burger King
	Steak and Ale
	Le Chateau
	Poppin Fresh Pies
	Bennigans
Marriott Corporation	Hot Shoppes
	Roy Rogers
	Marriott In-flite Services
	Marriott Hotels
	Marriott's Great America Theme Parks
	Contract Food Services
	Farrell's Ice Cream Parlours
	Charley Brown's
	Charley's Place
	Casa Maria
	Bob's Big Boy
	Phineas
	Gino's
SAGA Corporation	Straw Hat Pizza
	The Velvet Turtle
	Stuart Anderson's Black Angus
PepsiCo	Pizza Hut
	Taco Bell
General Foods	Burger Chef
General Mills	Red Lobster
	York Steak House
Royal Crown Cola	Arby's
Heublein	Kentucky Fried Chicken
	Zantigo's

Table 2.3. Interrelationship of the Corporate Mating Game.

reaction? Changes must be well planned and implemented with care if they are to meet with consumer acceptance and financial success. With change a constant part of the foodservice industry, it is difficult for a manager to devise new marketing techniques. Here are a few samples:

- One restaurateur wanted to establish a high level of perceived value in the minds of his patrons, so he offered complimentary spaghetti and meatballs to children under 10 who dine with their parents.
- Another manager decided to offer a break to those patrons who paid with cash. He offered them a four percent discount if meals were paid for with cash instead of credit cards.
- One enterprising manager of a hospital foodservice operation implemented a complimentary glass of wine with patient dinners, and the response was overwhelmingly positive.
- Another hospital foodservice manager developed a series of special dinners for parents of newborn children, including steak Diane and other gourmet meals. Results of this program have been very good, and it has since been expanded to include a wider variety of patients.

The major foodservice marketing thrusts for the years ahead may be the ones you read about in the trade journals, but each manager needs to identify a target market and develop a plan for appealing to that particular market.

Marketing plays an important role in the profit planning of any foodservice operation. Commercial operations must undertake efforts to generate a continuous flow of new consumers and stimulate as large a percentage of repeat patronage as possible. Even nonprofit operations need to allocate resources for marketing efforts when planning for budget expenditures. These operations normally expend money for special events to maintain a customer interest, and they conduct surveys of patrons and other marketing activities.

The old phrase, "In order to make money, you have to spend money," rings true for marketing. Every day, a typical American consumer is exposed to hundreds of advertisements and personal marketing efforts for a wide range of products and services. Given this deluge of information and organized persuasion, it is difficult for the average consumer to develop a strong allegiance (brand loyalty) to any one foodservice operation. It is therefore important for all foodservice managers to engage in organized and well-planned marketing campaigns. The simple fact remains that those managers who fail to implement some type of marketing program are likely to fail to achieve the highest level of success possible.

The amount of money allocated for marketing activities varies greatly in the foodservice industry. Typically, marketing efforts account for one to six percent of gross sales. The lower figures may apply to noncommercial operations or those that are so well established that they find themselves operating in a relatively noncompetitive environment. Operations that are newly established or that function in highly competitive markets may spend more than six percent of total sales for marketing efforts. No formal guidelines can be used to determine an ideal amount to allocate for marketing. Instead, each manager must carefully plan a marketing program that will achieve the desired results without being wasteful.

It is highly desirable that a manager or group of managers establish a firmly defined marketing budget that allocates specific dollar figures to specific activities (e.g., radio advertising and consumer surveys) for well-defined periods, such as monthly intervals. In this manner, a plan or frame of reference is created, and managers are able to gauge the extent to which they are following the predetermined plan. Marketing budgets can be either fixed or flexible. Fixed budgets use dollar figures, which are precise and not subject to change even though sales volumes may vary. Flexible budgets, on the other hand, are normally based on two or more projected levels of sales and would allow more flexibility, as may be necessary in certain competitive situations. The budgetary process is discussed in greater depth in Chapter 10.

Managing Personnel for Improved Marketing

Management assumes a series of important responsibilities in the marketing efforts for a foodservice organization. If an organization is to achieve its desired objectives, the manager must make serious efforts to carry out these specific responsibilities.

First, the management establishes and maintains the tone for the entire operation. Employees look to the manager to set an example for them to follow and to set performance standards. For example, everyone has been in restaurants where all the service personnel seemed happy and were smiling. The orders were taken efficiently, and perhaps the service person engaged in some suggestive selling. The food and beverage items were served in the proper manner, and maybe, just maybe, customers were persuaded by the waiter or waitress to have belt-tightening desserts. Dining out in this manner is extremely pleasant. What makes some restaurants a pleasure to go to, and others seem like an ordeal? The management sets the tone and is responsible for these activities. A manager can and must convey the marketing concept to the employees and must also teach them to engage in suggestive selling and other marketing activities.

Second, a manager is responsible for his or her own personal development. Managers can easily become so wrapped up in day-to-day operational activities that they fail to engage in self-development. If managers do not undertake some type of self-directed development, however, chances are that they will stagnate and lose some of their effectiveness on the job. For this reason it is important for managers to belong to professional organizations through which they can meet and talk with other managers. In this way, they can discuss common problems and perhaps learn about possible solutions. There are numerous professional organizations that a manager might choose to join. The National Restaurant Association (N.R.A.) is perhaps the best-known association. A manager might also consider a state or local restaurant association. In addition, most localities also support chapters of the International Food Services Executives Association (I.F.S.E.A.), which normally holds monthly meetings in an area. In addition, a manager should also make an honest effort toward education. It would be desirable for a manager to attend yearly one or two seminars related to specific operational problems. Such seminars are sponsored by numerous groups, including professional associations and colleges and universities.

Third, if managers are to achieve the highest possible level of marketing success, they must pay particular attention to the selection process for guest-contact employees. Employees who deal directly with guests must be able to make guests feel welcome and appreciated even under the most trying of circumstances. It takes a special type of person to do this successfully. For this reason, the screening process by which guest-contact employees are selected must be examined closely. Too often, managers simply hire the first applicant or hire an individual without checking any of the applicant's credentials or references. This practice can be termed "the warm body approach to staffing." Often, the first individual who applies for a position is hired, and the results are often regrettable. Not all individuals are suited for guest-contact positions, and therefore some effort must be made to screen out those individuals who would have a negative impact on internal marketing efforts.

Fourth, a manager must assume responsibility for the development of the entire staff. All employees need initial training and refresher training to learn new skills and refine older skills. In addition, training serves as a motivating tool, showing that management does indeed care and wants the operation to be the best possible. One of the most common refresher in-service training activities is in the area of wine service. Many employees do not feel totally comfortable with their knowledge of wines and wine service. As a result, they fail to promote wine as actively as they should, simply because they lack the self-confidence. It is normally quite simple for a restaurant manager to arrange an employee wine seminar with the cooperation of a local wine purveyor from whom wine is purchased on a regular basis. Purveyors are usually helpful in arranging and conducting such seminars, and the results from this type of training can be very positive. Employees are motivated and this obviously has a direct effect on sales and profits.

Fifth, management must acknowledge that the guest-contact employees are the first-line salespeople. They deal personally with every guest, and they represent the operation's manager and owners. In the eyes of the guest, these employees are the restaurant. A manager must devise strategies to motivate these employees. Again, no single strategy will work for all individuals in all situations, and a manager must devise new motivational techniques and strategies. Broadly defined, motivational techniques can be divided into two categories, monetary and nonmonetary rewards. Monetary rewards involve money or something of value, which is awarded to the employee, while nonmonetary rewards are intangible. Both of these techniques can be used either separately or in combination. Table 2.4 illustrates potential motivational techniques.

Table 2.4. Possible Monetary and Nonmonetary Motivational Techniques.

Monetary	Nonmonetary
A 10-dollar bonus to the employee who sells the most desserts each week	Acknowledging either orally or in writing outstanding employee performance
An incentive whereby an employee receives 25 cents for each carafe of wine sold	Expanding an employee's job responsibilities because of outstanding performance
A weekend trip for two at a resort to the employee who sells the most bottles of a special wine over a two-month period of time	Allowing an employee to take a more active role in the planning or decision-making process of the organization
A 10-dollar award to every employee who provides a sales lead that results in a banquet or catering function being cooked	Implementing employees' suggestions and giving them full credit for the ideas
	An "Employee of the Month Award" for outstanding work

Motivation of employees is extremely important because of the effect it has on the entire staff and on sales and profits. For these reasons, managers who want to achieve satisfactory results should devote time to this important area.

Summary

This chapter provides an overview of marketing in the foodservice industry. In addition to the marketing function, managers are also held responsible for operations, finance, administration, and research and development.

Historically, foodservice organizations have adopted a growth strategy founded on rapid growth and expansion in the number of units. This rapid expansion has been studied and is incorporated in the model illustrating the product life cycle. This cycle has five stages—introduction, conservative expansion, rapid expansion, plateaued maturity, and decline or regeneration. The experts do not all agree about the relative merits and weaknesses of the product life cycle, but managers who use it must develop marketing strategies appropriate for each of its stages.

Current marketing thrusts include the need for research and development that leads to innovation and a position of strength in the marketplace. The expansion of large corporations into the foodservice industry marks a turning point for the independent operator, who may be forced to modify operating and marketing practices in order to survive in the coming years. Rapidly changing consumer tastes are also likely to dictate changes that managers will need to make so that foodservices can remain competitive. In addition, escalating costs of operation may dictate an increased shift toward more self-service and other changes in the delivery systems employed by operations today.

Marketing must assume a role in the profit planning for all foodservice operations. Foodservice managers must engage in marketing activities if they are to prosper and achieve desired financial goals. In some instances, firms may allocate more than five percent of total sales to the marketing effort. It is important that this money be budgeted in an organized manner if its maximum use is to be assured.

Management must assume responsibilities for the marketing efforts of the organization and its employees. The responsibilities having a direct bearing on marketing include establishing and maintaining the tone of the operation, personal development, recruiting and selecting the best possible guest-contact employees, training and development of the entire staff, and acknowledging the importance of guest-contact employees by using motivational techniques to encourage their achievements.

Questions for Review and Discussion

1. What are the major functions a foodservice manager engages in? Briefly discuss each function.
2. What are the five stages in the product life cycle?
3. What are the strengths and weaknesses of the product life cycle concept?
4. Do you think that the rapid growth strategy was a wise strategy for corporations to have followed? What type of strategy do you believe will be the best to follow in the next five to ten years?
5. What do you think will be the major marketing thrust in the next five to ten years?
6. How much time and effort do you think firms should devote to research and development? Do you believe that the return on investment is worth the cost of engaging in this activity?
7. If a manager wanted to obtain the very best possible guest-contact employees, how do you believe that he or she should go about recruiting these individuals?
8. What motivational techniques would you employ if you were the manager of a large foodservice operation?

Notes

1. "The 17th Annual 400 Report," *Restaurants and Institutions,* Vol. 89, No. 1, July 1, 1981, p. 49.

Chapter 3

Establishing a Marketing Plan

Chapter Outline

This chapter will introduce the concept of strategic planning as it pertains to the marketing function. A model for strategic planning will be introduced and discussed at some length, and aspects of this model will be discussed in greater depth in the chapters that follow. The model is designed to provide an overall framework into which material in later chapters can be placed. The chapter is divided into the following major sections:

Introduction

Planning for Effective Marketing

- types of planning
- advantages and disadvantages associated with planning
- an example of poor marketing planning—a mini case study

A Systems Model for Developing a Marketing Plan

- introduction of strategic marketing
- strategic marketing model
- why some plans fail

Summary

Introduction

Each year the process of successfully marketing a foodservice operation becomes more difficult. New types of foodservice operations loom on the competitive horizon as either direct or indirect competitors. Consider, for example, the tremendous growth throughout the foodservice industry in the 1970s. Several of today's well-established and well-recognized chain operations were launched during the past decade. As these chains rapidly expanded, hundreds of independent operations and small chains were forced to appraise the competitive environment and develop strategies to allow them to counteract this new competition successfully. Many of these independent and small chains, however, were unsuccessful in their efforts. What caused these operations to fail?

Numerous factors contribute to the failure of a foodservice operation; such factors include employee theft, inconsistent quality of the product-service mix, and poor location. In addition, poor marketing planning and execution often contribute to operational failures. This means that management has simply failed to anticipate the impact that increased competition would have upon the organization. This failure results in a lack of contingency planning, and the result is the failure of many foodservice organizations.

An old saying that still holds true today indicates that there are three types of companies: those who make things happen, those who watch things happen, and those who wonder what happened. Those companies in the first group are generally actively engaged in planning. They have established corporate objectives, which in turn lead to the formation of overall strategies that serve as the basis for day-to-day operations. The truly successful companies are those that never lose sight of the organization's objectives and overall strategies. Becoming overly concerned with day-to-day operations is a major pitfall and is often the downfall of many foodservice organizations. The result is much like the phrase "You can't see the forest for the trees." Managers become so engrossed in the various aspects of operations management that they fail to see the overall picture. They are not aware of trends, and when the competitive environment does change, they are not prepared for it.

Successful planning is a key element in the financial success of all foodservice organizations. Those organizations that allocate resources (time and money) for planning are much more likely to perform better than those that do not.

Planning for Effective Marketing

Types of Plans

Consider two levels of management: operations, and multiunit or corporate. The planning that takes place at each of these levels pertains to a variety of managerial functions, including marketing. Specific marketing-planning efforts are related to each of these levels.

Operational marketing planning is planning undertaken by management at the individual unit level. The unit management must formulate a market plan to serve as a guide for the marketing activities during the next year or two. This type of consideration might include the following questions: What types of advertising are planned? What in-house promotions are scheduled? Within small chains and independent operations, the unit management is often granted great autonomy. Within larger chain organizations, most aspects of the marketing function are tightly controlled, and the management of an individual unit assumes the role of implementer rather than planner. This is done to assure coordination of marketing efforts and consistency throughout the chain.

Multiunit marketing planning is planning undertaken by a multiunit organization or a chain. Within organizations of this type, all aspects of the marketing function are the responsibility of the corporate director of marketing. This individual, working in conjunction with others, is responsible for planning and implementing the marketing program for several units. In addition, the unit management must be supplied with input for planning the local marketing program. Inherent in the responsibilities at the multiunit level is the coordination of marketing activities for the various units with the marketing activities of the entire organization. Certain economies of scale become available to multiunit operations, particularly in the area of advertising.

Strategic marketing planning involves the establishment of long-range objectives and a long-range marketing plan. The top management of the organization, working in conjunction with the owners or board of directors, must establish broad-based long-range objectives. Questions concerning the long-term future of the organization must be addressed. These might include the following: To what new target market(s) should we appeal? At what rate should we develop new units? By what methods should we strive to raise the volume of sales within our existing unit(s)? The plans formulated by this group should serve as the basis for all other marketing decisions, for the objectives established by this group have implications for all management decisions. The strategic options from which the organiza-

Table 3.1. Market Expansion Opportunities.

	Existing Product-Service Mix	New or Modified Product-Service Mix
Existing Market Segments	Market penetration	Product-service mix development
New and Revised Market Segments	Market development	Diversification

tion may choose are shown in Table 3.1. The four options are (1) market penetration, (2) product-service mix development, (3) market development, and (4) diversification.

A market penetration strategy is selected when the existing product-service mix is sold to the existing market segments. In an effort to increase sales, management attempts to increase the rate of repeat patronage, building on a solid base of clientele. Another part of this strategy is to increase initial patronage among those members of existing markets who have not previously patronized the foodservice operation. This is done by drawing patrons away from competing operations, thereby increasing the market share. The overall goal is twofold: to increase sales and to increase market share. This strategy is commonly used during periods of economic uncertainty, such as rapid inflation. As it becomes more expensive to borrow capital for physical expansion, one of the best ways to grow is to increase sales within existing units. In this manner, a larger percentage of the increased sales will eventually become profits.

Product-service mix development involves using marketing information concerning the unmet needs and wants of existing market segments. New products and services are introduced in an attempt to increase sales. No foodservice operation can remain unchanged for too long and expect to continue to prosper. Markets change, consumer needs and wants change, and so too must the product-service mix of any foodservice organization. Consider, for example, the product-service mix development of any of the fast-food chains. New menu items have been added continually over the years to increase unit sales and expand the total market. New meals, such as breakfast, were successfully introduced adding significantly to total sales of the individual units and the total corporation. In some cases, the addition of breakfast increased total sales volume by more than 25 percent. New service aspects, such as inside seating, drive-through windows, and electronic cash registers were added to speed up customer service. Product-service mix development should be an ongoing aspect of any marketing program.

Market development as a strategy has proven to be very successful during the last 20 years. It involves expansion into new market segments using the existing product-service mix. As foodservice chains open and are successful, management usually begins to look for new markets. New units are constructed, and soon a regional and, perhaps eventually, a national chain has emerged. The undisputed leader in this area is, of course, McDonald's with well over 6,000 units worldwide.

Finally, a diversification strategy can be employed, but normally only by the largest of foodservice organizations. Diversification occurs when the organization purchases or takes control of other firms. These firms may or may not be in the foodservice industry. The most common form of diversification within the foodservice industry occurs when a foodservice firm seeks to control its suppliers and distributors. In this manner, the firm can lower its operating costs and increase profits. If a foodservice firm has sufficient size and is financially stable, this can be a very successful strategy.

Many foodservice organizations, particularly small independent operations, often do not take the time or make the effort necessary to develop adequate strategic marketing plans. Without such plans, the marketing strategy can easily become reactionary; the organization merely reacts to each new competitive force and lacks an overall sense of direction and purpose. Conversely, an organization that develops well-defined strategic marketing plans has laid the groundwork necessary for a proactive marketing effort, one that sets the pace rather than merely reacting to what competitors do.

Advantages to Planning

Formulating an organized and well-conceived marketing plan can have a tremendously positive impact on a foodservice organization. First, it helps the organization cope with change more effectively. If the competitive environment changes rapidly, an organization with some contingency planning will be able to effectively deal with the change.

Second, planning related to the marketing function helps assure that the objectives the organization establishes are either achieved or modified. The plans formulated serve as guides used to achieve the objectives. If, in some unforeseen circumstances, the objectives cannot be achieved, revised objectives and plans can be formulated. This is done after a very careful analysis of the situation pertaining to the reasons that the original objectives could not be achieved.

Third, establishing a marketing plan aids management in decision making. The established plans can easily serve as a point of reference for management to consult when confronted with a difficult decision. Given the alternative choices, managers can ask which one will contribute the most to the achievement of their objectives.

Fourth, the development of both short- and long-range marketing plans aids management in the eventual evaluation of the marketing efforts. Results of marketing efforts can be compared against projected results, and by doing so, management establishes a control process for the marketing function. Just as management is concerned with the financial progress of an organization and compares the actual performance against that which was budgeted, so too management assesses the degree to which the marketing objectives have been achieved.

Disadvantages to Planning

Establishing a marketing plan is not without its drawbacks. First, establishing objectives and formulating a marketing plan is very time consuming. The time that management invests in planning can be expensive, and the results of planning must be cost-effective. The overall benefits of these efforts, however, normally far exceed the cost to the organization.

Second, if plans are poorly conceived or are based on false assumptions, they can be inaccurate or ineffective. For this reason, some managers feel that planning is of little value. Additionally, unplanned scenarios can develop rapidly, rendering marketing plans much less effective.

A Mini Case Study

Poor Marketing Planning at XYZ Fast-Food Company

Several years ago, a fast-food company located in the western part of the United States specialized in hamburgers and fried chicken. Business was brisk, and the small company began to expand, first to 10 units, then 15 and eventually 35 units. With the opening of each new unit, the owners proudly felt that with the additional profits from each new unit, rapid expansion was just around the corner. When there were a total of 35 units in the chain, the owners seemed ready to embark on a major expansion program. They had gained recognition in one of the national trade journals as one of the growth chains, and the future looked bright.

Beneath the veneer of rapid expansion, however, lay many problems at the core of the organization. First, the owners of the firm were proud entrepreneurs, individuals who spent most of their time dealing with the operating problems of each of the 35 individual units. Little time had been devoted to long-range planning, and as a result, the company lacked a unified well-defined plan for the future. Second, sites for all the units had been selected without considering future shifts in population. Failure to consider these population trends had resulted in several units' falling well below sales projections. Third, no overall advertising and promotional strategy had been formulated. Instead, each individual unit manager was instructed to "run a few newspaper advertisements with coupons when business was slow."

Despite the existing and potential problems, which may appear evident, the owners did not perceive any major problems. Decreasing sales at one or more units were discounted with "the economy is hurting everyone," or "the weather's been bad," although at the same time, other fast-food chains prospered and were rapidly expanding in the same geographic area. Finally, while other successful fast-food chains offered a highly selective menu strongly supported by regional and national marketing programs, this small chain offered a diversified menu (by fast-food standards) and lacked a unified marketing program. As a result, the target market was not narrowly focused. The owners were attempting to be "all things to all people."

Unfortunately, a declining spiral had been set in motion, and despite top management's efforts, the organization eventually filed for bankruptcy. With some careful thought and diligent planning, the situation might have been avoided.

Questions for Consideration

1. What marketing errors did management make?

2. How should each of these decisions have been approached? Why?

3. Why type of planning efforts might have been undertaken? How could this have been done?

A Systems Model for Developing a Marketing Plan

Establishing and implementing a marketing plan is not a difficult task. It is, however, time consuming and requires a considerable amount of in-depth thought if it is to be sufficient for any real value.

One of the major problems for many foodservice managers is that an overall comprehensive marketing plan is never fully developed and implemented. To accomplish this task, managers must draw information from several sources and combine it into a unified and logical plan. Many foodservice managers are unable to accomplish this task, and therefore the marketing efforts of the organization never fully realize their potential.

For this reason, this chapter approaches the task of developing a marketing plan from a systems perspective. Using a systems approach provides both a visual and a descriptive step-by-step planning and implementation process that a manager can use to develop a marketing plan for an organization. This planning system moves the initial planning through final evaluation of the results. The systems model is illustrated in Figure 3.1.

Two major aspects must be considered when formulating strategic marketing plans; these are the current situation and the desired market position. An analysis of the current situation involves careful consideration of several questions, including the following: Where are we now? Where will we be if we continue on our present course and our environment remains unchanged or changes in the manner we predict? What are the most significant activities of our competitors? Considering the second aspect requires asking where the firm desires to be 2, 5, or even 10 years from now. This look into the future should expand beyond 1 year and should yield long-term plans. Those companies that do not look carefully into the future are often those that become overly involved in the day-to-day operational concerns and the activities of the current marketing program.

By examining the current situation and the desired future marketing position, a gap between the two should be evident. This gap is called the *strategic gap*. The goal of strategic planning is to conceive and implement a plan that will allow the organization to reduce or eliminate the strategic gap by moving the current situation toward the desired market position.

The Strategic Marketing Model

1. **Input from environmental scanning and marketing information systems.** Fig. 3.1 shows that input from environmental scanning and a marketing information system influences each step of the model. Managers who formulate marketing plans for the future do not do this in a vacuum. All foodservice operations, large or small, publicly or privately owned, gourmet or fast-food, nonprofit or for profit, are all subject to influences from the environment. Failure to account for these influences can be disastrous. Determining the impact that these environmental factors will have on the strategic plans of a foodservice organization is indeed difficult and will require considerable time and study. The term *environmental scanning* is used to describe the process whereby the environment is examined and the most significant events are noted.

Figure 3.1. A Strategic Marketing Model.

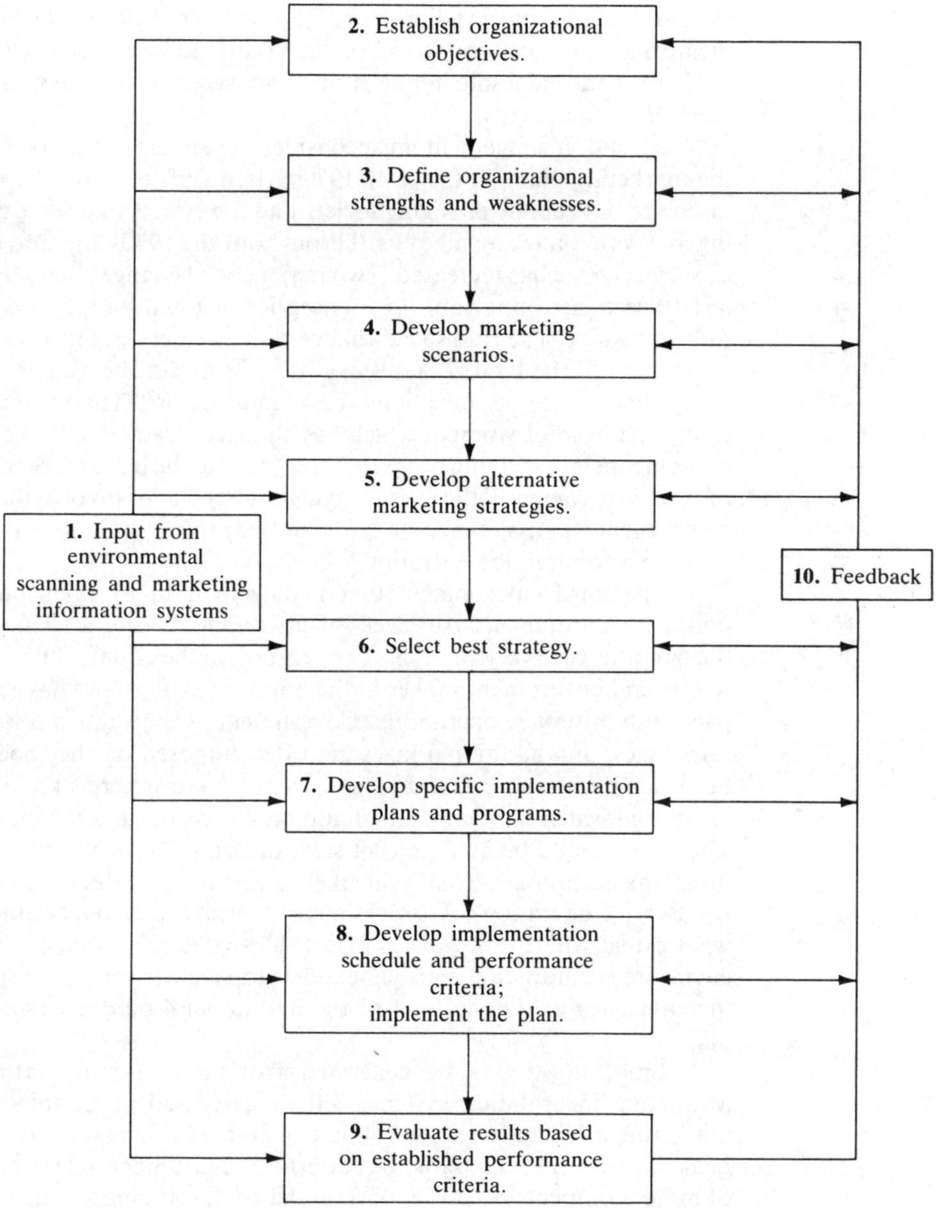

The environmental variables are categorized as economic, social, or political components of the system. First, management must take into account the relative state of the economy within the geographic area in which the organization operates. What are the trends for future business growth, consumer spending, population changes, and other economic indicators? On a broader scale, what are the national economic indicators projecting? What effect will changes in these indicators have on the foodservice organization? Reviewing trade journals and other business and economic publications can serve as an invaluable resource for foodservice managers.

Second, management must consider the effects of the social environment on the marketing plan. In the early 1970s Alvin Toffler wrote *Future Shock,* which discussed our rapidly changing society and the effects that these changes were having and would have on all of us. Throughout the 1970s and into the 1980s the rate of social change has increased. Two major social changes that have occurred in the last 10 years are important for foodservice, yet many foodservice managers have failed to adapt. The first social change is the tremendous growth in the number of individuals in the United States over the age of 50; this is a growing market that many foodservice organizations continue to ignore. The second change is in the traditional role of women, which has changed dramatically, yet many managers planning their marketing programs are ignoring the large market segment made up of working women. Other social changes to consider involve the role that federal government will assume in the 1980s and beyond. What impact will these changes have on a foodservice operation?

The third environment that management must take into account is the political environment. All levels of government have a tremendous impact on the operation of every foodservice operation in the country. For example, changes the federal government makes in the minimum wage laws have an immediate impact on foodservice operations. Government at the state and local level controls sales taxes, and additional taxes are often imposed on the foodservice industry. For example, suppose that the state sales tax is four percent and the local government is considering adding an additional 4 percent sales tax on restaurant meals. The result would be an 8 percent sales tax on restaurant meals. When this additional tax is imposed, what is the likely effect on the sales volume of an individual foodservice operation? As prices increase because of the additional sales tax, to what extent will this negatively affect sales volume? Based on the analysis of the environment, how can management develop a marketing program to maintain or increase sales volume in light of the additional 4 percent restaurant meals sales tax?

Input must also be generated from a marketing information system. Marketing information systems will be discussed in Chapter 4. In general, a marketing information system should generate information concerning consumer behavior patterns, demographic patterns of consumers, sales trends, and activities of major competitors. It is important, when developing a marketing plan, to have available current information that can serve as the basis for sound marketing plans.

2. **Establish organizational objectives.** Based on the environmental scanning and the marketing information system, management is now ready to establish marketing objectives. Objectives serve several functions. First, they enable management to come to some consensus concerning the goals of the organization. Second, responsibility for specific objectives can be assigned to various managers, thereby establishing accountability. If a specific manager is assigned the responsibility for following through and seeing that the objective is completed, the results are likely to be more positive than if no one individual is assigned responsibility. Third, establishing objectives with the input of all management personnel serves as a brainstorming and motivational device. By allowing each individual to have input into formulating the organizational marketing objectives, individuals develop allegiance for the objectives because they have played important roles in establishing them. As a result, managers are likely to work more diligently in attempting to achieve stated objectives.

The formulation of good objectives will take time, and care should be taken to assure that the objectives are workable. Several characteristics of good objectives are

- Operational objectives should be specific and well understood. They should not be broad and difficult to define. Everyone involved in formulating the objectives should clearly understand the precise objectives toward which the organization seeks to move. For example, the objective "to increase sales within the next six months" is so unspecific as to be meaningless.
- Objectives should identify expected results. If at all possible, they should be quantitative so that no gray area will exist for purposes of evaluation. By stating the objective in quantitative terms, the expected results are more readily understood. For example, the objective "to increase the number of dinner patrons by 15 percent on Monday, Tuesday, and Wednesday evenings" is a well-stated quantitative objective.
- Objectives must be within the power of the organization to achieve. When establishing objectives, management must keep in mind the relative abilities of the organization. For example, the objective "to open 10 new units within the next 18 months" would make little sense if the organization had only 6 units and lacked the necessary capital to undertake such a large expansion program.
- Objectives must be acceptable to the individuals within the organization. The management must come to a consensus concerning the objectives. It is extremely difficult for an organization successfully to achieve the stated objectives if the managers with input into the formation of the objectives do not agree. The extra time spent at this stage in achieving a consensus will make the remaining planning and implementation steps proceed more smoothly.

3. **Define organizational strengths and weaknesses.** Once the organizational objectives are formulated, management should critically examine the organization for its strengths and weaknesses. It is at this point that management must be extremely critical in asking, "What do we have or offer that is different, unique, or excellent in comparison with the competition?" Management must also

examine the organization's shortcomings by asking, "What do we have or offer or do that is below average?"

The process of identifying organizational strengths and weaknesses is similar to examining a balance sheet with assets and liabilities. The strengths can be used in promotional efforts, while at the same time, management makes every effort to correct or neutralize the weaknesses. Many managers find it difficult to identify an organization's weaknesses clearly. They tend to overlook negative factors because these may, in some cases, be a negative reflection on an individual manager.

In addition, it is also an excellent practice to examine the corresponding strengths and weaknesses of major competitors. It is relatively easy to identify specific areas in which a distinct competitive advantage or weakness is evident. These can then be either exploited or corrected as the situation warrants.

As a minimum, the evaluation of the organization's strengths and weaknesses should consider the following areas:

- Personnel at all levels should be evaluated, with particular emphasis placed on guest-contact employees. Are the employees as competent as they should be? Do they need additional training? Are suitable replacements readily available from the local labor pool?
- Physical facilities are a major part of the product-service mix. What is the condition of the building exterior, the interior decor, furnishings, and appointments? Is the number of seats available adequate? Should the seating configuration be changed?
- The financial status of the organization should also be considered, including past, present, and future performance.
- The quality of the product-service mix should be critically examined. Are the menu items prepared and presented properly at all times? How might the product-service mix be improved? What are the sales trends for all menu items?
- Are the current marketing activities producing the desired results? Should the emphasis be changed? How could marketing resources be used more effectively?

4. **Develop marketing scenarios.** The development of scenarios involves discussions of "what if" situations. For example, what if the major competitor launches an advertising blitz that reduces sales volume by 15 percent? What if inflation exceeds 12 percent during the next year? What if unemployment in the area increases by 2 percent during the next six months because a major manufacturing plant is closed? The development of such scenarios is a form of contingency planning in which management attempts to anticipate possibilities and then formulates plans to deal effectively with the situation that each scenario presents.

A common method of contingency planning involves the use of sales forecasts. In order to develop an effective marketing plan, an accurate projection of sales is necessary. Data supplied by a marketing information system are used to project the number of covers to be served, the average check, and the total sales volume. These projections are usually based upon historical sales data. The use of a computer in simulating sales projections is of tremendous potential value. Certainly in the coming years, the computer will become more common in the industry. Even small hand-held calculators, however, have the capability of doing linear regression and trend line analysis. These functions can be of significant value to management when projecting future trends. The advent of inexpensive personal computers for business applications is also a significant development.

Tables 3.2 and 3.3 illustrate sales projections for a table-service operation. This operation is open from 11:30 A.M. until 10:00 P.M. and uses the same menu

Table 3.2. Sales Projections.

	Expected Number of Covers Served		Expected Check Average		Days Open per Year		Projected Total Revenue
Optimistic Projection							
Sunday	200	×	8.25	×	52	=	$ 85,800
Monday	245	×	8.25	×	52	=	105,105
Tuesday	245	×	8.25	×	52	=	105,105
Wednesday	250	×	8.25	×	52	=	107,250
Thursday	290	×	8.25	×	52	=	124,410
Friday	440	×	8.25	×	52	=	188,760
Saturday	415	×	8.25	×	52	=	178,035
	2175			Projected annual revenue			$894,465
Moderate Projection							
Sunday	175	×	8.25	×	52	=	$ 75,075
Monday	210	×	8.25	×	52	=	90,090
Tuesday	210	×	8.25	×	52	=	90,090
Wednesday	215	×	8.25	×	52	=	92,235
Thursday	250	×	8.25	×	52	=	107,250
Friday	395	×	8.25	×	52	=	169,455
Saturday	370	×	8.25	×	52	=	158,730
	1825			Projected annual revenue			$782,925
Pessimistic Projection							
Sunday	150	×	8.25	×	52	=	$ 64,350
Monday	175	×	8.25	×	52	=	75,075
Tuesday	175	×	8.25	×	52	=	75,075
Wednesday	180	×	8.25	×	52	=	77,220
Thursday	210	×	8.25	×	52	=	90,090
Friday	350	×	8.25	×	52	=	150,150
Saturday	325	×	8.25	×	52	=	139,425
	1565			Projected annual revenue			$671,385

Table 3.3. Projected Annual Revenue With Assigned Probabilities.

	Projected Annual Revenue		Probability Assigned		Weighted Projected Annual Revenue
Optimistic Projection	$894,465	×	0.30	=	$268,339.50
Moderate Projection	$782,925	×	0.60	=	469,755.00
Pessimistic Projection	$671,385	×	0.10	=	67,138.50
			1.00		$805,233.00

during the entire time. In Table 3.2 the expected number of covers served has been projected for optimistic, moderate, and pessimistic levels of sales. The expected number of covers served is determined using the sales histories supplied by a well-organized marketing information system and the input from environmental factors.

The expected number of covers served is then multiplied by the expected check average. The check average figure is based on historical data and the expected menu price increase for the coming period (in this case one year). These figures are then multiplied by the number of days that the operation is open per year, and the result is the projected total revenue figure. By projecting sales revenue for three separate volumes, management is able easily to determine a projected range of sales. In Table 3.2, the projections of annual revenue range from a low of $671,385 to a high of $894,465.

Table 3.3 illustrates how management can carry these projections one step further in more finely tuning the operation. Each projected annual revenue figure is assigned a probability that indicates the relative likelihood of the pessimistic, moderate, and optimistic projections. In the example, the pessimistic figure is assigned a probability of 0.10 or 10 percent, the moderate figure is assigned a probability of 0.60 or 60 percent; the optimistic figure is given 0.30 or 30 percent. These assigned probabilities must add up to 1.00 or 100 percent. How are these probabilities assigned? Each represents management's best estimate of the likelihood of a given sales projection's being correct. The probabilities are assigned based on historical data, marketing research, and judgment.

The projected revenues are then multiplied by the assigned probabilities, and these answers are added together to provide a weighted annual revenue figure. This figure ($805,233 in the example) represents management's best projection for revenue during the next 12 months. The projected annual revenue range ($671,385–894,465) and weighted projected annual revenue figure ($805,233) can then be used to prepare budgets and other financial forecasts.

5. **Develop alternative marketing strategies.** Based on the scenarios conceived in the previous step, management should formulate a number of marketing

strategies to respond adequately to each of the scenarios and to allow the organization to gain the maximum competitive advantage from each.

All management personnel with marketing responsibilities should be involved in a series of brainstorming sessions designed to get as many alternative strategies recorded as possible, for only when all potential ideas are explored will the very best strategy or combination of strategies emerge. It is important, however, that suggested strategies be evaluated for the contribution they will make to the achievement of the organization's overall objectives, both short- and long-term. Any strategy that is selected will potentially affect the organization's objectives, and only those strategies that contribute positively to these objectives should be considered.

6. **Select the best strategy.** Based on brainstorming sessions and discussions to date, the management group should work toward a consensus regarding the most desirable strategy or combination of strategies. It is unlikely that any one alternative strategy will satisfy all the marketing objectives of the organization. For this reason, management must further evaluate the relative merits of each proposed strategy. Some give and take among individuals is desirable, as the goal of this discussion is group consensus. The group consensus process of combining strategies to produce the best overall strategy is more desirable than having one individual make all the marketing decisions. The process allows the thoughts and opinions of many individuals to be incorporated into the final decision.

It is also a sound management practice to involve managers without specific marketing responsibilities in these decisions, for their input can prove to be invaluable. For example, if a change in menu content is deemed desirable from a marketing point of view, what effect will this have on the operational aspects of the organization? An operations manager will know the implications of such a change.

7. **Develop specific implementation plans and programs.** Unless plans are properly implemented, the results are often less than fully successful. Once the best strategy (or combination of strategies) is selected, management must develop an implementation plan. This plan should focus on: who will assume responsibility for implementing the individual components of the overall strategy; specifically, how each individual component will be implemented; what needs to be accomplished prior to implementation; and where each component will be implemented.

By themselves, strategies and plans are of little value to a foodservice organization; it is not until these plans are implemented that positive results will occur.

8. **Develop implementation schedule and performance criteria; implement the plan.** Following the development of the marketing strategies and before implementing the plans, two activities should be completed. First, an implementation schedule should be developed. Not all the strategic plans can be implemented at the same moment. Instead, an orderly timetable or schedule should be established to show, in detail, when the specific aspects of the plan will be implemented.

Second, a series of performance criteria for evaluating the relative success of the strategic plans should be established. Performance criteria should be precise so that the marketing plan can be carefully evaluated. For example, performance criteria should be carefully established for degree of consumer satisfaction, market share, product-service mix, quality assurance, sales volumes, and advertising effectiveness. Specific sales objectives should be established based on breakeven analysis and other measures of financial performance. The performance criteria should be established in relation to current and future environmental trends. Are the desired performance criteria going to be satisfactory in times of economic instability, inflation, recession, or growth? It is extremely important that the performance criteria be clearly defined prior to implementation of the plan, for without clearly defined criteria, evaluation becomes subjective and not nearly as meaningful as it should be.

9. **Evaluate results based on established performance criteria.** After the plan has been implemented and has been in place for a significant period of time, an evaluation should be conducted. The results of the plan should be evaluated in light of the established performance criteria. These results should also be evaluated for the degree to which they contribute to the achievement of the organizational objectives (see step 2 in Figure 3.1).

10. **Feedback.** It is important that this model not be viewed as a purely linear process. It is possible, and in many cases desirable, to recycle through various steps of the process. As the environment changes or the results are not what is anticipated, management should return to the appropriate step to reformulate marketing strategy. This strategic marketing model is best viewed as a dynamic model, one with sufficient flexibility to allow for changes in strategies or implementation schedules due to ever-changing environmental and competitive conditions.

Why Some Plans Fail

Despite the best efforts of management planners and all those involved in the planning process, some plans fail to fully achieve the desired results. Why do some plans fall short of the desired objectives? Based on the findings of several research studies, the following are the most common reasons why some plans fail:

– Strategic planning is not integrated into the day-to-day activities of the marketing function. In these cases, the plan is seen as an end in itself, and the plan is not made operational. Plans that are carefully developed but sit on a shelf and are not used are almost worse than no plans at all. The planning process is a dynamic, ongoing process as Figure 3.1 illustrates. Plans should be implemented, evaluated, revised, and implemented again. Only when this cycle is ongoing can planning truly succeed.

- The planning process is not understood by the planners. It is important that the planning group carefully work through all of the steps of the entire model. Sometimes, managers want to jump ahead and draw conclusions before all environmental variables are considered and before a clear consensus has been formed. This tendency should be avoided at all costs, for the results are usually less than desirable. Every member of the planning team must fully understand the steps involved in the planning process and should actively contribute during each step.
- Lack of input from nonmarketing managers. For a marketing plan to succeed, it must be implemented in part by managers who have major responsibilities in areas removed from the marketing function. The plan must have the input of these managers, for if the plan is conceived by a small group and without the input and support of those who will in part implement it, the probability that the plan will fail increases.
- Financial projections are not plans. Some foodservice organizations make projections or forecasts for sales and label this activity planning. Projections by themselves should not be equated with plans. Only when clearly defined strategies are identified for achieving the desired sales projections does planning take place.
- Inadequate input and lack of consideration of all variables the environment may present can be a cause of failure when formulating a plan. Although it is impossible to consider all the variables, the real danger is not too much information, but too little. Managers often want to rush to a conclusion rather than consider the information readily available. Again, this information comes from environmental scanning and marketing information systems.
- Planning focus is placed too heavily on short-term results. The emphasis should be placed on formulating plans that will allow the organization to move toward the successful achievement of long-term objectives. Too frequently, the emphasis is placed on short-term profits at the expense of long-term objectives and profits.

Of course, hundreds of other reasons might also explain why plans sometimes fail to achieve the desired results. If, however, the members of the planning group focus their attention clearly on the initial stages of the planning model, the later stages will become much easier to complete, and the chances for success will also increase. The tendency to avoid is to rush through the initial steps in order to produce results.

Summary

This chapter focused on the necessary steps for formulating a strategic marketing plan. An example of a fast-food chain illustrated the disastrous financial results that can occur when an organization does not engage in either short- or long-range marketing planning. Planning for effective marketing includes operational and multiunit, or corporate levels of marketing planning. Although there are several advantages and disadvantages to planning, several research studies have clearly demonstrated that those organizations engaging in marketing planning hold a decisive advantage over the competition and exhibit improved financial performance.

The last section of the chapter introduced the concept of strategic planning. Strategic planning includes three important concepts: (1) analysis of the current situation, (2) the desired market position, and (3) the strategic gap. A multistep strategic model provides managers with a procedure to follow in formulating marketing plans. Common reasons for the failure of marketing plans can be identified, but by referring to the model outlined here, managers can avoid common mistakes.

Questions for Review and Discussion

1. What makes an organizational objective a good one?
2. What are the strengths and weaknesses of a systems approach, such as the one outlined in this chapter?
3. What differentiates among the various levels of marketing planning?
4. Compare and contrast the systems model for developing a marketing plan with the techniques used by an organization with which you are familiar.

Further Reading

Stapleton, John, *How to Prepare a Marketing Plan* (London: Gower Press, 1971).

Vesawich, Peter C., "The Execution and Measurement of a Marketing Program," *Cornell Hotel and Restaurant Administration Quarterly,* May 1979, pp. 41–52.

Chapter 4

Marketing Information Systems for the Foodservice Industry

Chapter Outline

This chapter focuses on the marketing informational needs of foodservice managers. It introduces and discusses the concept of marketing information systems and the uses of these systems.

The chapter is divided into the following major sections:

Introduction
- the critical need for information
- definition of marketing information systems
- the components of a marketing information system

Use of Marketing Information Systems
- timely uses for a marketing information system
- three requirements for a successful marketing information system

Internally Generated Marketing Information
- sources of information
- use of point-of-sale information

Externally Generated Marketing Information
- sources of information
- primary and secondary data

Market Research Methodology
- research methodology
- sampling methodology
- survey instrument design

The Marketing Audit

Summary

Introduction

The Critical Need for Information

Throughout the 1970s, the United States experienced an information explosion, and all industries made rather substantial advances in information collection, analysis, storage, and retrieval. The foodservice industry was very much a part of this trend. As the environment in which foodservice organizations operate becomes more complex and more competitive, the information needs of these organizations become more complex. Those organizations that are able to collect, analyze, store, and retrieve information most effectively and efficiently are likely to be the most successful organizations in the 1980s and 1990s.

In making effective marketing decisions, management needs information about the marketing environment in which the organization must function. Without the proper types of information available on a timely basis, management is more likely to make decisions that will adversely affect the performance of the organization.

A simple example will illustrate this point. Suppose that the management of a small restaurant chain must make a decision concerning the allocation of the advertising budget among the available media for the upcoming quarter. Two of the advertising objectives of this restaurant are (1) to reinforce the chain's high level of perceived value among current customers, thereby increasing the rate of repeat patronage by 10 percent and (2) to increase by 10 percent the number of customers who are patronizing one of the chain's restaurants for the first time. To make an effective decision about media allocation, the management of this chain has specific informational needs. Here management needs access to the following types of information: (1) characteristics of the current clientele, (2) characteristics of the target market segments most likely to patronize the chain's restaurants for the first time, (3) media habits of both of these groups, and (4) characteristics of the consumers of all available media (television, radio, print, etc.) and the individual media vehicles (for example, individual radio stations).

Without this specific information available on a timely basis, the management of this restaurant chain will be forced to make a less than fully informed decision. The results of a less-informed decision could directly and adversely affect the advertising effectiveness of the organization and indirectly affect the financial performance of the organization.

All too often, management is forced to make critical decisions without the necessary marketing information. Most managers are not satisfied with the quality and quantity of information available to them. They must frequently work with too much of some types of information and too little of others. What type of information is needed if management is to make informed decisions? A broad overview of the information needs of management is shown in Table 4.1. This list is by no means all inclusive, but it is shown here to provide a starting point for the development of a list of information needs specific to an individual foodservice organization. Some types of information may be critical to one organization, yet of little value to another. Each foodservice organization should compile a list of information needs and then design and implement a method for collecting this information.

Initially, management needs information that will provide insight into the needs and wants of both current and potential customers. These insights allow management to understand the customer better, and they aid in developing a product-service mix with a higher probability of satisfying the customers. Generally, management focuses on demographic, geographic, psychographic, and behavioristic variables, as shown in Table 4.1. Information related to these four variables will allow management to have a sufficient understanding of the target market segments. Other information concerns include marketing activities of direct and indirect competitors, in-

Table 4.1. An Overview of the Information Needs of Foodservice Managers.

Type of Information	Example
Demographic variables	Age, sex, income, occupation
Geographic variables	Location of home and office
Psychographic variables	Indicators of life style and personality
Behavioristic variables	Frequency of dining out, expenditure habits, restaurants frequently patronized
Perceptions of food and beverage quality	Portion size, price, value
Competitive situation	Analysis of actions taken by direct and indirect competitors
Macroenvironment	Economic, political, social situations
Sales histories	Analysis of business patterns and forecasts

fluences of the macroenvironment, and sales histories and trends for each foodservice facility within the organization.

Definition of Marketing Information Systems

A *foodservice marketing information system* is a structured organization of people and procedures designed to generate a flow of information from inside and outside the operation. This is the data to be used as a basis for marketing decisions. Marketing information systems is a broader and more encompassing term than market research. Research indicates that information is collected for a specific reason or a specific project; the major objective is one-time use. For example, a potential foodservice owner may undertake a feasibility study and use market research to determine whether to build a new restaurant. Such an information-gathering study is designed to answer a very specific question and is not intended to be used for other purposes.

A *marketing information system,* on the other hand, is an ongoing data-gathering process involving initial data collection as well as routine and systematic data-collection procedures. For example, a manager may choose to survey the consumers who patronize the restaurant. This systematic and routine information gathering is not intended to be used to address one specific question but is instead a part of an overall system to monitor the degree of marketing success that the operation is able to achieve.

A marketing information system involves four basic criteria:

1. A structured organization or established system of people and information-gathering procedures
2. A system designed to generate a continuous flow of information to provide accurate and current marketing information for management
3. Information gathered from inside and outside the organization, involving external information-gathering methods, such as consumer surveys, and internal information-gathering methods, such as employee meetings, patron comment cards, and in-house consumer surveys
4. Information compiled so that management can use it as a basis for marketing decisions.

It would be extremely difficult and quite hazardous for the management of a foodservice organization to make decisions without accurate and up-to-date marketing information. Professional management demands that decisions be founded on sound information. Managers who are able to use information as the basis for marketing decisions are likely to make better and more consistent decisions. The McDonald's Corporation serves as a good example. For many years, this corporation has relied upon a widespread marketing information system that has generated information used in the decision-making process. The resulting decisions have consistently been very good and have thereby allowed McDonald's to establish and maintain a leadership position in the fast-food segment of the industry. This is not to say that a very good marketing information system alone will allow an organization to achieve financial success, but it would be of tremendous benefit to management.

The Components of a Marketing Information System

If a marketing information system is to be fully effective, information relative to the environment in which the foodservice organization operates must be available on a timely basis. The basis for this data collection is environmental scanning. *Environmental scanning* is a term used to describe a process whereby variables that could affect a foodservice organization are given a quick evaluation. Based on this initial evaluation, those with the greatest potential impact (positive or negative) are examined in greater detail. From a theoretical standpoint, if management is to make a rational decision, all information that could affect the foodservice organization should be examined and evaluated. Realistically, however, this is not possible because of the finite limits on the valuable resources of time, money, and personnel. Instead, only those environmental variables that appear to be the most important or most critical are examined in greater detail.

In short, a marketing information system that uses environmental scanning provides an overview of the entire environment as well as further detail concerning those variables within the environment that are most critical to the successful operation of a foodservice organization.

Within the environment in which a foodservice organization functions are three subenvironments. These subenvironments are (1) the macroenvironment, (2) the competitive environment, and (3) the organizational environment. A conceptual model of the components of a marketing information system is shown in Figure 4.1. Data are generated for each of the

Figure 4.1. Components of a Marketing Information System.

```
┌─────────────────────────────────────────────────────────────┐
│                    Environmental scanning                    │
└─────────────────────────────────────────────────────────────┘
```

Macroenvironment	**Competitive environment**	**Organizational environment**
Economic effects	Monitor actions of	Internally generated
Legislative effects	direct and indirect	marketing information
Governmental agency	competitors	Point-of-sale information
effects	Market research	Sales histories and
Demographic effects	activities	trends
Sociocultural effects	Marketing audits	

```
              ┌──────────────────────┐
              │ Marketing information │
              │     compiled and      │
              │      summarized       │
              └──────────────────────┘

              ┌──────────────────────┐
              │ Marketing trends evaluated │
              └──────────────────────┘

              ┌──────────────────────┐
              │ Marketing plans formulated │
              └──────────────────────┘
```

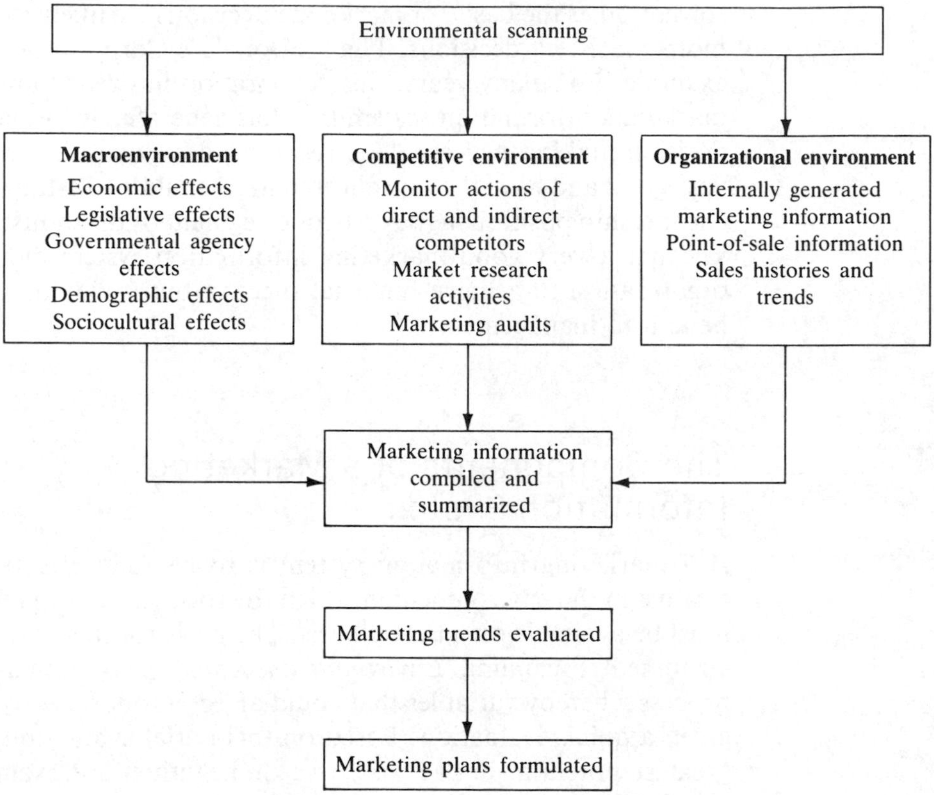

three subenvironments through an environmental-scanning process. The data are then compiled, summarized, and stored until needed by management. At the appropriate time, management can readily retrieve data summaries, evaluate marketing trends, and formulate marketing plans and strategies. The overriding objectives of a marketing information system are (1) to collect relevant data concerning each of these subenvironments, (2) to compile, summarize, and store the data, and (3) to have data readily available for management on a timely basis.

The *macroenvironment* concerns the broadest possible effects. Macroenvironmental effects are those that the individual foodservice organization is almost powerless to control; they include economic, legislative, governmental agency, demographic, and sociocultural effects. As conditions change within the macroenvironment, the management of foodservice organizations should collect data concerning these changes. Knowledge of existing conditions will provide a basis for calculating the impact that these variables will have on the operation of a foodservice organization. For example, if the inflation rate exceeds 10 percent during the next year, what impact is this likely to have on sales volume? If the federal government reduces the personal income tax rate, what will be the most likely impact? As nearly 20 percent of the population moves each year, how will these demographic changes affect a foodservice organization? These are the influences that the management of a foodservice organization is virtually powerless to control. At best, management can monitor the variables of the macroenvironment and can gauge the effects that they might have on the macroenvironment.

The *competitive environment* immediately surrounds the foodservice organization. The organization exerts some degree of control over this environment, but it can never control it totally. The major concern for management is to monitor closely the marketing and operational actions taken by direct and indirect competitors. Attention should be focused initially on changes made in the marketing mix, menu prices, and sales volume as measured in both dollars and in customer counts. Exact figures are not likely to be available, but all competitors should be monitored closely so that management can be prepared for changes before they occur or at the time they occur, rather than weeks or months later. By monitoring competition in this way, an appropriate competitive response can be readied, thereby gaining a differential competitive advantage.

The two other aspects of the competitive environment for a marketing information system are market research activities and marketing audits. *Market research* encompasses a wide range of activities undertaken to generate information about a specifically defined problem. *Marketing audits* are evaluations of the effectiveness of current marketing practices.

The third subenvironment that is a part of a marketing information system is the *organizational environment*. Data collection in this environment involves examining all relevant information sources within the foodservice organization. The basis for data collection in this environment is sales histories, although information can be generated from other sources as well. Sales histories are records of all sales, broken down by menu group and menu item. Only when managers have access to records of previous sales are they able to make informed decisions concerning the product-service mix for the organization.

Use of Marketing Information Systems

Timely Uses for a Marketing Information System

The overall purpose of a marketing information system is to provide accurate and timely information that management can add to the decision-making process. This information can be used in many situations, including

- Decisions concerning market segmentation
- Decisions involving advertising and promotional efforts
- Decisions involving capital investment and expansion of existing units or construction of new units
- Decisions concerning changes in menu offerings
- Identifying new or different sales opportunities
- Decisions concerning hours of operation
- Decisions involving changes in design, decor, and atmosphere
- Decisions concerning the market position of an organization.

The use of a marketing information system should allow a foodservice manager to speed up the reaction time to changing market conditions, thereby allowing the organization to gain a competitive advantage.

Three Requirements for a Successful Marketing Information System

For any collected information to be useful to foodservice management, it should fulfill three requirements.

The Marketing Information System Should be Objective.   Management should be able to quantify and analyze the information gathered. Management needs as much purely objective data as possible in order to make sound decisions. For example, which of these two statements seems to provide the best-quality information for decision-making purposes?

- *Statement A:* "As the owner of this restaurant, I think we should modify our menu so that we can appeal to more family business."
- *Statement B:* "A recent study has indicated a 10 percent increase in the number of families with children under the age of 10 in our area."

Statement B would appear to be more objective and offer quantitative data on which to base a decision. Statement A is, on the other hand, merely a statement of opinion and is not supported by any quantitative data.

Too many foodservice managers rely heavily on subjective opinion for decision-making purposes. As a result, their decisions are often incorrect. Decisions based on purely personal opinion are often less than successful when implemented. Decisions based on a combination of data and managerial thought generally yield higher-quality decisions.

The Marketing Information System Should be Systematic.   The marketing information system is not an on-off process; it is a system that should be designed to provide a continuing information source for a foodservice manager. By gathering information in a systematic and continuous manner, more and better information is available to a foodservice manager.

The Marketing Information System Should be Useful.   Many studies produce information of little value, and this is obviously not the purpose of a marketing information system. One rule of thumb to follow is this: Collect, compile, and store information only if it is used actively; do not collect information and then file it away without using it. This is a needless and expensive waste of time and effort, yet many foodservice operators, in attempts to gather any quantitative information, maintain data that are never used and are truly useless.

For example, one foodservice manager invested approximately 30 minutes per day tabulating and recording information regarding the number of customers served in each hour of operation. The manager in question continued to have his staff complete these tabulations for one year, yet he had not used the information once. At the end of the year, this manager had invested 182.5 personnel hours in tabulating time. Information of this type can be extremely useful, especially for decisions regarding expansion or redefinition of meal service periods. However, if the information is not used on a regular basis, it makes little sense to invest time and money in data collection.

To determine the usefulness of gathered information, an information flow chart should be considered. An information flow chart is a method of monitoring the usefulness of information gathered for analysis and interpretation. An information flow chart is used for the same basic purpose as a time and motion study in evaluating effectiveness. Each time information is compiled, transported, inspected, analyzed, delayed, stored, or discarded, a symbol is used to represent this change. The symbols most commonly used are

Operation or compiling of paper   ○

Transportation   →

Inspection or analysis   ▭

Delay   D

Storage   ▽

Discarding and throwing away   ⊤

A flow chart is most useful in evaluating how information is compiled and used. Is the information gathered and used to analyze the operation? Is the information actively used in the decision-making process? If information is merely gathered and then filed or stored, as was the case in the preceding example, then there is no need to spend time and effort in collecting the information in the first place.

Figure 4.2 illustrates a simplified information flow chart. This chart il-

Figure 4.2. Simplified Informational Flow Chart.

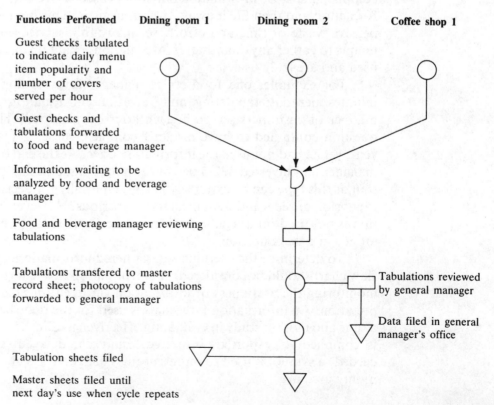

| Functions Performed | Dining room 1 | Dining room 2 | Coffee shop 1 |

Guest checks tabulated to indicate daily menu item popularity and number of covers served per hour

Guest checks and tabulations forwarded to food and beverage manager

Information waiting to be analyzed by food and beverage manager

Food and beverage manager reviewing tabulations

Tabulations transfered to master record sheet; photocopy of tabulations forwarded to general manager

Tabulations reviewed by general manager

Data filed in general manager's office

Tabulation sheets filed

Master sheets filed until next day's use when cycle repeats

lustrates the flow of guest checks and data involving three restaurants located within a single facility.

Internally Generated Marketing Information

The component of a marketing information system that is the simplest to design and implement is an internal system, or the component designed to collect data from within the organizational environment. When considering the organizational environment, management need only be concerned with information available from within the physical confines of the organization's restaurant(s). This component of a marketing information system requires less time and money than does the competitive environment, or externally generated marketing information. The internal component of a marketing information system is very valuable to management because it provides a wealth of information.

Sources of Information

Management has three main sources of internal marketing information. They are (1) sales histories, (2) hourly employees and management staff, and (3) consumers who patronize the facility.

Sales Histories. No rules can tell a manager exactly what records should or should not be maintained. The management of every foodservice organization must make this decision based on individual needs. The records maintained may be simple tabulations, such as customer counts for all meal periods, or they may be a tabulation of sales for each menu item over a specified period of time, such as one month. With the easier access to computers provided by time sharing and the greatly reduced cost of micro and personal computers, today's foodservice manager should seriously consider implementing a more sophisticated computer system. The cost of storing data by computer has been reduced significantly, making this a very feasible alternative for a great many foodservice managers. By using computer tabulation and storage, a manager allows both more complete tabulation of data and nearly instantaneous recall. It is obvious that, with accurate information readily available, a manager is more likely to consult such marketing information prior to making a marketing decision.

Employees and Management Staff. All too often foodservice management ignores the wealth of information that is informally gathered by hourly employees, such as service people, hosts, and hostesses. These individuals are in constant contact with a restaurant's clientele, yet they are rarely asked to relay customer comments and reactions to operational changes, such as new menu items or decor changes. These employees represent an excellent source of information, although the information they provide may not be totally objective. It is a good idea for management to meet with employees on a regular basis and discuss problems and opportunities.

Studies done by Frederick Herzberg[1] and others have shown that employees like to feel recognized by their supervisors as important. Mere recognition by a superior is one of the leading motivators according to Herzberg. Consequently, two advantages are to be gained by meeting with the employees. First, useful marketing information may be gained by management, and second, the meetings serve as a motivator for all employees. All employees need to be exposed to some motivation techniques, although many managers ignore the simple and basic needs of employees as individuals.

The subject of employee meetings is, of course, the responsibility of each individual manager, but the following list of questions provides several possibilities:

- Who are our present customers?
- Where do they live?
- What is their approximate socio-economic level?
- Where else do they go to eat and drink?
- What new features and menu offerings might our present customers like?
- To what new or different market segments might our restaurant appeal?
- What are the wants and needs of these new segments?
- Will this new potential market segment mix with our current clientele?
- How does our restaurant compare with others in the area?
- What do other restaurants offer that we do not and that consumers find attractive?
- Is the food quality as high as it should be?
- Is the service as friendly and prompt as possible?
- How do the building appearance and decor compare with the competition?

This is just a beginning for a foodservice manager. A creative manager could easily add dozens more questions that might serve as a starting point for an informal discussion.

Consumers Who Patronize the Facility.   The focus of the marketing concept is the foodservice operation's clientele. All aspects of the entire foodservice operation should be aimed at satisfying these individuals. The purpose of using an internal marketing information system is to solicit opinions and comments from the current clientele. This can be done in a number of ways, such as having the manager talk with a few of the customers or having service personnel check with the customers. One method used frequently is the *comment card.* This is a card given to the customers after they have finished the meal; its purpose is to solicit their opinions and comments concerning the foodservice operation's food quality, service, decor, and other factors.

All three internal sources of marketing information are very valuable. Together they can provide a great deal of useful information with which to make decisions. Historically, foodservice managers have failed to use these sources to maximum advantage, but the current competitive situation in the foodservice industry dictates that all sources of information be used to gain a competitive advantage and to earn maximum financial rewards.

Use of Point-of-Sale Information

During the latter years of the 1970s and early 1980s many foodservice organizations purchased point-of-sale (POS) terminals and electronic cash registers (ECRs). Manufacturers of POS equipment have continued to improve the product. Not only does this equipment make a foodservice operation function more smoothly, but it is also capable of providing a good deal of useful marketing information to management as well. Simple tabulations that previously took many hours to complete are now readily available because of microprocessor technology.

From an operational point of view, POS equipment with microprocessor technology offers the following features and advantages:

- **Price lookups.**   This feature prevents over- and undercharging of customers. This is a very common problem, as errors in guest-check tabulation frequently occur. Errors occur in approximately 10 percent of all guest checks because of addition errors, item prices not included in the check total, and transposition errors. Figures 4.3 and 4.4 illustrate a POS machine and the keyboard of a recent model of a POS machine that features a ''paging'' format. A microswitch paging keyboard allows the user access to as many as 200 departments with just

50 department keys, thereby reducing the chances that an error will be made. Figures 4.5 and 4.6 illustrate common mistakes that occur when guest checks are hand written and hand tabulated. Figure 4.7 illustrates a guest check produced by a POS terminal.

Figure 4.3. An Electronic Cash Register.
(Courtesy of Litton, Sweda International, Inc.)

Figure 4.4. A Paging Keyboard of an Electronic Cash Register.
(Courtesy of Litton, Sweda International, Inc.)

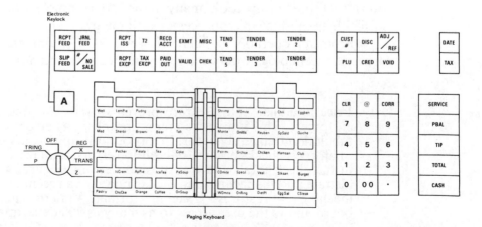

TOTAL LIQUOR
TOTAL FOOD BEFORE TAX 1470
399347
SALES TAX 89
NO. OF GUESTS 3 SERVER NO 9 TOTAL 1559
LIQUOR 195 195
SALESPERSON TYPE TRANS.NO. STORE TERM. DATE
3 0020 230085 SEP0280
DEPT./CLASS DESCRIPTION QUAN./TAX AMOUNT
103 RESTAURANT
103 14.70
SUBTOTAL 14.70
TAX .89
TOTAL 15.59
TOTAL LIQUOR 380
FOOD ITEM CHARGE
345
345
335
150
110
185
1470
Thank You—Have a Nice Day TOTAL FOOD 1559
F1581 (1-80)

UNDERCHARGE

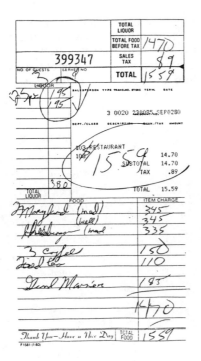

Forgot to charge for liquor..$3.90.

Figure 4.5. A Miscalculated Guest Check.
(Courtesy of Litton, Sweda International, Inc.)

TOTAL LIQUOR
TOTAL FOOD BEFORE TAX 13.50
393847
SALES TAX 81
NO. OF GUESTS 3 SERVER NO 6 TOTAL 14.31
LIQUOR
SALESPERSON TYPE TRANS.NO. STORE TERM. DATE
3 0028 230085 SEP0480
ACCOUNT NO.
DEPT./CLASS DESCRIPTION QUAN./TAX AMOUNT
103 RESTAURANT
103 1 13.50
SUBTOTAL 13.50
TAX .81
TOTAL 14.31
TOTAL LIQUOR
FOOD ITEM CHARGE
salad bar 4.25
salad bar 4.25
4.45
tossed salad
boiled
iced Tea 55
coffee 50
Thank You—Have a Nice Day TOTAL FOOD 13.50
F1581 (1-80)

UNDERCHARGE

Mistake in addition.
Should be $14.00..
undercharge $.50.

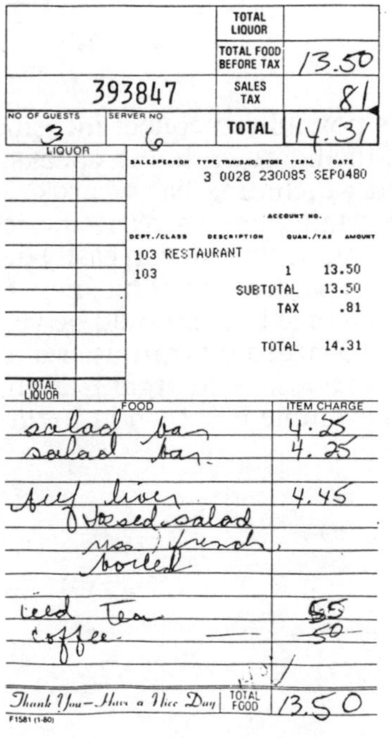

Figure 4.6. A Miscalculated Guest Check.
(Courtesy of Litton, Sweda International, Inc.)

– **Guest-check tracking.** To ensure accuracy when the previous balance is picked up, POS equipment can maintain a record of all outstanding guest checks. In addition, the machine will automatically begin printing on the guest check just below where it had previously printed, thereby providing a much more legible check. An example is shown in Figure 4.7.

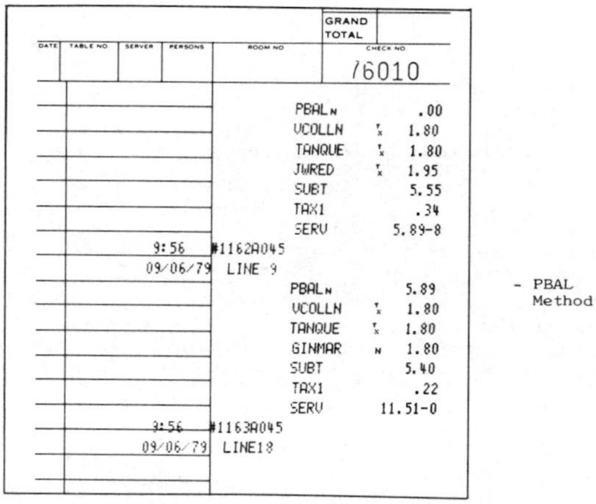

Figure 4.7. A Guest Check Printed on an Electronic Cash Register as Part of the Precheck Function.

(Courtesy of Litton, Sweda International, Inc.)

– **Multiple tendering.** It is possible to collect information for several different types of tender, including cash and checks, and several different types of credit cards, including bank cards (Visa and Mastercard) and travel and entertainment cards (American Express and Diner's Club). In this way, management can easily determine whether the dollar amount or relative percentage of business for any one credit card or type of tender has changed. This could be very important, for the commission percentage charged by various credit cards differs, as does the time it takes for a foodservice organization to receive credit for a credit card sale. An example is shown in Figure 4.8.

SWEDA INTRODUCES		
MODELS 4615-4625		
XXXX		
	(#01)	
	(#02)	- Register Requested
	(#32)	
TTL		
CID		
	586.03	- Cash-in-Drawer
0CART	0.00%	- Percent of Daily Sales*
	.00	- Miscellaneous Tender
7CHEK	5.94%	- Percent of Daily Sales
	95.84	- Check Tender
0PO		- Paid Outs of Cash,
	.00	Check and Miscellaneous
6RA		
	376.50	- Received on Account
1TIP		
	5.00	- Tips (Prints if tips net CID)
SUBT		
	310.37	- Subtotal
4AMEX	3.83%	- Percent of DSLE
	61.75	- Charge Tender
3VISA	5.45%	
	87.92	
2DNRS	2.43%	
	39.25	
3MAST	66.32%	
	1069.83	
0HOUS	0.00%	
	.00	
1MISC	2.43%	
	39.17	
0PKCH		
	.00	- Pick ups of Charges
1TIP		
	5.00	- Tips
2SERV		
	17.88	- Service Total
1CKPD		
	7.98	- Checks Paid Total
@CKPD		
	7.98	- Average Check Paid•
TTL		
	1613.19	- Total
	(#01)	
	(#02)	- Registers polled
	(#32)	
10:15 #0106 032		
10/29/79		
THANK YOU		

*Percent of Daily Sales = Tender Total ÷ Daily Sales
•Average Check Paid = CKPD ÷ CKPD Counter

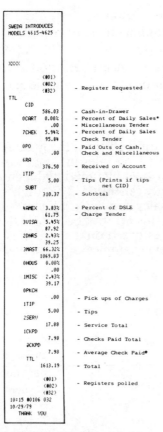

Figure 4.8. A Summary Tender Report.
(Courtesy of Litton, Sweda International, Inc.)

- **Check endorsement.** Checks can be endorsed at the time they are accepted, thereby increasing security and saving time. An example is shown in Figure 4.9.

FOR DEPOSIT ONLY FIRST NATIONAL
ACCT #123/456/789
CHEK 28.00
10/12/79#0508F001

Figure 4.9. Check Endorsement.
(Courtesy of Litton, Sweda International, Inc.)

For a marketing information system, POS equipment also offers many advantages. POS equipment can provide a great deal of useful marketing information at a very low cost. The initial purchase price is well within the affordable range for nearly all foodservice organizations. The types of marketing information readily available and the uses for this information are outlined as follows:

- **Sales histories.** Without question, the greatest value of POS equipment is the manner in which sales information can be collected. Reports that break down sales by individual menu items and by department group can be easily generated. The total dollar value of sales and percentage of total sales for each item are also readily available. Management can use this information to evaluate menu sales trends and menu item changes based on a solid sales history. Figures 4.10, 4.11, and 4.12 illustrate examples of these types of reports.

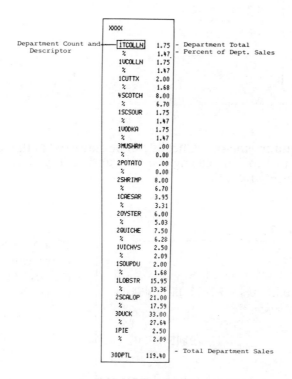

Figure 4.10. A Full Department Report.

(Courtesy of Litton, Sweda International, Inc.)

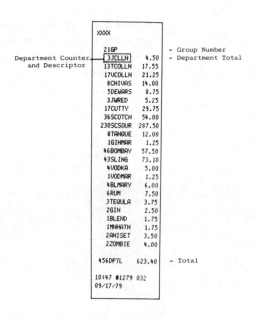

Figure 4.11. A Department Group Report.
(Courtesy of Litton, Sweda International, Inc.)

Figure 4.12. An Individual Department Report.
(Courtesy of Litton, Sweda International, Inc.)

– **Service personnel productivity.**   Service personnel assume the critical function of personal selling. Through the suggestive-selling efforts of these individuals, total sales volume and the average guest check can be increased. Not all sales personnel, however, are equally successful in these efforts. Figure 4.13 illustrates a productivity report for service personnel. This report provides the following information for each service person: total individual sales for the shift, percentage of total

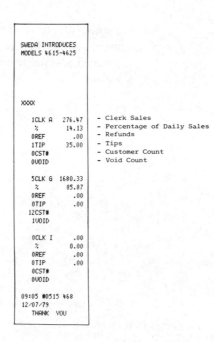

```
SWEDA INTRODUCES
MODELS 4615-4625




XXXX

   1CLK A   276.47
      %       14.13
   0REF         .00
   1TIP       35.00
   0CST#
   0VOID

   5CLK G  1680.33
      %       85.87
   0REF         .00
   0TIP         .00
   12CST#
   1VOID

   0CLK I       .00
      %        0.00
   0REF         .00
   0TIP         .00
   0CST#
   0VOID

09:05 #0515 468
12/07/79
   THANK  YOU
```

- Clerk Sales
- Percentage of Daily Sales
- Refunds
- Tips
- Customer Count
- Void Count

Figure 4.13. A Serviceperson's Productivity Report. (Courtesy of Litton, Sweda International, Inc.)

restaurant sales generated by each service person, refunds, dollar value of tips, customer count, and void count. By carefully studying this report, management can identify weak service personnel and take corrective action.

These examples represent only a portion of the total information-generating capacity of POS equipment. POS equipment presents foodservice managers with the opportunity to collect a wealth of valuable marketing information to facilitate marketing decision making and improve the marketing effectiveness of any foodservice organization.

Externally Generated Marketing Information

While externally generated marketing information is extremely valuable, it is normally not collected on a daily basis, as is the case with internally generated marketing information. This is due to a much larger investment of time, money, and other scarce resources that externally generated information requires.

Sources of Information

Management should consider using a wide variety of sources of external marketing information. Literally, thousands of sources of external information are available, and these sources are limited only by management's own efforts to locate them. Following are a few sources typically viewed as sources of external marketing information:

- Trade associations, such as the National Restaurant Association or the International Food Service Executives Association
- City Chambers of Commerce or local planning boards
- Trade journals and periodicals, such as *Food Service Marketing, Restaurants & Institutions, Restaurant Hospitality, Nation's Restaurant News,* and *Restaurant Business*
- University bureaus, foundations, and the Cooperative Extension Service
- Government publications concerning population and retail business census data
- Small Business Administration publications
- Syndicated services, such as Harris or Gallup Polls, Target Group Index, or W. R. Simmons
- Public or university libraries
- City convention or visitor bureaus

A number of guidelines should be followed when collecting external information. If these guidelines are not followed, much time, effort, and money are likely to be wasted. They are outlined as follows:

- **State known facts.**   Before undertaking an external study, make an accounting of all data currently available. It makes little sense to conduct an extensive study or pay to have one conducted only to produce information that is available from existing sources. By stating all known facts, management establishes a base from which to work. This base may easily be established by looking at all internal sources previously discussed and collecting all data available internally before proceeding with more expensive, external information-gathering techniques.
- **List specific goals and objectives.**   Once a base of information has been established, a plan must be formulated. Goals and objectives are the basis for this plan. Without goals and objectives, an external study could easily go astray and would not yield the information needed by a foodservice manager. The manager needs to ask, "What do I want to learn? What types of information about my clientele, my competition, or my own operation would be most useful?" Having answered such

questions, an operator can begin to formulate potential questions for a survey to provide the desired information.

– **Collect all relevant data.**   At this point the actual legwork must be done to ensure an adequate sample. The information gathered must be both valid and reliable. *Validity* is the degree to which the data gathered measure what they are supposed to measure. *Reliability* is the degree with which data consistently measure whatever they measure. Data collection is extremely important and is not a process to be treated lightly. The information generated will only be as accurate and valid as the procedures used to generate the information. For this reason, great care must be taken to assure that the information is gathered correctly.

–**Summarize the data and analyze the situation.**   No matter what data collection methods are used, some type of summary and analysis must be done to reduce the data into a manageable package. This may then be used by management to make a wide variety of decisions.

Primary and Secondary Data

Primary Data.   Primary data are original research done to answer current questions regarding a specific operation. An example is a foodservice manager who attempts to ascertain consumer attitudes toward new menu offerings or solicit consumer perceptions of increased menu prices or different portion sizes. This type of data is very pertinent to an individual operation but may not be applicable to other situations.

The advantages to primary data include

– **Specificity.**   These data are tailored to one operation only and can provide excellent information for decision-making purposes.
– **Practicality.**   Just as the data are geared toward one operation, they can provide solid "real life" information and a practical foundation to be used in the decision-making process.

Drawbacks to using primary data include

– **Cost.**   For an individual manager, gathering primary data is extremely expensive. To gather primary data even from a city of 100,000 people may prove to be a monumental task for an operator and cost too much time and money.
– **Time lag.**   Marketing decisions often must be made quickly, yet it requires a good deal of time to conduct a thorough information-gathering study. While a manager is collecting the data, the competition may be driving the foodservice operation into bankruptcy.

- **Duplication.** While primary data are geared toward a specific operation, other sources of existing data may closely duplicate the information collected and would therefore be appropriate for decision-making purposes. This duplication of effort is very expensive and primary data collection should therefore be undertaken only after all secondary data sources have been exhausted.

Secondary Data. This type of data is information already available from other sources. It may include such information as a nationwide average guest-check figure for various types of foodservice organizations, growth patterns of a city, or existing consumer attitude surveys. The National Restaurant Association has published a series of consumer attitude surveys that pertain to many facets of the foodservice industry. Information concerning these surveys may be obtained by writing to the National Restaurant Association, 311 First Street, N.W., Washington, D.C. 20001.

A shrewd foodservice manager will make a thorough check of all available secondary data sources before undertaking primary data collection. Secondary data can save many personnel hours and a great deal of money. The major advantages of using secondary data are

- **Cost.** It is much less expensive to obtain information from existing sources than to develop entirely new data. These existing sources may require a nominal charge for the information, but it will be much less than the cost of undertaking primary data collection.
- **Timeliness.** Secondary data are available almost instantaneously. A foodservice operator can have access to data very quickly and therefore does not have to wait weeks or perhaps months for primary data to be collected, tabulated, and analyzed.

By using secondary data whenever possible, a manager saves the frustration of designing the data-collection instrument, pretesting the instrument, devising a sampling plan, gathering the data, checking the data for accuracy and omissions, tabulating the data, and summarizing and analyzing the data. Instead, a manager can merely locate the appropriate source and extract and record the information desired. This process can be completed in a few hours or days, while primary data collection can take weeks or months to complete.

Secondary data collection is not, however, without drawbacks. These include

- **Limited applicability.** A restaurant manager has no assurance that information gathered by others will be applicable to a particular foodservice operation. For example, information gathered in New York about the popularity of a specific menu item may not be useful to a manager located in the Midwest. Information that pertains to one operation may apply only to that operation and can be of limited value to anyone else.

– **Information frequently out of date.**   Managers need current and accurate information on which to base decisions. All too often, secondary data are not as useful as they might be merely because they are not current. For example, a consumer attitude survey concerning restaurant price and value perceptions conducted four years ago would be of little use to a foodservice manager making plans today. During the four years, a great many changes in consumer attitudes are likely to have taken place. These changes in attitudes will make the original data outdated and useful only in a historical sense. If a foodservice manager were to make use of less than timely data, the results are likely to be less than satisfactory.

– **Reliability.**   Whenever a foodservice operator uses secondary data as the basis for a decision, the manager runs the risk that the information may or may not be reliable and accurate. A manager would do well to ask, "Who collected the data and what method of data collection was used?" Information is only as good as the individuals who collect it and the methods they use. If a study is administered in a haphazard manner, the results and conclusions should be viewed with caution.

Market Research Methodology

Research Methodology

Market research efforts are undertaken to answer a wide variety of questions. Such questions might include, "Where do my customers live? How frequently do people dine out in this area? In what types of restaurants do they most frequently dine? If the seating capacity of restaurant X is expanded by 20 percent, what impact will this have on sales and profits?"

Conducting a market research effort is not an inexpensive proposition, and when research is undertaken, care must be taken to assure that the proper methods are used. This remains true whether the foodservice organization conducts its own market research or relies on external consultants. Market research data are only as good as the methodology used. If poor methodology is used, the results are not likely to describe the situation accurately. If this is the case, marketing decisions based on this information are not likely to be the most appropriate decisions.

Following are six steps that will generally ensure that the outcome of the research project will accurately reflect the true situation:

1. **Define the problem.**   Before initiating any market research effort, the problem should be clearly defined. What does the research effort propose to do? What types of questions need to be asked? What solutions are sought? A strong tendency among all researchers, especially novice researchers, is to rush into data collection without giving adequate thought to defining the problem. This tendency should be vigorously avoided. A small amount of time spent in defining and refining the problem will save many hours of time later on.

2. **Conduct a preliminary investigation.**   The purpose of this step is to save both time and money. Little can be gained by researching an area or problem that has been researched before. Therefore, all internally generated marketing information should first be examined to collect data that may be relevant to the stated problem. Second, all available secondary data should also be reviewed for the same reason. These two generic types of information should save a great deal of time and are likely to produce a few tentative answers to the research problem. These tentative answers can then be tested in later steps.

3. **Plan the research.**   Based on the defined problem and the data collected from secondary sources, plans should be formulated concerning the method by which further data should be collected. Numerous methodologies are commonly used; they include questionnaire surveys, sales forecasts, consumer motivation research, as well as quantitative methods.

4. **Collect the data.**   Once the research has been planned, the data should be collected in the manner prescribed. No shortcuts should be taken; a slow, systematic approach is best. Every effort should be taken to avoid contamination of the data by extraneous variables.

5. **Analyze the data.**   As statistical procedures have become more sophisticated, so too have the approaches to data analysis. Procedures that used to take hours of calculations by researchers can now be done in a matter of seconds or minutes with the use of computers. The general rule in analyzing data is to complete the relatively simple analysis before advancing to the more sophisticated.

6. **Summarize the data and reach conclusions.**   Based on the five previous steps, management should now have a clear picture of the problem, the key variables, the relationships among these variables, and the courses of action available. In many cases, the decision will be clear-cut; in other cases, managerial judgment will be the deciding factor. The important point to remember is that by engaging in a methodical approach to the research effort, better decisions are likely to result.

Step 3 involves a research plan. Following are three common approaches to a research plan: (1) the experimental method, (2) the observational method, and (3) the survey method.

The *experimental method* is the most formal of the three methods and finds only limited use in the foodservice industry. When using this method, a researcher divides the sample of people into groups and exposes each group to a different treatment. For example, McDonald's Corporation uses cities across the country as test-market centers. In each of these centers, McDonald's introduces or "test-markets" new products to obtain customer reaction to new items and to project future sales of these items. Sales may then be compared with other test-market centers to determine popularity of new and old items and to decide which products will be introduced systemwide. It is quite expensive to conduct this type of study, and it is also quite difficult to control all external variables that may affect the outcome of the experiment. For example, such external variables as the weather or the advertising efforts of competitive foodservice operations could easily have an effect on the sales volume of new products. Because of the expense, only the large chains are able to conduct such studies on a regular basis.

Many large chains, such as McDonald's, Burger King, and Wendy's, are continuously conducting experimental test-market studies. These studies allow these foodservice giants accurately to predict the future sales of a new product. McDonald's and Burger King test-marketed a steak sandwich entree for some time, with the hope that it would increase the check average and allow them to appeal to a wider targeted market. At the same time, Wendy's test-marketed a salad bar in order to diversify the menu and broaden market attraction. A corporation that has the financial size and stability needed to engage in test marketing is able to gain additional competitive advantage.

The *observational method* involves observing consumer behavior and making organized notes to document or record the observed behavior. When doing this type of research, it is important that all individuals acting as observers record their observations in the same manner. Therefore, if more than one individual is recording observations, it is imperative that a common method of observing behavior and recording information be established. This is done to assure consistency among the different observers. The observational method will not be effective unless it is carried out in this way.

The observational method might be used to record observed reactions of consumers to various personal selling approaches. Suppose a manager instructed the service personnel to use three different sales approaches for the promotion of wine. Each service person would then be instructed to record both the approach used and the customer's reaction. After a period of time, perhaps two weeks, the manager could then compare the recorded information of all service personnel and might better determine which promotional technique would likely be most effective for future use.

Such information is easily used in the foodservice industry, but the observational method is not without its drawbacks. The major drawback is that it is difficult to observe and document all relevant customer behavior. It is also difficult to instruct and train all the observers so that all of them observe and record information in exactly the same manner.

When used properly, the *survey method* can gather a great deal of useful information for a foodservice manager. The survey method is adaptable to a variety of situations and is relatively inexpensive. Surveys may be accomplished using a number of different methods, including telephone surveys, direct mail surveys, or personal interviews.

Telephone surveys are the easiest to implement and produce very quick results. One major advantage to this type of survey is the cost. No travel is involved, and a single individual may contact and solicit answers from a large number of people in a fairly short period of time. On the other hand, there is no face-to-face contact, and people are often not inclined to answer questions over the phone. The reliability of the answers received over the telephone is also in question.

Direct mail surveys are used a great deal too. They offer ease of completion and moderate cost, but they present two major drawbacks. First, the rate of return is normally quite low. Often, less than 25 percent of the surveys are properly completed and returned, and it is extremely hazardous to base business decisions on such a small return. The risk always exists that those individuals who returned the surveys are atypical and may not provide answers and opinions that truly represent the majority of the targeted market segment. Second, direct mail surveys do not allow any in-depth questioning, and they do not allow follow-up questions. The respondent merely sees the written questions and has no opportunity for clarification. This may make it more difficult to generate answers that reflect the complexity of opinion within the targeted market segments.

Personal interviews allow more in-depth questioning. An interviewer normally uses a guide sheet to direct the interview and may adjust the questioning to focus on a point of special interest or to follow-up an answer given by the respondent. There are two drawbacks to personal interviews as a surveying technique. The major drawback is cost. It is extremely expensive to have an interviewer spend a long period of time with one individual in order to gather information. An in-depth interview can last as long as two hours; hence the number of individuals that can be interviewed is limited, and the cost per interview is quite high. The cost of travel also makes this type of survey expensive. Second, a good deal of interviewer training must be done so that interviewers are effective. In addition, supervision is required in order to have control over the interviewers.

Step 5 of the six-step research methodology is data analysis. The most basic approach to data analysis is to calculate the relevant measures of central tendency such as the *mean* (arithmetic average), the *median* (midpoint), and the *mode* (the most frequently selected response). Additionally, the measures of variability should include the *range* (difference between the highest and lowest score, such as a 1–10 rating) and the *standard deviation* (the distribution of scores on both sides of the mean).

Once these calculations are completed, cross tabulations are often performed to determine whether a relationship exists. Correlation coefficients can be calculated to describe not only the relative strength of the relationship but also whether it is positive or negative. For example, suppose a foodservice market researcher wanted to determine whether there was a relationship between annual income in dollars and the number of times per week that adults dine outside the home. The results of the research study might indicate a high positive correlation (+0.90) between annual income and the number of times per week adults dined outside the home. This means that as annual income rises, so too does the number of times that an adult dines outside the home. A negative correlation is just the opposite; if the relationship in the example were a high negative (−0.90) correlation, the number of times per week that adults dine outside the home would decrease as annual income increases. Correlation coefficients can range from −1.00 to +1.00. The larger (closer to 1.00) the correlation coefficient (positive or negative), the stronger the relationship.

Multivariate statistical techniques are also commonly used in marketing research. These techniques include multiple regression analysis, discriminant analysis, and factor analysis. *Multiple regression analysis* seeks to analyze the influence that one or more variables, independent variables, have on another variable, the dependent variable. For example, what influence does radio advertising have on sales volume? *Discriminant analysis* seeks to classify variables rather than assign a numerical value. For example, what are the traits or characteristics of those individuals who dine outside the home more than 10 times per week on average? *Factor analysis* is a statistical technique used to discover a few basic factors that may explain intercorrelations among a large number of variables.

Statistical procedures are very useful in analyzing data, but managers must also rely on critical thinking and the role of intangibles in reaching their conclusions.

Sampling Methodology

Market research data are often based on *probability sampling;* a relatively small sample is randomly selected, and the results from this sample are generalized to the larger population. It is imperative that the market researcher select the random sample with care, for errors in sample selection can affect the results and hence the generalizations. The three sampling methods pertinent to a foodservice operation are (1) simple random sampling, (2) cluster sampling, and (3) systematic sampling.

For any of these methods, the first requirement is to define the population from which to gather information. The *population* is simply a definition of the group of individuals from which to gather information. For example, two specific populations might be (1) all males and females between the ages of 20 and 26 who are not married and (2) all males and females who earn more than 12,000 dollars per year and work within one mile of our restaurant.

The next step or requirement is to determine the number of individuals to survey. This is known as the *sample size*. The size of the sample really depends on the risk a foodservice manager is willing to assume. As more individuals are surveyed, the degree of risk is reduced because the information gathered is more likely to represent the entire population, or universe. The risk is reduced because the information gathered tends to be more valid and reliable as more individuals are surveyed. But the question arises: How many people should be surveyed? This is not an easy question, and there is no set answer. The sample size necessary is directly related to the size of the population. As the number of individuals in the population increases, the percentage of the population included in the sample decreases. The following examples illustrate this point.

Population Size	Necessary Sample Size
500	217
5,000	357
50,000	381
100,000	384

Having identified and defined the population and determined the number of individuals to be surveyed, the next steps are to select the individuals and implement the survey. If a survey is to have any usefulness, it must be implemented with great care. A poorly chosen sample is not likely to produce information that represents the opinions of the entire population. Without information that is truly representative of the entire population, it is extremely difficult to make a sound decision. Any decisions based on insufficient or inaccurate data are tenuous at best.

One of the most popular methods of sample selection is *random sampling*. This method allows each and every member of a population an equal chance of being selected. Random sampling is probably the best method for a foodservice manager to use when undertaking a survey. It does not guarantee a representative sample, but it comes as close as any available method. The steps in selecting a random sample are

1. Identify and define the population.
2. Determine the desired sample size.
3. List all members of the population.
4. Assign each member of the population a consecutive number starting with one.
5. Select an arbitrary number from a table of random numbers. Random numbers tables are easily generated by computer program, and can also be found in research methodology textbooks. One excellent source is *Foundations of Behavioral Research,* 2nd Edition, by Fred N. Kerlinger (New York: Holt, Rinehart, and Winston, Inc., 1973). The number will correspond with the numbers assigned in Step # 4.
6. Repeat Step 5 until enough individuals are selected to complete the desired sample size.

Another sampling method that a foodservice manager should consider is cluster sampling. *Cluster sampling* involves the use of previously formed groups rather than separately chosen individuals. If a manager surveyed all the consumers who patronized a particular foodservice operation on a given day or during a specific meal period, this would be a cluster sample, and the patrons would be the cluster. The manager has no control over the selection of the individuals that make up the cluster but uses the entire cluster as a sample. Similar clusters might be all the individuals who live in one apartment building or in series of buildings.

Systematic sampling is also of potential interest to a foodservice manager. *Systematic sampling* involves using an existing listing of names (often in alphabetical order) and selecting a representative sample from these names. The steps are

Step	**Example**
1. Identify and define the population.	1. The entire population of city XYZ, population 100,000.
2. Determine the desired sample size.	2. The approximate sample size for a population of 100,000 is 384 individuals.
3. Obtain a list of the population.	3. *Source:* Telephone directory
4. Determine k by dividing the size of the population by the sample size.	4. $k = \dfrac{100,000}{384}$ $k = 260.$

Step	Example
5. Start at a random point near the top of the list.	5. Randomly selected name near the top of the list.
6. Take every *k*th name on the list until the desired sample size is reached.	6. Every 260th name until the desired sample size is reached.

Survey Instrument Design

Survey questionnaires are commonly used by market reseachers within the foodservice industry because they are relatively inexpensive, and with them, a broad range of information can be collected. Surveys can be used in direct mail, personal interviews, and telephone interviews. The design of surveys, however, is by no means a simple task. It may appear to be fairly easy to jot down a few questions and develop a survey instrument, but this is far from the truth. The design of a successful survey instrument is a difficult task, and a great deal of time and thought needs to go into development. Following is a series of questions to help a survey instrument designer begin.

- Who does what, when, where, and how?
- What do the respondents know about the subject?
- How do the respondents feel about the subject?
- Why do the respondents act or feel the way they do?

When developing a survey instrument, the instrument designer should make it as clear and as interesting to follow as possible. By starting the survey with easy, yet interesting questions, the designer allows the respondent to become involved and respond to all of the questions on the survey instrument. Two types of questions may be included in a survey; these are the open-ended and the closed-ended question. An open-ended question might read like this: "Please offer any comments and suggestions as to how we might improve our restaurant." (This is followed by a few lines for writing.) On the other hand, a closed-ended question might look like the following example:

Please check the box that most closely represents your feelings.

	Excellent	Very Good	Average	Fair	Poor
Quality of food					
Quality of beverage					
Quality of service					

Both types of questions are widely used and offer certain advantages. An open-ended question allows the respondent to reply with a personal touch, given a few brief lines in which to write the answer, but this type of survey does make tabulation of responses more difficult. On the other hand, a closed-ended question is easy to tabulate, but the respondent has very little choice of response and merely decides the most appropriate preworded answer. Open-ended questions are most effective if used to determine subjective opinions, while closed-ended questions are best for gathering objective information and facts.

Surveys are used for a multitude of reasons, and it is difficult to establish any concrete rules that will apply in all situations. The following general guidelines however, apply to the construction of all survey instruments.

- Avoid the use of technical language. Ask the questions using language the respondent understands and is familiar with.
- Avoid long and wordy questions. These will tend to discourage the respondent and may reduce the number of respondents to a written survey.
- Avoid questions that are vague and general in nature.
- Avoid including more than one idea per question.
- Avoid personal questions that might embarrass the respondent.
- Avoid putting any personal bias into the questions.
- Make sure that you fully understand the purpose of the question, for if you do not, the respondent is not likely to understand the question.
- In closed-ended questions, provide a "don't know" or "no opinion" response where appropriate.
- All responses in a closed-ended question should be mutually exclusive.
- The number of choices in a closed-ended question need not be limited to five or six responses; a larger number of responses can be used where appropriate.
- Indicate very clearly in the directions the number of choices a respondent should check for a closed-ended question.
- Avoid talking down to the respondent.
- Watch for words and phrases that have more than one meaning, as this can confuse the respondent.
- Questions of a personal nature are generally less threatening if they are placed toward the end of the survey.

Surveys are extremely useful to the management of a foodservice organization. They can help gather a great deal of useful information about present and potential patrons. The appendixes of this chapter contain examples of survey instruments used to gather marketing information.

The Marketing Audit

In recent years, the term *marketing audit* has been used more frequently by owners and managers of foodservice organizations. What does the term mean? How can a marketing audit be used? Should all types of foodservice operations engage in marketing audits? A marketing audit is simply a tool used to examine and evaluate the effectiveness of an organization's marketing strategies and practices. In an audit, management takes a broad view and seeks to analyze the organization's performance against prestated objectives as well as environmental conditions.

To achieve maximum use, it is recommended that foodservice operations undertake a marketing audit in a systematic way and on a regular basis. The vast majority of foodservice firms should plan to conduct an audit on at least an annual basis. Each manager must determine precisely the marketing elements that are to be subject to an audit. The following is a suggested list of components for a thorough marketing audit:

- **Marketing environment audit.** It is advisable to begin with a brief study of the macroenvironment in which the foodservice operates; this means looking at the large-scale economic, social, political, and technological factors that play on the industry. In addition, the microenvironment should also be reviewed; this means examining the competitive environment that immediately surrounds the foodservice operation. This study should consist of markets, consumers, and competitors.
- **Marketing strategy audit.** In light of environmental conditions, the firm's marketing strategies must be carefully reviewed. Goals and objectives related to marketing must be reviewed carefully to determine (1) whether the goals are still appropriate and (2) the best strategies for successfully achieving goals if the goals are still appropriate. During the 1960s and 1970s most large foodservice firms were devoted to a strategy of rapid expansion as the best route to financial success. This strategy, however, is now being questioned, and increasing individual unit efficiency and productivity is instead being viewed as the best strategy for the 1980s and beyond.
- **Marketing sales effectiveness audit.** Consumer reaction to the sales and marketing efforts must be studied carefully. How effective are the service and sales personnel? Do they really serve the needs of the foodservice operation's consumers? Do they adequately engage in personal selling of the products and services offered?
- **External and internal marketing productivity audit.** Efforts that have been undertaken to increase sales must be examined. All advertising and promotional efforts must be examined carefully to determine which efforts yield the best results per dollar spent. Zero-based budgeting is a technique that might prove to be very useful in this effort.

In addition, marketing audits can prove to be extremely useful. Marketing audits can be used to

- Search for new opportunities to pursue
- Search for weaknesses within the organization that should be eliminated
- Provide current information about the micro- and macroenvironments.

Marketing information systems should be designed for the purpose of producing data that are useful to a foodservice manager. This information can be used as a basis for decisions. This information should not, however, be used as the sole determining factor when making any decision. Two other factors, experience and intuition, also come into play when making a decision. If all decisions could be based solely on information produced by marketing information systems, there would be no need for managers. Instead, machines could be used to tabulate the information and predict the correct answer. Managers, however, have far too many uncontrollable variables to contend with in gathering marketing information. For this reason a foodservice manager must view the situation by considering (1) marketing information, (2) previous experience in similar situations, and (3) intuition as to what the future holds. Based on these three factors, a decision must be made, and the foodservice manager must accept the final responsibility for the decision.

Summary

A foodservice marketing information system is a structured organization of people and procedures designed to generate a flow of data from inside and outside the operation. It is used as a basis for marketing decisions. A marketing information system can be used in many ways by a resourceful foodservice manager. It can, for example, be an information source for decisions related to market segmentation, advertising, and menu item changes. A marketing information system makes use of environmental scanning of three subenvironments: (1) the macroenvironment, (2) the competitive environment, and (3) the organizational environment.

Marketing information systems involve both internally and externally generated marketing information, each with its own unique set of sources for information and its own methodology for obtaining necessary information. Data collected may be classified as either primary or secondary. Primary data result from original research, while secondary data are information taken from sources that already exist in printed form. The methodology used to design and implement a research study is critical to the success of the research efforts. A six-step approach to research methodology is a useful guide.

Survey design is extremely important, for the techniques used will affect the validity and reliability of the information generated by a survey instrument. For this reason, the individual who designs a survey instrument must pay particular attention to several key guidelines.

Finally, the marketing audit can be a very useful tool for a foodservice manager. An audit can identify potential strengths and pinpoint existing weaknesses that a manager can work toward improving. Just as other types of audits, such as financial audits, have tremendous value to a manager, so too does a marketing audit, which critically examines the marketing function of a foodservice organization.

Appendix 4.1
National Restaurant Association
Customer Attitude Questionnaire

We would appreciate it if you would take a few minutes to complete the following questionnaire so that we can find out more about our customers.

1. Which of the following best describes where you were just prior to coming to this restaurant?   (Check one)

(4) _____   1 At work
    _____   2 At home
    _____   3 Shopping
    _____   4 Social or recreational activity
    _____   5 Travel or vacation
    _____   6 Other, please specify _____

2. Which of the following best describes where you will go immediately after you leave this restaurant? (Check one)

(5) _____   1 Work
    _____   2 Home
    _____   3 Shopping
    _____   4 Social or recreational activity
    _____   5 Travel or vacation
    _____   6 Other, please specify _____

3. Excluding this restaurant, what is your favorite restaurant for dinner?   (Please give full name of restaurant.)

_____

4. Please compare this restaurant with the favorite dinner restaurant you have mentioned for each of the categories listed below. (Check under the appropriate word how you feel this restaurant compares with your favorite one.)

CHARACTERISTICS	MUCH BETTER	BETTER	SAME	WORSE	MUCH WORSE
(6) Service	( )	( )	( )	( )	( )
(7) Cleanliness	( )	( )	( )	( )	( )
(8) Quality of food	( )	( )	( )	( )	( )
(9) Menu variety offered	( )	( )	( )	( )	( )
(10) Employee friendliness	( )	( )	( )	( )	( )
(11) Atmosphere	( )	( )	( )	( )	( )
(12) Convenience of location	( )	( )	( )	( )	( )
(13) Value for the price	( )	( )	( )	( )	( )

5. How many people are in your party today?

(14) _____ 1 One   _____ 4 Four
     _____ 2 Two   _____ 5 Five
     _____ 3 Three   _____ 6 Six or more

6. How often do you eat at this restaurant?

(15) _____ 1 More than once a week
     _____ 2 About once a week
     _____ 3 About every 2–3 weeks
     _____ 4 About once a month
     _____ 5 About once every 2–3 months
     _____ 6 Less than once every 3 months
     _____ 7 First visit

7. Who chose this restaurant for today's meal?

(16) _____ 1 Myself
     _____ 2 Another family member
     _____ 3 Co-worker
     _____ 4 Friend
     _____ 5 Other, please specify _____

The last few questions are just for classification purposes. All answers will be confidential.

8. How old are you?

(17) _____ (1) 18 to 24   _____ (4) 45 to 54
     _____ (2) 25 to 34   _____ (5) 55 to 64
     _____ (3) 35 to 44   _____ (6) 65 or older

9. Are you a male or a female?

(18) _____ 1 Male   _____ 2 Female

10. How many members are there in your household?

(19) _____ 1 One person   _____ 4 Four persons
     _____ 2 Two persons   _____ 5 Five or more persons
     _____ 3 Three persons

11. How many wage earners are there in your household?

(20) _____ 1 One   _____ 2 Two   _____ 3 Three or more

12. What is the best description of your occupation?

(21) _____ 1 Sales   _____ 7 Management/
     _____ 2 Clerical   Administration
     _____ 3 Farmer/Rancher   _____ 8 Service Worker
     _____ 4 Self-Employed   _____ 9 Housewife
     _____ 5 Professional/   _____ 10 Retired
              Technical   _____ 11 Student
     _____ 6 Government   _____ 12 Other, please
                                          specify _____

13. What is your approximate household income?

(22) _____ 1 Under $10,000   _____ 4 $20,000 to $24,999
     _____ 2 $10,000 to $14,999   _____ 5 $25,000 to $29,999
     _____ 3 $15,000 to $19,999   _____ 6 $30,000 and over

Reprinted from: *Market Research for the Restaraunteur.* Courtesy of: The National Restaurant Association, Washington, D.C.

Appendix 4.2 Telephone Survey

Courtesy: Robert Harr, Vice President, Holiday Central Commissary.

Name _____ Telephone No. _____ Area _____

Hello is Mr. _____ or Mrs. _____ there?

(If _____ is not at home, terminate and call back later.)

My name is _____ and I am doing research for the restaurant industry and would like to ask you a few questions. Do you mind?

1. Do you or your family ever dine out for dinner in the _____ area?
   Yes___ No___
   a. If yes, would that be yourself? ___ Your family? _____ or both? _____
   b. If yes, approximately how often per month? _____ dinners

2. Approximately what price per person do you spend when dining out for dinner? _____.

3. In order of importance, what three restaurants do you normally visit for dinner in the _____ area?

Why these restaurants? (Ask separately)

1. _____   1. _____
2. _____   2. _____
3. _____   3. _____

4. I would like to read you a list of foods and ask you which do you think is the most healthy, natural and nutritious:

   a. Most nutritious.   b. Which is the least healthy, natural and nutritious?

   _____ Roast Beef   _____ Roast Beef
   _____ Hamburgers   _____ Hamburgers
   _____ Roast Chicken   _____ Roast Chicken
   _____ Barbecued Pork   _____ Barbecued Pork
   _____ Barbecued Chicken   _____ Barbecued Chicken
   _____ Broiled Fish   _____ Broiled Fish

5. Have you ever patronized a restaurant that served Barbecued Ribs and Chicken?
   Yes _____ No _____. If yes, about how often? _____ If no, would you mind telling why you haven't? _____

6. Which restaurant did you last patronize for dinner? _____

7. What did you like best about _____ ? _____

8. What did you like least about _____ ? _____

9. How would you rate _____ on the following categories in terms of poor, fair, good, and superior?

                                    Poor   Fair   Good   Superior
   a. Quality of food served
   b. Selection of the menu
   c. Size of portions served
   d. Courtesy of all employees
   e. Speed & attentiveness of service
   f. The prices
   g. Overall cleanliness of restaurant
   h. Decor

10. For poor/fair ratings ask: why do you consider them to be poor/fair? (Probe for details.)

   _____

   If menu selection, what item is wanted? _____

11. Is there anything you would like to see changed at _____ ?
     Yes _____ No _____. If yes, what? _____

12. What do you feel would be the advantage of a restaurant featuring Roast Chicken and Barbecued Ribs? None _____
     Other _____

(IF NONE SKIP TO QUESTION 17 & CONTINUE)

13. What additional menu items do you feel that a restaurant offering Roast Chicken and Barbecued Ribs should have? _____

14. What price range do you feel that a restaurant offering Roast Chicken and Barbecued Ribs should have? _____

15. Could you describe the style of service that a restaurant offering Roast Chicken and Barbecued Ribs should have? _____

16. What type of person do you feel this type of restaurant would attract?
     _____

17. In what range does your age fall?   18–34 _____ 35–39 _____ 40–49 _____
     50–59 _____ 60 + _____

18. This is an optional question that you *do not* have to answer, it pertains to your total household income. I would like to read you some ranges and ask you to stop me when I get to your range, O.K.?
     under $8,000 _____   9–12,000 _____   13–16,000 _____   17–20,000 _____
     21–25,000 _____   26–30,000 _____   31–34,000 _____   35–40,000 _____
     40,000 + _____   refused _____

19. How many adults (over 21) in your household are employed? _____

20. What is your zip code? _____

21. How many persons under 18 are living in your household? _____ None __

22. Could you describe what you consider to be the ideal restaurant for dinner?
     _____

23. What radio station do you regularly listen to? _____

Questions For Review and Discussion

1. Why would it be useful for a foodservice organization to implement a marketing information system?

2. Cite those sources for internal and external marketing information that you consider to be the best. Discuss the advantages and disadvantages to these sources.

3. Differentiate between primary and secondary data, including their advantages and disadvantages.
4. Discuss the three methods for collecting marketing data. Which method would work best in a specific situation with which you are familiar?
5. How is random sampling done?
6. If you were hired by a foodservice firm and were asked to design and implement a marketing information system, how would you approach the task?
7. What role should a marketing information system play in the management of a foodservice establishment?

Notes

1. Frederick Herzberg, "One More Time: How Do You Motivate Employees?" *Harvard Business Review,* Vol. 46, No. 1 (January–February 1968), pp. 53–62.

Further Reading

Anonymous. *Market Research for the Restauranteur* (Washington, D.C.: The National Restaurant Association and Technomic Consultants, 1981).

Churchill, Gilbert A., Jr., *Marketing Research Methodological Foundations,* 2nd Edition (Hinsdale, Illinois: The Dryden Press, 1979).

Cundiff, Edward W., Richard Still, and Norman Govoni, *Fundamentals of Modern Marketing,* 2nd Edition (Englewood Cliffs, New Jersey: Prentice-Hall, 1976).

Dillman, Don A. *Mail and Telephone Surveys: The Total Design Method* (New York: John Wiley and Sons, Inc., 1978).

Donnelly, James H. Jr., *Analysis for Marketing Decisions* (Homewood, Illinois: Richard D. Irwin, 1970).

Kerlinger, Fred N., *Foundations of Behavioral Research,* 2nd Edition (New York: Holt, Rinehart, and Winston, Inc., 1973).

Thompson, Howard A., (Ed.), *The Great Writings in Marketing* (Tulsa, Oklahoma: Petroleum Publishing, 1976).

Chapter 5

Market Segmentation and Positioning

Chapter Outline

For any foodservice organization to achieve the highest possible level of success, management must have a clear understanding of the market segments that it serves. This chapter focuses on market segmentation, positioning the product-service mix in such a way so as to gain the maximum competitive advantage, and measuring the market demand.

The chapter is divided into the following sections:

Introduction
- the nature of segmentation
- segmentation variables
- criteria for effective segmentation

Positioning the Product-Service Mix
- positioning defined
- constructing the space of the product-service mix

Measuring Demand
- evaluating market segments
- forecasting methods

Two Often-Ignored Consumer Markets
- working women
- individuals over 49

Summary

Introduction

The Nature of Segmentation

Most foodservice organizations serve the needs of a fairly wide variety of client groups. These groups include those who are young and old, wealthy and not so wealthy, men and women, and people from all ethnic backgrounds. National foodservice chains serve the needs of client groups living in all 50 states, and most take into consideration the sometimes not-so-subtle differences among those living in the East, South, Midwest, and West. Differences in geographic location, demographic variables, life style, and consumer behavior add special challenges to the marketing of the product-service mix of a foodservice organization.

One of the ways that marketing managers have long used to handle this problem is to segment the market into smaller homogeneous groups. Therefore, a simple definition for *market segmentation* is pursuing a marketing strategy whereby the total potential market is divided into homogeneous subsets of customers, each of which responds differently to the marketing mix of the organization.

Figures 5.1, 5.2, 5.3, and 5.4 illustrate the concept of market segmentation. Figure 5.1 illustrates a market that is not segmented, one in which no attempt has been made to divide the entire market into homogeneous subsets. Figures 5.2 and 5.3 illustrate markets that have been segmented by age and annual income, respectively. Figure 5.4 illustrates a market that has been segmented using both age and income as criteria. It is, as this chapter will show, a common marketing practice to segment markets based on a variety of criteria.

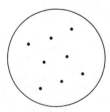

Figure 5.1. A Nonsegmented Market.

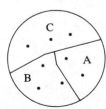

Figure 5.2. A Market Segmented with Age as the Criterion (A = 18–34, B = 35–49, C = above 49).

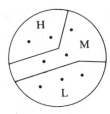

Figure 5.3. A Market Segmented by Annual Income (H = High, M = Moderate, and L = Low).

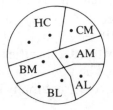

Figure 5.4. A Market Segmented by Annual Income and Age.

Why segment the market? Many owners and managers of foodservice organizations ask this question. Often, they believe that they are trying to appeal to all potential consumers and that by segmenting the market they will weaken their competitive position. They believe that if they segment the market and aim their marketing and promotional efforts squarely at a few segments, their sales volume will fall.

This approach really misses the reasons for segmentation. Segmentation, when done properly and when based on solid data, can actually improve sales and profits because it allows the organization to target specific segments that are much more likely to patronize the organization's facilities. At the same time, segments that hold little potential receive little or no attention and scarce marketing resources are not used chasing after market segments with little sales potential. The basic approach to segmentation is to put the resources where the markets are. Advertising dollars should not be allocated for attracting market segments that do not hold the potential for a substantial volume of business.

Marketing managers hold that no single homogeneous market exists for any product or service. This is also true of the foodservice industry. Think for a moment of McDonald's, Burger King, Steak and Ale, Red Lobster, Houlihan's, and Howard Johnson's. Initially, each may seem to be appealing to a mass market that includes nearly all consumers in the United States, but this is simply not the case. Each of these foodservice organizations has clearly defined several market segments as either primary or secondary. All of their marketing efforts evolve from their segmentation of the total market into clearly defined segments. For example, the television commercials run by the large foodservice chains are clearly aimed at specific targeted market segments, and the programs on which they appear are carefully chosen to deliver the largest number of individuals from the specific targeted markets and at the highest cost efficiency.

By segmenting the market, different product-service mixes can be promoted to meet the needs of the different segments. For example, a cocktail lounge manager may appeal to a variety of market segments by varying the type of entertainment offered. One manager in particular was able to increase sales volume by more than 40 percent simply by establishing specific nights of the week as "jazz night," "fifties night," "disco night," and "blues night." Each of these "nights" offered a specific type of entertainment that appealed to specific clientele. The approach proved to be very successful because the operator was able to attract many more customers.

Segmentation Variables

Five basic variables used by marketing managers typically segment consumer markets. These variables are geographic, demographic, psychographic, and behavioristic variables and benefit segmentation.

A *geographic variable,* as the name implies, relates to the geographic area in the country in which the consumers who make up the segment reside. Markets are often segmented by region of the country, such as the New England, Mid Atlantic, North Central, and Pacific regions. Segmentation is also often accomplished by examining the population of a given area. Standard Metropolitan Statistical Areas (SMSAs) are used to classify urban areas by size and type. Figure 5.5 illustrates a SMSA map of the United States. Geographic segmentation can also be accomplished outside the SMSAs by use of county size, labeled A, B, C, and D. This type of segmentation may be of particular value to a chain organization seeking to expand. Certain minimum population figures may have been established for consideration in the site selection process, and examining SMSAs and county size maps would be of particular value.

Markets are often segmented according to *demographic variables.* Demographic segmentation is based on statistical data related to such factors as age, sex, annual income, family size, stage in the family life cycle, educational level achieved, occupation, ethnic factors, religion, nationality, and social class. When the foodservice industry is considered in light of these variables, certain trends emerge. For example, different age groups are more likely to patronize specific types of operations. Young singles may be heavy users of singles' bars and discos, while married couples in their 40s and 50s are much more likely to belong to country clubs. As annual income

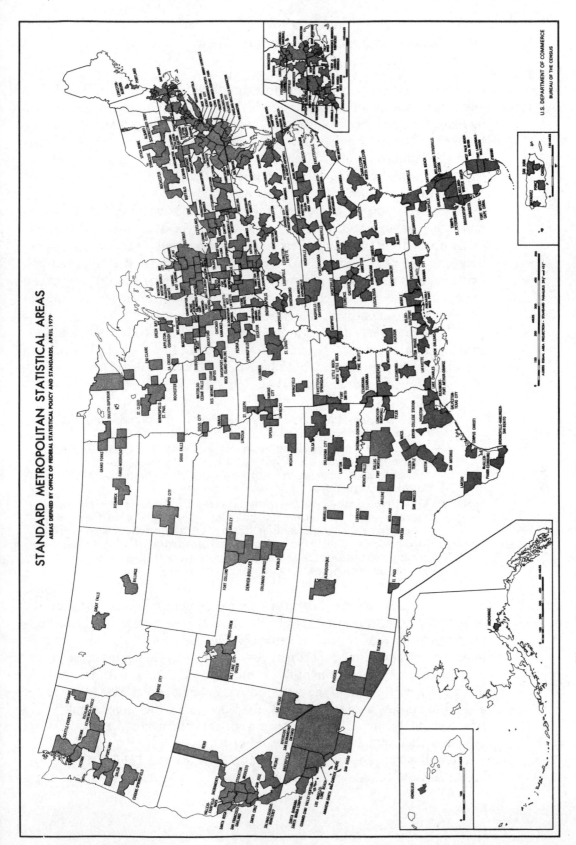

Figure 5.5. A Standard Metropolitan Statistical Areas Map for Market Segmentation.

increases, this normally leads to more dining outside the home. Family size and stage in the family life cycle also influence dining habits. As family size increases, the number of times per week that the family dines outside the home decreases. As individuals and couples progress through the family life cycle, dining habits will change substantially. For example, couples with young children dine out less frequently than do other groups, such as older married couples without preschool children.

Segmentation by demographic variables is very common. It allows marketing managers accurately to describe the type of clientele desired. It is easily understood by nonmarketing managers as well. Demographic classifications are also widely used by various media to describe viewers, listeners, and readers. In this way a foodservice marketing manager can easily match the desired market segment with the most heavily used media, thereby increasing advertising effectiveness.

Psychographic variables are also commonly used to segment markets. Psychographics refer to segmentation based on life style, attitudes, and personality. Psychographics have been defined by Emanuel Demby as having the following characteristics:

1. Generally, psychographics may be viewed as the practical application of the behavioral and social sciences to marketing research.
2. More specifically, psychographics is a quantitative research procedure that is indicated when demographic, socioeconomic, and user/non-user analyses are not sufficient to explain and predict consumer behavior.
3. Most specifically, psychographics seeks to describe the human characteristics of consumers that may have bearing on their response to products, packaging, advertising and public relations efforts. Such variables may span a spectrum from self-concept and life style to attitudes, interests and opinions, as well as perceptions of product attributes.[1]

Psychographics are used primarily to segment markets, but they can be used for other purposes as well. Psychographics are useful when selecting advertising vehicles, as the vehicle(s) selected can be matched with the interests, attitudes, and personalities of the targeted market segment. Psychographics are also helpful when designing the advertising itself. Illustrations, pictures, and the actual copy can be designed with the needs of a specific market segment in mind. By pinpointing the targeted market in this manner, the advertising and promotional efforts are likely to be more effective, thereby increasing sales and profits.

To illustrate the use of psychographic research, Table 5.1 describes both male and female psychographic groups. These groups resulted from

Table 5.1. Male Psychographic Groups.

Group I   The Quiet Family Man (8% of total males)

He is a self-sufficient man who wants to be left alone and is basically shy. Tries to be as little involved with community life as possible. His life revolves around the family, simple work, and television viewing. Has a marked fantasy life. As a shopper he is practical, less drawn to consumer goods and pleasures than other men.

Group II   The Traditionalist (16% of total males)

A man who feels secure, has self-esteem, follows conventional rules. He is proper and respectable, regards himself as altruistic and interested in the welfare of others. As a shopper he is conservative, likes popular brands and well-known manufacturers.

Group III   The Discontented Man (13% of total males)

He is a man who is likely to be dissatisfied with his work. He feels bypassed by life, dreams of better jobs, more money, and more security. He tends to be distrustful and socially aloof. As a buyer, he is quite price conscious.

Group IV   The Ethical Highbrow (14% of total males)

This is a very concerned man, sensitive to people's needs. Basically a puritan, content with family life, friends, and work. Interested in culture, religion, and social reform. As a consumer he is interested in quality, which may at times justify greater expenditure.

Group V   The Pleasure-Oriented Man (9% of total males)

He tends to emphasize his masculinity and rejects whatever appears to be soft or feminine. He views himself as a leader among men. Self-centered, dislikes his work or job. Seeks immediate gratification for his needs. He is an impulsive buyer, likely to buy products with a masculine image.

Group VI   The Achiever (11% of total males)

This is likely to be a hardworking man, dedicated to success and all that it implies, social prestige, power, and money. Is in favor of diversity, is adventurous about leisure time pursuits. Is stylish, likes good food, music, etc. As a consumer he is status conscious, a thoughtful and discriminating buyer.

Group VII   The He-Man (19% of total males)

He is gregarious, likes action, seeks an exciting and dramatic life. Thinks of himself as capable and dominant. Tends to be more of a bachelor than a family man, even after marriage. Products he buys and brands preferred are likely to have "self-expressive value," especially a "Man of Action" dimension.

Table 5.1 *continued*

Group VIII   The Sophisticated Man (10% of total males)

He is likely to be an intellectual, be concerned about social issues, admire men with artistic and intellectual achievements. Socially cosmopolitan, with broad interests. Wants to be dominant and a leader. As a consumer, he is attracted to the unique and fashionable.

Female Psychographic Groups

Group I   The Conformist (8% of total females)

This woman is conventional, is quite rigid and intolerant when it comes to change. She likes the familiar and finds reassurance in familiar brand names. She takes pride in hunting down bargains.

   She belongs to the lowest educated group, lowest socioeconomic status, and the oldest group in this sample.

Group II   The Puritan (13% of total females)

This is an unpretentious woman, who likes her conventional role of the ideal mother and housewife. She is trusting and altruistic and tends to be more religious than the other women. She likes well-known and time-tested products.

Group III The Drudge (16% of total females)

This woman tends to feel lonely and insecure. She has a hard time coping with life. She tries to please her family but finds little satisfaction in daily life. If she buys brands and products that are well known, it gives her a sense of doing the right thing.

Group IV The Free Spender (9% of total females)

This is an outgoing woman who enjoys life, tends to be happy, likes to be with people. Likes a beautiful home, beautiful clothes. Shopping is an important part of her life; she is an impulsive spender and likes good things, especially if she can show off with them.

Group V   The Natural, Contented Woman (8% of total females)

She enjoys life, likes the simple, readily available things, likes the outdoors, has a friendly, casual relationship with her friends, neighbors, and everyone else. She likes functional things, as a shopper, but is not necessarily price conscious.

Group VI The Indulger (16% of total females)

This kind of woman usually finds housework boring: she escapes from daily pressures by acquiring material things. She likes things which enhance her ap-

Table 5.1 *continued*

pearance, such as clothing, jewelry and cosmetics. She likes to be the center of attraction, has little capacity for extending herself for the welfare of others. Shopping is her main activity; she tends to be an impulsive buyer. Her taste runs toward the popular and the conspicuous. She is romance oriented.

Group VII   The Striving Suburbanite (17% of total females)

Very accomplished homemaker. Tends to have broad social and community interests, but no interest in a career. Is status conscious and seeks self-improvement. When shopping, she is likely to be very selective, likes the special and exceptional things, but is not price conscious.

Group VIII   The Career Seeker (13% of total females)

This woman is likely to reject the housewife roles in favor of a career. Tends to feel liberated, likes to cultivate her intellect, and wants to feel important in life. Is an impulsive buyer, spends money freely, and likes attractive things.

This is the best educated group, with the highest socioeconomic status, and although 83% of them are married, they have the lowest proportion of marrieds among them.

From: *Marketing Today: A Basic Approach,* Second Edition, by David J. Schwartz, © 1973, 1977 by Harcourt Brace Jovanovich, Inc. Reprinted with permission of the publisher.

research done by the Consumer Opinion Research Panel, Inc. As can be easily seen in Table 5.1, psychographic segments are more subjective than demographic segments. The division of the markets into segments is not based solely on easily quantified variables, such as age, sex, or income. Rather, the division is based on less easily defined factors, such as life style, attitudes, and personality.

The fourth segmentation variable is the *behavioristic variable.* Behavioristic segmentation focuses on the behavior that consumers exhibit in the marketplace. For example, what benefits do different consumers seek when dining out—economy, prestige, or convenience? How loyal are foodservice consumers? Are they easily swayed by the advertisements of competitors, or are they very loyal repeat patrons? How frequently do they dine out? Would they be considered light, medium, or heavy users of various types of foodservice facilities? What are their most commonly cited reasons for dining outside the home?

Each year, more and more research is undertaken to understand more fully the field of consumer behavior. Potentially, behavioristic variables represent an excellent segmentation variable, for as data are collected concerning the manner in which consumers actually behave in the foodservice marketplace, the data will allow foodservice managers to gain a better understanding of consumer behavior. As marketing managers better understand consumers, this will facilitate the development of product-service mixes that will better satisfy the needs of consumers. Selected aspects of consumer behavior are discussed in greater depth in Chapter 6.

Finally, market segmentation can be based on the benefits that consumers are seeking. These benefits are expressions of the needs and wants of consumers. If management is fully able to appreciate and understand these needs and wants, then advertising can be pinpointed to discuss and to stress the benefits that the targeted market seeks. In this manner, consumer behavior can be influenced. Market research can identify the benefits that are important to various types of consumers. This marketing information allows management to segment the market based solely on benefits sought rather than on demographic, psychographic, or other variables. For example, those who value a fun-filled dining atmosphere as the most important benefit when dining out would be grouped together as a separate and unique market segment, regardless of other segmentation criteria. The challenge for the foodservice manager who uses this segmentation method is to link the benefits sought with the media used.

Criteria for Effective Segmentation

As foodservice marketing managers attempt to segment a given market, they have many methods by which this can be accomplished. As the segments are divided, however, how is a marketing manager to know whether a given segment holds significant potential? When any segmentation activities are undertaken, three criteria should be used to evaluate the market segments. Each of the segments should satisfy the following criteria:[2,3] (1) substantiality, (2) measurability, and (3) accessibility.

First, the size of the segment must be reasonably substantial. As the market is segmented, the foodservice manager is following the product-service mix or the promotional mix to meet the needs of the individual segments. The size of each of these segments must be large enough to warrant this special attention. For example, segmenting the market into segments based on marital status and number of children seems logical because a substantial number of individuals would fall into each category. Segmenting the market into two segments for college graduates who had obtained master's degrees and doctoral degrees would not be logical because the number of individuals in each of these categories would not be substantial.

Second, each of the segments should be measurable. The overall size of all segments should be measured in numbers as well as in purchasing power. Minimum cut-off points should be established relative to the size of the segments. If the number of consumers within a given segment falls below the cut-off point, segments can simply be combined.

Third, the segments must be accessible. They must be possible to reach through advertising and promotion. Without accessibility, there is very little point to segmenting the market at all, as a major purpose for segmenting the market is to isolate substantial segments and expose the segments to advertising and promotion related to specific aspects of the product-service mix. Without accessibility, this is not possible, and segmenting the market is of little value.

Positioning the Product-Service Mix

Positioning Defined

What does it mean to position the product-service mix? Of what value is positioning to foodservice managers? Positioning the product-service mix involves two important considerations: (1) the consumer's perception of the major subjective attributes of the product-service mix and (2) the distinction, if any, between this perception and reality.[4] Unlike tangible physical products, such as automobiles and washing machines, which are ''owned,'' the product-service mix of a foodservice organization is purchased and consumed simultaneously. It is a blend of both tangibles and intangibles, but the mix itself is largely intangible.

According to Lewis, three key elements should be considered when positioning decisions are made. They are (1) the perceived image of the organization, (2) the benefits offered by the organization, and (3) the product-service mix differentiation.[5] First, positioning a foodservice organization entails establishing and measuring the consumers' perceived image of the organization. This image can be either positive or negative. It can accurately reflect the nature of the organization's product-service mix, or it may be inaccurate. The most important thing for foodservice management to remember is that in order to position the operation's product-service mix successfully, a clearly perceived image must be established in the consumer's mind. Another aspect of the positioning of the product-service mix that management should consider is that the perceived image alone does not lead to purchasing behavior. Consumers simply hold a perception of the organization, and this image, no matter how positive, will not by itself lead to increased sales.

Second, management should carefully inventory all of the benefits offered by the organization. Because one of the methods used to segment a market is the benefits sought by consumers, it is the benefit dimensions that are the key to increasing sales, although perceived image, the first element, is important. Simply stated, consumers look at any foodservice organization's product-service mix and ask, "What will this foodservice operation do for me?" All consumers have needs and wants that they seek to satisfy, and they select foodservice operations to satisfy these needs. The important thing for foodservice marketing managers is to package the benefits offered clearly to demonstrate to sometimes-wary consumers that the organization can and will satisfy their needs. All advertising should emphasize these benefits and offer support. This support must convince consumers that they will indeed receive the stated benefits. The foodservice marketing manager must also work closely with the managers responsible for operations to assure the product-service mix and benefit package are delivered as promised. Nothing will undercut the efforts of a foodservice marketing effort more quickly than failure to deliver the product-service mix as promised through advertising and promotion.

Third, the positioning statement should differentiate the organization's product-service mix from direct and indirect competition. For many years, foodservice managers have advertised and promoted "fine food," "prompt, courteous service," "elegant atmosphere," and "top-flight entertainment." As might be expected, these promotional approaches are not as effective as they might be. Consumers usually do not believe these statements because they have heard them many times before and have often found themselves disappointed when they patronized advertised foodservice operations. Also, these statements do little to separate the organization's product-service mix from the direct and indirect competition. If many foodservice organizations are promoting "fine food" or similar benefits, then all the advertising is basically the same. The key to success in positioning is to establish some unique element of the product-service mix and promote it. This allows management to differentiate the product-service mix from the competition and thereby gain a competitive advantage. This approach is called "establishing a unique selling proposition," or "USP." With a USP, every effort should be made to link the benefits with tangible aspects of the product-service mix. In this way, consumers have something tangible with which to associate the foodservice operation.

Positioning is a very important aspect of the marketing efforts of any foodservice organization. The positioning statement, and thus the advertising message, should clearly reflect image, benefit package and support, and differentiation of the product-service mix. Only when all three of these elements are reflected in the advertising and promotion of the organization can the full potential of the organization be realized. The positioning statement should be supported with tangible clues, rather than the intangible and ineffective "fine food" or "excellent service," for this will add credibility to the advertising message.

Constructing the Space of the Product-Service Mix

A technique that has enjoyed wide acceptance is the use of spatial models or maps to represent the product space. These maps represent a graphic representation of the various product-service mixes perceived by consumers. These consumer perceptions can be based on a wide variety of critera. The purpose for using spatial product-service maps is

1. To learn how the strengths, weaknesses, and similarities of the different product-service mixes are perceived.
2. To learn about consumers' desires and how these are satisfied or unsatisfied by the current market.
3. To integrate these findings strategically to determine the greatest opportunities for new product-service mixes and how a product or its image should be modified to produce the greatest sales gain.[6]

Figure 5.6 provides a hypothetical example of a product-service market map. This market map has been constructed based on two variables: the perceived quality of the product-service mix and the perceived value provided by the product-service mix. A considerable amount of consumer research must be done before a map of this type can be constructed. The following are questions for which marketing managers typically seek answers:

– How do consumers perceive the existing product-service mixes available in the marketplace? These product-service mixes can be evaluated for a wide variety of variables, including price, value, atmosphere, food quality, beverage quality, entertainment, and level of prestige.

- How does my product-service mix compare to the product-service mix of direct and indirect competitors?
- What benefits are consumers using when judging the similarities and dissimilarities among the various product-service mixes?
- How does my product-service mix compare with the consumers' perceptions of the "ideal" product-service mix?
- Are there areas within the product-service map for which there is significant consumer demand but no real offering in the product-service mix? This would indicate significant demand for which no product-service offering was available.

Figure 5.6. A Marketing Map for a Product-Service Mix.

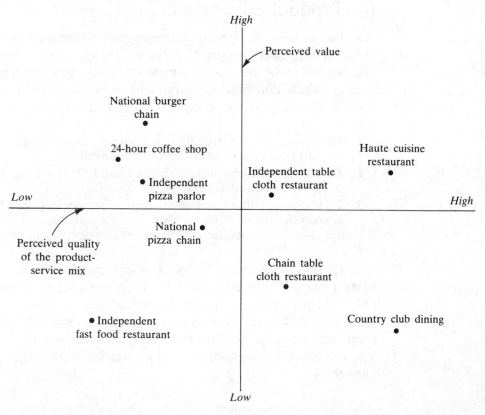

Several methods can be used to construct a product-service marketing map. Among the most common methods are similarity/dissimilarity data, preference data, and attribute data.[7] *Similarity/dissimilarity data* are concerned with consumers' perceptions of the attributes of the product-service mix. Consumers are asked to compare and contrast a variety of product-service mixes. For example, consumers might be given the names of three restaurants and asked to select the two that are most similar. *Preference data* involve asking consumers to indicate their ideal facilities or preferences for specific types of foodservice operations. They might be asked to rank-order a list of restaurants or rate a specific restaurant on a 1-to-10 scale. *Attribute data* involve the marketing manager's determining in advance the attributes of the product-service mix that consumers value (this is normally based on previous research). The marketing manager might then ask consumers to rate a given restaurant based on a series of attributes.

These approaches enable the marketing manager to understand the various market segments more fully. The techniques used require statistical techniques, such as multiple discriminant analysis, multidimensional scaling, and factor analysis. These methods are more thoroughly discussed in *Market Structure Analysis,* written by James Meyers and Edward Tauber.

What are the managerial implications of using product-service market maps? Management can use these maps in several ways. First, market maps are used to determine the position in the market that will produce the largest dollar volume of sales and profits. Second, market maps are often used to help management decide how the product-service marketing mix might be changed or modified to improve the level of consumer satisfaction and to increase sales and profits. Third, these maps are used to indicate marketing opportunities where consumer needs are not currently being satisfied by competitors. This approach assists management in developing new product-service mixes.

Measuring Demand

Evaluating Market Segments

Determining the sales potential of a given market segment or an entire market for any given product-service mix is an extremely difficult task. Computer models and statistical approaches have facilitated the process somewhat, but it is still very difficult to account for all of the variables that can influence consumer demand. Even the very best of forecasts may be subject to a margin of error of two percent in either direction. Obviously, other forecasts may be off the mark by a much greater margin, but management must have some knowledge of the level of market demand in order to plan for short- and long-term contingencies as well as day-to-day operations. Without reasonably accurate forecasts, management must operate "by the seat of the pants." The demands of the 1980s will not permit this sort of approach.

Swartz has defined market demand as people, purchasing power, and motivation.[8] This definition makes it easy to see that many variables can affect the demand within any given segment. Such variables as consumer motivation are often difficult to quantify. Kotler defines market demand in the following manner: "Market demand for a product is the total volume that would be bought by a defined customer group in a defined geographic area in a defined period in a defined marketing environment under a defined marketing program."[9] Only when clear definitions are available for each of these variables can market demand be calculated precisely.

Forecasting Methods

This textbook will provide no more than an overview of methodology by which market demand can be calculated. Foodservice managers should, however, be able to study a forecast and understand the basic methodological approach used. If further study of methodology is warranted, a textbook or other resources devoted solely to this subject area should be consulted and studied with care.

The most common method used to forecast market demand is to base the expected future demand on the past sales histories. Point-of-sale information, as discussed in Chapter 4, serves as the foundation for accurate forecasting. This information asks such questions as, "Where do our customers come from? How much do they spend? How often do they dine out? Do they pay cash for their meals or use another form of payment?" Forecasts based on this type of information are usually trend-line analysis. Today, microcomputers have greatly facilitated the process of forecasting demand.

Market demand for a new product-service mix is much more difficult to determine with any degree of certainty. The total potential market for any product or service is based on three factors: (1) the number of customers given certain assumptions about the marketplace, (2) the number of times the average customer will dine in the particular foodservice operation during a specified period of time, and (3) the average check per person.

For example, if the total number of customers is 50,000, the average number of times per year in which a customer dined in the operation per year is four, and the average check per person is 8 dollars and 50 cents. The total market demand would be 1,700,000 dollars, as shown in Figure 5.7.

Figure 5.7. Calculation of Total Market Demand.

Total market demand		Number of customers in market		Frequency of dining out in the specific foodservice operation		Average check per person
	=	50,000	×	4	×	$8.50
	=	$1,700,000				

Consumer surveys related to purchase intentions are also commonly used to determine market potential. These surveys are typically based on information related to past and anticipated consumer behavior. Consumers indicate how they have behaved in the past or what their purchasing intentions are for the future. While this method has the advantage of gaining information directly from consumers, it also has its drawbacks. For example, consumers may not accurately recall some of their past purchasing behaviors, or they may not actually behave in the manner they anticipate in the future. If this occurs, the accuracy of the forecasts would be subject to error, and this is especially likely for foodservice customers. Purchasing decisions related to foodservice consumption are often impulse decisions without the amount of consideration that most consumers give, for example, to the purchase of an automobile. Because foodservice customers' decisions are often made "on the spur of the moment," it may be difficult for consumers to identify their future purchasing behavior accurately.

Expert opinion has a place in forecasting market demand. The opinions of experts are often the result of detailed study of such variables as economic effects and level of competition. Each year, forecasts are prepared by the National Restaurant Association and other professional associations that forecast sales and demand for specific geographic regions of the country and for the entire industry. These forecasts can be used as gross estimation of future demand. Expert opinion may also be available through workshops, seminars, or trade publications. Expert opinion can be collected fairly quickly and at a relatively low cost. Data of this type may, however, be subject to error. Such data are more reliable for aggregate forecasting rather than for forecasts related to geographic areas and specific foodservice operations.

Another commonly used method for developing sales forecasts is *test marketing*. This method allows management to gauge consumer purchasing behavior on a limited basis within a small-scale test area. The design of the test-market study can be very complex, so it must be well planned. Kotler raises several questions to consider when planning test marketing:

- How many test sites should be selected? As more sites are used, the accuracy of data will increase, but the time and expense of establishing test-market sites should be weighed carefully.
- What sites should be selected? No one site is perfect, but the sites selected should represent the larger market.
- For how long should test marketing be conducted? To measure accurately not only initial purchase rates but also repeat patronage, the test-market study will need to be run for a reasonable length of time.
- What information is desired? As with any research study, clearly defined objectives are needed before initiating the study.
- What action should be taken? Data supplied by the market test should give some clue as to the market potential of the product or service. Rates of initial purchase and repeat patronage are useful, as are other forms of data. Management must, of course, still make the hard decisions.[10]

Test marketing is a very useful tool to forecast total market demand based on a small-scale setting. Many extraneous and often uncontrollable variables, however, can influence the test marketing activities of the organization. These variables might, for example, include national, regional, and local economic conditions as well as actions taken by competitors.

Finally, a wide variety of statistical approaches can also be used. These methods include many sophisticated approaches using computer resources, and they allow management to isolate single variables and determine the impact that changes in each variable will have on total market demand. A detailed step-by-step approach to determining market demand can be found in *The Owners and Managers Market Analysis Workbook* written by Wayne A. Lemon; it is an excellent resource.

Determining total market demand is an important marketing function because so many other assumptions are based on its forecast. Foodservice managers should be able to examine forecasts for market demand and understand their uses and their limitations.

Two Often-Ignored Consumer Markets

The marketing efforts of many foodservice organizations are based on the assumptions that (1) the primary target markets are under 40 years of age, (2) marketing efforts should be aimed at males, and (3) the emphasis should be on youth and the image of youth. For many operations, these assumptions are normally successful, but the foodservice industry has, for the most part, ignored two potentially important markets. These are (1) working women and (2) those individuals over the age of 49.

Working Women

It is very easy to fall into the trap of stereotyping individuals, placing people in categories based on personal perceptions and assuming that all women are such and such and all men are something else. Some people assume, for example, that women select the color of the upholstery while men select the make and model of an automobile. Many people believe this stereotype, yet research indicates that a full 40 percent of all purchases of new cars are made by women. Stereotypes can be very dangerous to the marketing manager, for they often cloud perceptions of reality and cause major errors in judgment.

Within the American life style, a quiet revolution has taken shape. Women are working outside their homes in greater numbers each year, and this is having a major impact on the foodservice industry. Comparing the number of women working outside the home with housewives points out a marked contrast with the early 1970s. In 1971, housewives outnumbered working women, but by the late 1970s, the ratio of working women to housewives has shifted so that 55 percent were working women and 45 percent were housewives.[11] Just why are so many women working outside the home? There are, of course, hundreds of specific reasons, but they generally fall into two broad areas: economic motivation and personal motivation.

Economic motivation is, of course, very strong. In lower-economic groups, the economic motivation is simply to "make ends meet," or to survive. The working woman often heads a household or finds that two incomes are needed to maintain a standard of living. During the late 1970s and early 1980s, the annual inflation rate was more than 10%, while personal incomes rose by only seven to eight percent per year. As a result, both real income and the standard of living declined. In higher-income groups, the woman's salary increases the standard of living, thereby allowing the household to engage in new activities, such as dining outside the home more frequently.

Personal motivation is also very strong for many women. Many women engage in employment simply to have a job, but an increasingly large percentage of women are engaged in career advancement. This is especially true of those individuals who are college graduates, as college-educated people are more likely to have a career orientation. In addition to a career orientation, personal motivation for many women is manifested through broadening horizons, contributing to self-image, and gaining a sense of satisfaction.

Individuals Over 49

A second major market that is often ignored by foodservice operations consists of those individuals over the age of 49. These individuals represent roughly 40 percent of the total population of the United States.[12] Again, many people harbor stereotypes of individuals over 49, and these are often not valid perceptions. Perhaps a more realistic view would lead to increased marketing success. Figure 5.8 illustrates the composition of the "over-49 market."[13]

Active and affluent people	40%
Homemakers	22%
Disadvantaged	17%
Active retireds	15%
In poor health	1%
Others	5%
	100%

Figure 5.8. Composition of the Over-49 Market (Percentages have been rounded).

Adapted from Rena Bartos, "Over 49: The Invisible Consumer Market," *Harvard Business Review,* Vol. 58, No. 1, January–February 1980, pp. 140–148.

Given the composition of this market, it is active and affluent people, homemakers, and active retired people who represent the best possible markets for the foodservice industry.

Three major factors will influence the attractiveness and potential of this market. These are (1) economics, (2) available time, and (3) satisfactory health. As long as these groups are able to satisfy these three factors, they will represent a very significant target market. Several characteristics should be considered by the marketing manager:

- Individuals who are 50 to 65 years of age are normally still actively working and have reached the highest levels of their working careers. After 20 to 30 years in the work force, they have "made it." This results in higher salaries and increased status, which allow for more dining outside the home.
- Often, individuals over 49 have seen their children become more independent and/or leave home. They now have more free time than those with younger children. This increase in available time makes this market an excellent prospect for the foodservice industry. After many years of providing for their children, those over 49 who no longer have this responsibility often indulge themselves.
- Finally, those over 49 should not be viewed as social and economic outcasts, for they often have adopted the values and life styles of younger target markets. As the United States has evolved into a youth-dominated culture, many individuals over 49 have made changes in their value systems, attitudes, and behaviors too.

Foodservice operators should therefore look beyond traditionally targeted markets to achieve the highest degree of success possible. Such markets as working women and individuals over 49 need to be explored to the fullest possible extent. Each foodservice operation must find a market niche in which to achieve success, for attempting to appeal to vast market segments is not likely to lead to success. Bartos has outlined a simple process that allows a foodservice manager to reformulate targeted markets:[14]

- **Step 1: Reexamine the assumed market.**   A manager would be wise to look closely at the market segments to which the foodservice operation is addressing its efforts. Attention should be paid to changes in values, attitudes, life styles, and dining habits. Both primary and secondary data should be examined. (See Chapter 4 for information concerning primary and secondary data.)
- **Step 2: Evaluate the market potential of new target markets.**   All potentially targeted markets should be examined objectively to deter-

mine whether the potential is significant enough to warrant active solicitation.

- **Step 3: Develop a fresh perspective.**   Old ideas and thought patterns may need to be discarded so that new ideas and outlooks may be adopted. An organization needs to develop a fresh perspective if it is to succeed.
- **Step 4: Explore the attitudes and needs of the new group.**   This involves data collected from specifically targeted markets, as discussed in Chapter 3.
- **Step 5: Redefine marketing targets.**   Based on the appraisal of potential markets and the performance of existing markets, a shift in focus may be justified. Two cautions need to be considered: (1) "He who hesitates has lost," meaning that failure to move toward new markets may result in a lost opportunity, and (2) abandoning a successful targeted market for other potential markets may also result in failure, or "A bird in the hand is worth two in the bush."

Management of a foodservice operation, just as management of any business concern, requires decision making in an uncertain world. It is impossible to comprehend all the aspects of consumer behavior, but to make consistently high-quality decisions, management needs to use information, experience, and intuition.

Summary

This chapter has focused upon market segmentation and positioning. Market segmentation involves considering several segmentation variables, as well as segmentation criteria. Segmentation variables include geographic, demographic, psychographic, and behavioristic variables, and benefit segmentation variables. Criteria for effective segmentation are (1) substantiality, (2) measurability, and (3) accessibility.

Positioning of the product-service mix involves consideration of three separate elements: (1) the perceived image of the organization, (2) the benefits offered by the organization, and (3) the differentiation of the product-service mix. Constructing the space of a product-service mix involves market maps, which allow management to visualize the market. Maps can be used to pinpoint marketing opportunities, and they carry many other managerial implications.

The measurement of market demand includes several methods used to forecast market demand. Today's marketing managers should also consider markets less often targeted when reviewing forecasts and determining marketing strategy. Marketing managers often find success by carrying out a small market niche in which the intensity of competition is reduced.

Questions For Review and Discussion

1. What is market segmentation?
2. Of what value is market segmentation to management?
3. Cite and discuss the criteria for effective segmentation.
4. Cite examples for each of the segmentation variables.
5. Is it possible to oversegment a market? Why or why not?
6. Define positioning.
7. Of what value to management are product-service market maps?
8. By what methods can management measure market demand?

Notes

1. Emanuel Demby, "Psychographics and From Whence It Came," In William D. Wells, Ed., *Life Style and Psychographics* (Chicago: American Marketing Association, 1974), pp. 11–30.

2. E. Jerome McCarthy, *Basic Marketing,* 6th ed. (Homewood, Illinois: Richard D. Irwin, 1978), p. 203.

3. Philip Kotler, *Marketing Management: Analysis, Planning, and Control,* 4th ed. (Englewood Cliffs, New Jersey: Prentice Hall, 1980), pp. 194–212.

4. Robert Lewis, "The Positioning Statement for Hotels," Cornell and Restaurant Administration Quarterly, vol. 22, no. 1 (May 1981), pp. 51–61.

5. Lewis, "Positioning Statement."

6. Richard Johnson, "Market Segmentation: A Strategic Management Tool," *Journal of Marketing Research,* vol. viii (February, 1971), pp. 13–18.

7. Johnson, "Market Segmentation."

8. David J. Schwartz, *Marketing Today: A Basic Approach,* 2nd ed. (New York: Harcourt Brace Jovanovich, 1977), p. 101.

9. Kotler, *Marketing Management,* pp. 214–217.

10. Kotler, *Marketing Management,* p. 338.

11. Rena Bartos, "What Every Marketer Should Know About Women," *Harvard Business Review,* vol. 56, no. 3, May–June 1978, pp. 73–85.

12. Rena Bartos, "Over 49: The Invisible Consumer Market," *Harvard Business Review,* vol. 58, no. 1, January–February 1980, pp. 140–148.

13.   Bartos, "Over 49," pp. 140–148.
14.   Bartos, "Over 49," pp. 140–148.

Further Reading

Lemon, Wayne A. *Market Analysis Workbook*. New York: AMACOM, 1980.

Meyers, James, and Edward Tauber, *Market Structure Analysis* (Chicago: American Marketing Association, 1977).

Chapter 6

Understanding the Behavior of Foodservice Consumers

Chapter Outline

Marketing managers in other industries have for many years understood their clientele very clearly. A great deal of in-depth research has allowed those responsible for marketing automobiles, washing machines, toothpaste, laundry detergent, insurance, and most other products and services to understand the consumers who purchase these products and services. This knowledge enables marketing managers to develop sophisticated marketing programs aimed at very specific targeted market segments.

One of the most perplexing problems confronting foodservice managers is trying to understand why foodservice consumers behave as they do. This chapter explores several important aspects of consumer behavior.

The chapter is divided into the following major sections:

Introduction

Consumer Satisfaction in the Foodservice Industry
- techniques to assess consumer satisfaction
- the most common reasons for consumer dissatisfaction
- why consumers dine outside the home

Trends for Food and Beverage Consumption
- monitoring ever-changing consumer trends
- an example of the wine market

Models of Consumer Behavior
- seeking innovators and early adopters
- three traditional models of consumer behavior

A Contemporary Consumer Decision-Making Model
- extrinsic influences on consumer behavior
- intrinsic influences on consumer behavior
- understanding consumer decision making

The Role of the Dining Environment
- environmental design
- table-top architecture

Summary

Introduction

The foodservice industry is broadly based. It includes such restaurants as the 21 Club in New York, the thousands of McDonald's operations worldwide, college and university foodservice operations, and a variety of other types of foodservice operations. Each segment appeals to a different type of consumer.

For example, the individual patronizing a gourmet restaurant for dinner is satisfying certain wants, needs, and desires. These might include such ego-related needs as the need to be pampered or the need to feel important. This consumer might desire a food entree that is difficult to prepare and is only available at that particular type of foodservice operation. That very same consumer might at another meal period have needs, wants, and desires that are totally different. The consumer who needs a quick lunch delivered with efficient service in a sanitary environment might patronize a fast-food restaurant, such as McDonald's or Burger King.

Foodservice consumers will switch from one type of operation to another as their needs change at a particular meal or day of the week. Consumers cannot be tightly categorized as patrons for only one or two types of operations. Within a 12-month period, a single foodservice consumer is likely to be part of many different foodservice market segments.

One such industry segment is the continental or gourmet segment. Restaurants that are part of this segment feature a product-service mix emphasizing "haute cuisine," or fine dining. Restaurants of this type are highly labor intensive in both the production and service areas. This segment caters to the needs of a rather limited clientele, including those who not only have the financial means to patronize these operations but also appreciate the very finest preparation, presentation, and service. Guests are pampered and made to feel important, and this treatment is an extremely important element of the product-service mix. For many consumers, dining out at these foodservice facilities is a special occasion, and the management should therefore do everything possible to make the dining experience memorable.

Another segment of the foodservice industry is the specialty restaurant. This segment includes a broad range of operations, including those with a definite theme, such as Early American, German, or Italian. Restaurants that specialize in a particular category of menu items, such as beef or seafood, are also included in this category. This type of operation usually stresses both atmosphere and food quality equally. The type of food served often includes such meat items as steaks, chops, and roasts, as well as such seafood and shellfish as shrimp, lobster, crab, and stuffed sole. While the perceived value of the product-service mix of specialty restaurants is not as high as it is for the continental segment, the level of personal attention and pampering is still quite high. Restaurants that are a part of this segment often satisfy consumers' needs for food and beverage items that are not readily available at home. Another common need of these patrons is to relax and unwind after a long day. Dining out as a normal part of business activities is also common within this segment.

Still another important segment of the foodservice industry is the coffee shop. Coffee shops satisfy the important consumer needs for convenience, low-to-moderate price, and a relatively high level of perceived value. Coffee shops are often open longer hours to serve consumer needs during all meal periods. Many coffee shops operate 24 hours a day and feature continuous service of a breakfast menu along with lunch and dinner. Coffee shops rely on a high volume of customer traffic to produce a profit and therefore are able to maintain a lower level of profit per customer.

Cafeterias are a segment of the foodservice industry that continues to experience steady growth. They are either public or private. Public cafeterias, such as Morrison's and Duff's, satisfy the consumer need for a full meal at a very reasonable price. Many cafeteria operations feature an "all you can eat" special at an attractive price, thereby appealing to budget-conscious consumers. Private cafeterias are often operated on a contractual basis by very large foodservice organizations, such as ARA Services or SAGA Corporation. These cafeterias are normally located within a larger facility, such as a college or university, an office building, a manufacturing plant, a hospital, or a nursing home. These cafeterias are operated solely for those individuals who live or work within the larger facility. The cafeteria provides a high level of convenience and a high level price and value perception. In business and industry cafeterias, the company often subsidizes the cafeteria operation as an employee benefit, thereby raising the perceived value in the consumer's mind.

The fast-food segment of the industry has experienced the greatest growth in the last 10 years. Fast-food operations feature a limited menu, fast service, low prices, and counter self-service using disposable serviceware. The most noteworthy of the fast-food companies is, of course, McDonald's; its growth has been spectacular indeed, as seen in Table 6.1.

Table 6.1. McDonald's Unit Growth from 1967 to 1981.

Source: William Marks and Judy Wiley, "McDonald's Changing Image: Following, Leading, and Perfect Timing," *Restaurants & Institutions,* vol. 80, no. 8, October 15, 1977, pp. 114–115.

Courtesy of *Restaurants & Institutions* Magazine, A Cahners publication.

Year	Company-Owned Units	Total Systemwide Units
1967	235	967
1970	540	1,592
1973	941	2,717
1975	1,211	3,706
1976	1,337	4,178
1979	1,406	5,185
1980	—	5,747
1981	—	6,263

Other fast-food giants include Burger King, Wendy's, Hardee's, Kentucky Fried Chicken, Church's, Long John Silver's, as well as many other national and regional chains. Why have fast-food organizations been so successful? Fast-food operations have two very important attributes; these are convenience and a high level of perceived value. Fast-food stores are typically located in high-traffic, high-visibility locations where many potential consumers pass by each day. These stores provide a close-by, convenient place to dine for many individuals. Fast-food restaurants also offer a relatively low price and a high perceived value. It is possible to purchase a meal in almost all of them for less than three dollars per person, making these meals affordable for virtually everyone. In addition, for many consumers, the time associated with shopping in a grocery store, preparing a meal, and cleaning up is not equal to the value provided by fast-food restaurants. These consumers believe that, when the value of their time is included in the cost of preparing a meal at home, it is actually cheaper to dine at a fast-food restaurant.

Numerous studies have been undertaken in an attempt to determine the number of foodservice operations in each of the aforementioned categories. This has proven to be a difficult task and one always subject to challenge. Tables 6.2 and 6.3 provide information concerning the foodser-

Table 6.2. Average Dinner Check.
Courtesy: National Restaurant Association, 1979.

Check Average per Person	Percentage
No Answer	11%
Under $3.00	19%
$3.00–$4.99	27%
$5.00–$9.99	29%
$10.00–$14.99	11%
$15.00 or more	3%
	100%

Table 6.3. Sizes of Foodservice Organizations.
Courtesy: National Restaurant Association, 1979.

Sales Volume of Foodservice Organizations	Percentage
$1 million or less	58%
$1 million to $5 million	23%
$5 million to $10 million	3%
$10 million to $25 million	5%
$25 million to $100 million	2%
$100 million or more	1%
No answer	8%
	100%

vice industry. The data were compiled in a research study conducted by the National Restaurant Association. These two tables illustrate two important points about the foodservice industry, both of which are contrary to the beliefs of some individuals. First, the foodservice industry is made of many small organizations, with a full 58 percent of those surveyed having less than 1 million dollars in annual sales. In addition, 46 percent of those surveyed have per-person check averages of less than 5 dollars, while only three percent average more than 15 dollars per person. These figures are expressed in 1979 dollars and should be considered in light of the rate of inflation in menu prices.

Consumer Satisfaction in the Foodservice Industry

Management's ability to attain a high level of guest satisfaction has a direct and almost immediate impact on the sales volume of a foodservice organization. The management of each organization undertakes those activities that managers believe will contribute the most to overall guest satisfaction and profitability. How successful are these planned activities? What techniques are used in assessing guest satisfaction? How do organizations follow-up complaints or compliments? What operational characteristics have the greatest positive or negative impact on the guest?

Techniques to Assess Consumer Satisfaction

First, nearly all foodservice organizations seek to measure guest satisfaction through comment cards. While these cards sometimes do provide adequate information, far too often the information reflects the feelings of atypical consumers, for those individuals who complete comment cards often do not adequately reflect the feelings of the total clientele of a foodservice operation. All too often the information supplied by comment cards represents the feelings of the highly motivated guest, whose reaction may be either positive or negative. Figure 6.1 illustrates how those with either strong positive or strong negative feelings toward a foodservice operation are most likely to complete comment cards.

Figure 6.1. Comment Card Respondents Representing the Atypical Consumer. (It should be noted that only a small percentage of consumers fill out comment cards; these consumers tend to be highly satisfied or dissatisfied.)

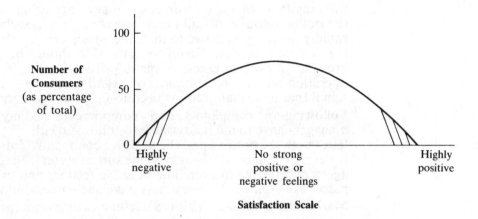

Those completing comment cards represent an atypical segment of the targeted market. A vast middle ground of typical consumers fail to use the comment card. In addition to comment cards, other measures of guest satisfaction often include

- **Spoken complaints and compliments.** These have the same drawbacks as comment cards in that most consumers will voice opinions only if they are highly motivated either positively or negatively. For example, many consumers who are dissatisfied with a meal will respond positively to both the service person and the cashier when asked, "Is everything OK?" As soon as these consumers leave the operation, however, they cannot wait to tell their friends what a terrible experience they had at XYZ restaurant. The result is negative word-of-mouth advertising, yet a positive measure of guest satisfaction because no complaints were registered.
- **Number of repeat customers.**   This can be a very accurate indicator of the degree to which a foodservice operation is satisfying its consumers. Information maintained in a marketing information system should provide the percentage of total consumers who are repeat guests. Many foodservice operations have developed standards that they attempt to achieve. For example, one manager's target is to have 80% of all guests be repeat guests. If the percentage falls below 80 percent, immediate management action is undertaken to increase the percentage of repeat patronage.

- **Sales trends.** As long as sales trends are increasing, it is safe to assume that guest satisfaction is also high and that the increasing sales are at least partly the result of positive word-of-mouth advertising. A foodservice manager must be careful, however, not to be lulled into thinking that volume (customer counts) is increasing simply because the dollar amounts of sales are increasing. It is possible in times of rapidly rising menu prices to have increasing dollar sales yet decreasing customer counts. Therefore, attention should be paid to "real growth," growth in excess of menu price increases. If a foodservice operation records three months of negative real growth, this should signal that immediate actions need to be taken by management.
- **Following-up complaints and compliments.** Many foodservice managers have found it advisable to follow-up either by telephone or letter both the positive and the negative comments. This may be done for every comment or through some sort of system. In this way, management attempts to overcome negative feelings and promote repeat patronage even when a guest may have had a poor dining experience.
- **Market share trends.** This is a useful measure for larger foodservice organizations. It measures the percentage of a particular market that the organization has captured. A declining market share often indicates poor guest satisfaction.
- **Shopping reports.** Many consulting organizations offer services known as "shopping." These are anonymous evaluations of the operation and include evaluations of food, beverages, service, atmosphere, and other qualities of the operation. They can serve a very useful function if properly performed. Before a foodservice manager contracts with a company offering shopping services, a thorough check should be done to assure the professional quality and reliability of the service.

The Most Common Reasons for Consumer Dissatisfaction

Guest satisfaction as it pertains to marketing is not a difficult subject to understand; it all revolves around the basics of sound management. Why then do so many foodservice operations fail to achieve success? No amount of professional marketing effort or intense advertising will draw consumers to a foodservice operation that is perceived to be low quality. What then turns people off?

A look at the basics shows that eliminating the major sources of guest complaints would be a major marketing advantage. National Restaurant Association studies indicate that the most frequent complaints are those listed in Table 6.4. The vast majority of problems with guest satisfaction relate to "people problems" involving poor treatment by the staff. Such

Table 6.4. Reasons For Consumer Dissatisfaction.
Source: Consumer Attitude Surveys, 1975, courtesy of National Restaurant Association.

Rank	Factor	Summary
No. 1	Food quality poor	Most annoying to 25 to 34 age group, annoyance increases with income
No. 2	Poor service	Most annoying to 35 to 44 age group, annoyance increases with income
No. 3	Too expensive	Most annoying to 35 to 44 age group, annoyance decreases with income, increases with household size
No. 4	Meals weren't well prepared	Uniformly annoying to most groupings, slightly more irritating to males
No. 5	Poor sanitary conditions	Most annoying to 35 to 44 year old group, more annoying as income increases
No. 6	Eating establishment too crowded	Most annoying to those under 25 and over 55, annoyance decreases with income
No. 7	Too noisy	Most annoying to persons over 45 and in 1 or 2 member households
No. 8	Waiters/waitresses were rude	Annoyance decreases with age, slightly more annoying to females
No. 9	Portions too small	Most annoying to 25 to 34 year olds, and larger households
No. 10	No place to park	Annoyance increases with age but decreases with income

Table 6.4. Reasons For Consumer Dissatisfaction (*continued*).

Rank	Factor	Summary
No. 11	Menus too limited	Annoyance increases with age, decreases with income
No. 12	Didn't have what was on the menu	Uniformly annoying to all segments studied
No. 13	Had to tip	Most annoying to persons over 55, most annoying to lower income groups and females
No. 14	Other people's children are a problem	Uniformly annoying to all groups

practices as keeping guests waiting in the lounge even though tables are available and failure of a service person to smile and make the guest feel genuinely welcome are to be avoided at all costs. Special attention must be paid to the development of "people skills" and "hospitality skills" for all personnel. First-class treatment by the staff can turn even an average meal into a memorable and positive experience. Poor treatment, however, can make even the finest of cuisine seem second rate. Surely, everyone can think of numerous examples to support this.

Why Consumers Dine Outside the Home

Literally, hundreds of reasons explain why people dine outside the home. The reasons vary depending on the season, month, day of the week, and time of day. A study conducted for the National Restaurant Association reveals the most frequently cited reasons for dining outside the home. These are shown in Table 6.5. It is important for management to be conscious of these reasons for dining out, for when advertising and promoting the foodservice operation, these are the points that should be stressed. Consumers have expressed these reasons and needs for dining out; the key is to demonstrate how a particular foodservice establishment can satisfy these needs better than the direct and indirect competition.

Table 6.5. Reasons for Dining Outside the Home.

Source: Consumer Attitude Surveys, 1975, courtesy of National Restaurant Association.

Rank	Reason	Summary
No. 1	Nobody has to cook or clean up	Importance decreases with age
No. 2	For a change of pace	Most important to families making $6,000 to 15,000
No. 3	For a treat	Most important to 25 to 34 year olds. More important to women than men
No. 4	Good way to celebrate special occasions	Importance increases with age, more important to men than women
No. 5	It's convenient	Most important to persons under 25 and 1 & 2 members in household
No. 6	Going out is a special occasion	Most important to 35 to 44 year olds, importance decreases with income
No. 7	For food not usually available at home	Importance increases with age and income. More important to females
No. 8	It's a good way to relax	Most important to under 25's and persons in upper income brackets
No. 9	The whole family enjoys themselves	Most important to 25 to 34 age group and larger households
No. 10	Spouse requests to eat out	Response provided by males approx. 2½ times more than females
No. 11	Enjoy good food	Importance increases with age
No. 12	It's a good way to entertain guests	Importance increases with age, most important in over $25,000 bracket

Table 6.5. Reasons for Dining Outside the Home (*continued*).

Rank	Reason	Summary
No. 13	Restaurant prices are reasonable	25 to 34 age group agreed least with this reason
No. 14	Business requires it	Importance increases with family income and household size, more important to male heads of households

Trends for Food and Beverage Consumption

Understanding consumer behavior and striving for increased levels of guest satisfaction are two admirable goals for any foodservice operation. One strategy for achieving these goals is to be innovative in food and beverage offerings. Each year new innovations and trends develop. A prudent foodservice manager seeks to identify trends and incorporate them into the menu wherever possible.

What are the current trends? Each year, more convenience foods are incorporated into the menus of foodservice operations. Although this trend was resisted for several years, the rising cost of skilled and unskilled labor has made convenience-food entrees an accepted norm. Managers cite a lack of skilled labor, a need for more menu variety, quality control, cost control, portion control, and fast preparation as the major reasons for using convenience foods. Suppliers of convenience foods also offer numerous marketing and merchandising aids that can prove invaluable to a foodservice manager.

Monitoring Ever-Changing Consumer Trends

Changing economic conditions, shifting consumer tastes, and other factors cause menu trends as well. The most successful merchandising trends of late have been shifts toward promoting freshness, variable portion sizes, special combinations of items, nutrition, and increased perceived value of price and portion size. These trends have been developing for some time and are now finding their way into the restaurant mainstream. The most successful operations are those that identify the trends as they develop and implement them into the operation. Every trend has a life cycle; some are long while others are very brief. The overall goal for any innovation should, of course, be to maximize the wealth of the owners of the firm.

Just as trends develop for food products, so too trends develop in beverages. Beverage trends tend to be more volatile, and their typical life cycles tend to be much shorter. During the 1950s and 1960s, consumption of alcoholic beverages was very stable. During the 1970s and into the 1980s, consumption patterns have shifted noticeably. Tables 6.6 and 6.7 illustrate the breakdown of food and beverage sales within the foodservice industry.

Table 6.6. Typical Percentages for Food and Beverage Sales.
Source: Restaurant Hospitality, vol. LXIV, no. 3, March 1980, p. 55.

Item	Percentage
Food sales	64.7%
Beverage sales	
Distilled spirits	17.4%
Beer	8.0%
Wine	5.9%
Nonalcoholic beverages	4.0%
Total	100.0%

Table 6.7. Typical Break-down of Alcoholic Beverage Sales.
Source: Restaurant Hospitality, vol. LXIV, no. 3, March 1980, p. 55.

Item	Percentage
Distilled spirits	55.6%
Beer	25.6%
Wine	18.8%
Total	100.0%

Several recent trends appear to be continuing. First, the relative percentage of sales of distilled spirits to sales of all alcoholic beverages has fallen somewhat as the percentage of sales of beer and wine has increased. Second, the sales of "whites" has increased tremendously. "Whites" are any lightly colored alcoholic beverage, such as vodka, tequila, and light rum. A very pronounced shift toward lighter drinks has increased the sales of vodka, tequila, and white rum, while the heavier and more traditional bourbons and blended whiskeys have fallen as a percentage of total sales. This trend is also noted in beer and wine sales. Several years ago, when light beer was first introduced in the marketplace, sales were very poor, partly because light beer was perceived as something less than beer by traditional beer consumers. Drinking light beer was not perceived to enhance the consumer's image. Then the Miller Brewing Company introduced "Miller Lite™." This product was introduced and marketed very professionally, and in a brief period of time, Miller Lite™ provided a significant amount of revenue for the company. Since this time, other brewers have developed light beers, and the competition in this market is extremely intense. It was believed five years ago that a foodservice operation that chose to sell draft beer needed to maintain two beers on draft, a popular and a premium brand. Today, if a manager does not also maintain a "light" beer on draft, a significant targeted market may be overlooked.

A similar success story is true for wine. Wine has become a very popular beverage. In recent years, the sales of house wines, bottled wines, and especially white wines have increased tremendously. Once a status drink, wine has become popular with nearly all socioeconomic groups. Advertising, promotion, and proper personnel training can remove much of the uncertainty that many consumers still experience when ordering wine.

One concept that many foodservice managers do not appreciate is the regional differences among beverage preferences. While stereotyping individuals based solely on geographic location may not be advisable, certain generalizations can be made. Table 6.8 illustrates that each region of the country has unique beverage preferences. Within each region, the recipe used in mixing the same named drink will also vary. For example, Figure 6.2 illustrates two types of Manhattans, one mixed in Knoxville and one mixed in Milwaukee. Both are generally accepted by consumers living within the geographic area.

Table 6.8. Alcoholic Drink Preferences By Region.

Source: Marvin Shanken, "Alcoholic Beverage Survey," *Institutions,* Vol. 85, No. 7, October 1, 1979, pp. 23–40. Courtesy: *Restaurants & Institutions* Magazine, A Cahners publication.

Most Popular Mixed Drinks: North East	Most Popular Mixed Drinks: North Central
1. Vodka martini	1. Whiskey/bourbon on rocks
2. Martini	2. Vodka martini
3. Other vodka drinks	3. Martini
4. Manhattan	4. Brandy drinks
5. Scotch and water	5. Scotch and mixer
6. Other Scotch drinks	6. Manhattan
7. Gibson	7. Vodka drinks
8. Scotch and mixer	8. Vodka and tonic
9. Fruit daiquiris	9. Fruit daiquiris
10. Sours	10. Whiskey/bourbon and mixer
Most Popular Mixed Drinks: **South**	**Most Popular Mixed Drinks:** **West**
1. Scotch and mixer	1. Vodka martini
2. Scotch and water	2. Margarita
3. Scotch on rocks	3. Scotch on rocks
4. Zombi	4. Whiskey/bourbon on rocks
5. Mai tai	5. Other whiskey/bourbon drinks
6. Other vodka drinks	6. Scotch and water
7. Rye drinks	7. Other Scotch drinks
8. Whiskey/bourbon and water	8. Other vodka drinks
9. Martini	9. Salty dog
10. Vodka martini	10. Vodka and tonic

Figure 6.2. Manhattans in Milwaukee and Knoxville.

Knoxville	*Milwaukee*
In a well-iced glass mix on the rocks:	In a well-iced glass mix on the rocks:
2 oz. bourbon whiskey	2 oz. brandy
1/2 oz. sweet vermouth	3/4 oz. sweet vermouth
2 dash bitters	Garnish with orange slice and cherry
Garnish with orange slice and cherry	

Two important points for every foodservice manager to consider when examining consumer behavior and trends are individual differences and personnel training. First, within each major geographic area and socioeconomic group, different consumption patterns and tastes in food and beverages exist. Foodservice managers must take these differences into consideration when making marketing decisions. Second, increased emphasis must be placed on training guest-contact employees. These individuals directly influence guests' impressions and directly affect the percentage of repeat guests. Training programs must emphasize a combination of efficiency and hospitality on the part of guest-contact employees. Personnel training and development are discussed in depth in Chapter 10.

An Example of
the Wine Market

Hundreds of publications provide information about consumer behavior that is potentially valuable to managers of foodservice organizations. Information is constantly published about frequency of dining out, tipping patterns, perceived values for dining out, and other concerns. One such concern is the market for wine, which provides an example of the type of consumer behavior information that is readily available. The following information is compiled from a series of articles written by Marvin Shanken which appeared in *Restaurant Hospitality* magazine. Mr. Shanken is the editor-publisher of *Impact,* a wine and spirits newsletter and *The Wine Spectator,* the wine newspaper. For further information concerning these two publications, write him at 305 53rd Street, New York, NY 10022.

Wine Trends From 1960 to 1980.   Wine has generally shown an explosive growth pattern during the last 20 years, as per-capita annual consumption of all types of wine has increased from 0.9 to 2.0 gallons. Marvin Shanken, a leading wine industry researcher, indicates however, that wine, and particularly table wine, may still be in infancy. Shanken confidently predicts that per-capita consumption will reach 4.3 gallons by 1990, well over twice the 1980 consumption rate and over three times the 1970 rate.[1]

Tables 6.9, 6.10, and 6.11 illustrate the tremendous growth of the wine market during the period from 1960 to 1980. At the same time that consumption was increasing, important shifts were taking place within the wine market. Of these shifts, the following are the most significant for the period from 1960 to 1979:

- Total consumption of wine in the United States increased from 163 million gallons to 444 gallons.
- The share of the total wine market captured by table wines increased from 32 percent to 74 percent.
- Within the table wine market, the white wine share of the total wine market increased from 17 percent to 49 percent.
- The imported wine share of the total wine market increased from 7 percent to 21 percent.

Table 6.9. The Wine Market—Consumption by Type from 1960 to 1980.
Source: Marvin Shanken, "Wine, Beer, Spirits: Trends and Predictions," *Restaurant Hospitality,* Vol. LXV, No. 3, March 1981, pp. 67-71. *Courtesy: Restaurant Hospitality.*

	Millions of Gallons		*Market Share*	
	1960	**1980**	**1960**	**1980**
Table	53	358.5	32%	75%
Dessert	87	45.2	54%	9%
Vermouth	7	8.7	4%	2%
Sparkling	4	29.8	3%	7%
Special natural	12	33.1	7%	7%
Total	163	475.3	100%	100%

Table 6.10. The Wine Market—Table Wines by Color.
Source: Marvin Shanken, "Wine, Beer, Spirits: Trends and Predictions," *Restaurant Hospitality,* Vol. LXV, No. 3, March 1981, pp. 67-71.
Courtesy: Restaurant Hospitality.

	Market Share			
	1960	**1970**	**1979**	**1980**
Red	73%	50%	30%	26%
White	17%	24%	49%	54%
Rose	10%	26%	21%	20%
	100%	100%	100%	100%

Table 6.11. The Wine Market by Point of Origin.
Source: Marvin Shanken, "Wine, Beer, Spirits: Trends and Predictions," *Restaurant Hospitality,* Vol. LXV, No. 3, March 1981, pp. 67–71.
Courtesy: Restaurant Hospitality.

	Millions of Gallons			*Market Share*	
	1960	**1980**		**1960**	**1980**
California	129	338.8		79%	72%
Other states	23	33.4		14%	7%
Imports	11	102.1		7%	21%
Total	163	474.3		100%	100%

The growth in the wine market, the table wine segment in particular and the white wine category specifically, is part of a much larger trend toward lighter alcoholic beverages or "white goods." The market share of "brown goods," such as bourbon and blended whiskey, fell substantially during the period from 1960 to 1979, while sales of "white goods," such as gin and vodka have increased dramatically, as shown in Table 6.12. Data about wine consumption for the year 1980 are summarized in Table 6.13. Highlights of this report include the following:

- Over 60 percent of all wine is consumed in the home, followed by parties (18 percent) and restaurants (16.4 percent).
- Nearly half (42 percent) of wine consumption occurs at dinner, yet 32.8 percent occurs in the evening, indicating significant consumption as a cocktail without food as a complement.
- Women consume slightly more wine than do men (51.9 percent vs. 48.1 percent).
- The age group from 30 to 39 consumes the largest percentage of wine followed by those from 40 to 49, 50 to 59, and 20 to 29.
- Wine consumption by household income is highest among those households with annual incomes in excess of 14,000 dollars and is particularly high in those households with annual incomes in excess of 25,000 dollars.

Wine Trends from 1980 to 1990.   Marvin Shanken (editor and publisher of *Impact*) predicts the following trends for the period from 1980 to 1990:

- Table wine will account for 90 percent of the wine market by 1990.
- White wine consumption will continue to increase, particularly as a cocktail consumed without food.
- Wine consumers will be influenced less by tradition and will select wine more for mood, occasion, and time of day.

The wine market is an expanding and shifting market. As per-capita consumption increases, definite trends become evident, and these trends will influence the decisions made by marketing managers.

Table 6.12. Trends of Major Liquor Market Segments from 1960 to 1979.
Source: Marvin Shanken, "Wine, Beer, Spirits: Trends and Predictions, *Restaurant Hospitality,* Vol. LXV, No. 3, March 1981, pp. 67–71.
Courtesy: Restaurant Hospitality.

	Market Share	
	1960	**1979**
"Brown goods" (bourbon, blends, Scotch, Canadian whiskey)	74%	47%
"White goods" (gin, vodka, rum)	19%	39%
Specialties (cordials, liqueurs)	7%	14%
Total	100%	100%

Table 6.13. 1980 National Wine Consumption (Percentage of Volume).
Source: Marvin Shanken, "Wine, Beer, Spirits: Trends and Predictions," *Restaurant Hospitality,* Vol. LXV, No. 3, March 1981, pp. 67–71. *Courtesy: Restaurant Hospitality.*

Region	Percentage of the Population	Percentage of Wine Consumption
Northeast	23.0%	28.6%
North Central	27.3%	19.3%
South	33.4%	21.9%
West	17.2%	30.2%

Table 6.13. *continued*

Location	Percentage of Wine Consumption
Home	60.7%
Restaurant/bar/club	16.4%
Party/other person's home	18.0%
Office/work/school	0.8%
Other	4.1%
Time of day	
Breakfast/morning	2.0%
Lunch	6.8%
Snack	16.4%
Dinner	42.0%
Evening	32.8%
Sex	
Male	48.1%
Female	51.9%
Age group	
Under 20	1.7%
20–29	17.7%
30–39	27.9%
40–49	22.2%
50–59	19.0%
60 and over	11.5%
Household income	
Under $14,000	18.5%
$14,000–$24,999	36.8%
$25,000 and up	44.7%

Models of Consumer Behavior

Foodservice consumers today are demanding more sophisticated dining experiences. Consumers are better educated, earn more money, and are more confident when dining outside the home. An increase in the concern about nutrition has partially sparked the growth of natural and healthy foods. Florence Skelly, a research specialist, reported in 1977 that research done by Yankelovich, Skelly, and White indicates that today's consumer is rejecting

- The Protestant concept of self-denial in favor of instant gratification
- Feeling responsible in favor of feeling terrific
- Planning in favor of improvising
- Complexity in favor of simplicity
- The nuclear family in favor of more individual living arrangements
- Study in favor of instant creativity
- Egalitarianism in favor of a return to class consciousness or status[2]

Seeking Innovators and Early Adaptors

Individuals have been classified according to willingness to change. Some are not upset by change, while others resist change in any form. Figure 6.3 illustrates how researchers have grouped individuals according to how they view change or innovation. When opening a new foodservice operation, it is very important that those individuals representing the "innovators" and "early adaptors" are reached by marketing efforts. These individuals offer excellent potential as early guests, for if they are satisfied, they will tell friends and associates, and in turn these people may become customers. People falling into the "early" and "late majority" categories will not usually try a new foodservice operation until they have heard positive comments from others. Chapters 9, 10, and 11 offer insights as to how a foodservice operator can reach out to the innovators and early adaptors.

Figure 6.3. Innovations.

Source: W.J.E. Crissey, et al., *Marketing of Hospitality Services: Food, Lodging, Travel* (East Lansing, Michigan: The Education Institute of the American Hotel and Motel Association, 1975), p. 43.

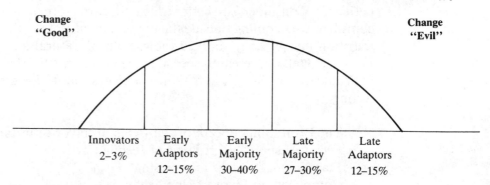

Three Traditional Models of Consumer Behavior

Researchers have for many years attempted to categorize, classify, and more thoroughly understand the behavior of individuals in the marketplace. Literally thousands of research projects have been undertaken, and these have led to a plethora of models. This section reviews three traditional models of consumer behavior. Alone, each model is not of great value, but taken together as a package, they provide considerable insight into the behavior of consumers.

Marshallian Economic Model. This model, based solely on economic variables, views consumers as very rational and motivated to consume. It holds that consumers carefully calculate the maximum use of their money to provide them individual happiness. It is not based solely on economic motivation, for if it were, the model would not explain why consumers dine away from home at all, as for the vast majority of people, it is more expensive to dine out. Instead the Marshallian model holds that utility factors, such as time and happiness, overcome the economic shortcomings of dining away from home. As a result, the individual chooses to dine out.

The Marshallian model advances several other hypotheses of consumer behavior in relation to a single product:

- As the price of a product or service is reduced, sales will increase.
- As the prices of competing products or services are reduced, sales of this product or service will decrease.

- As the prices of complementary products or services are reduced, sales of this product will increase. For example, if a fast-food chain lowered the selling price of french fries, this model would predict that sales of both hamburgers and french fries would increase.
- As advertising and promotional expenditures increase, sales will increase.

Pavlovian Learning Model. This model finds its origins in the experiments of Pavlov, a Russian psychologist. The model proposes that consumer behavior is learned through association. Behavior is conditioned by drives, cues, responses, and reinforcement.

Drives are defined as strong internal stimuli that may lead an individual to act. For example, within every person is the drive to eat. *Cues* are weaker stimuli found in the individual and the environment. These determine when, where, and in what manner an individual responds. For example, an individual may be driving in a car and hear a radio advertisement for a fast-food restaurant. This triggers the drive to eat and the individual may respond by seeking the foodservice establishment mentioned in the advertisement.

A *response* is an individual's overt reaction to the configuration of cues received. In the previous example, the individual's response may have been to seek the foodservice mentioned in the advertisement. Finally, *reinforcement* is anything that either positively or negatively influences or strengthens a response. It results in the likelihood that the response will be repeated or avoided, depending on positive or negative reinforcement, given a similar set of cues in the future. For example, if the response of seeking and patronizing a particular foodservice establishment were rewarded with a satisfying experience, then the next time an advertisement is heard, the response is likely to be positive. On the other hand, if the experience was unpleasant, each time the advertising stimulus is received, the individual remembers the unpleasant experience and responds negatively. Hence, it is very important that high-quality products and services be provided as reinforcement. If they are not, the individual presented with a marketing stimulus will respond negatively each time.

The Pavlovian model also holds that very strong cues must be used to overcome strong brand loyalties. For example, if a new foodservice operation is opening in an area where the consumers are very loyal to the direct competition, high levels of advertising would be necessary to induce patronage. In addition, the quality of the food and beverages would have to be perceived as superior to the direct competition in order to induce repeat patronage.

Veblenian Sociopsychological Model.   This model takes into account the influences on an individual by the social environment. Consumer behavior is not influenced by economics or internal needs, but it is influenced by social pressures. This model holds that an individual's culture, subculture, social class, reference groups, and peer groups hold primary influence in consumption decisions.

This model is supported by the evidence. Many consumers will not patronize a new foodservice operation until they receive positive information from others. Many individuals actively avoid novel situations, such as dining out at a new foodservice establishment, instead relying on the experiences of others as a basis for decision making. The Veblenian model illustrates why it is important to reach those individuals who are leaders of formal and informal groups, for directly and indirectly they influence the behavior of many others. The use of reference groups is also important. Most individuals aspire to be members of groups that are higher in socioeconomic status, and they use the members of these groups as role models. Therefore, inducing the patronage of one group should lead to patronage from others.

A Contemporary Consumer Decision-Making Model

When consumers make decisions concerning the purchase of goods and services, a very complex decision-making process takes place. Numerous variables influence this decision-making process, as the many models of consumer behavior demonstrate. Figure 6.4 pulls together several theories into a contemporary model that shows both extrinsic and intrinsic influences on consumer behavior.

This model illustrates the two major components of the decision-making process, extrinsic influences, or those external to or outside the individual, and intrinsic influences, or those internal to the individual.

Extrinsic Influences on Consumer Behavior

Culture is the first of four major extrinsic influences. It is defined as those patterns of behavior and social relations that characterize a society and separate it from others. It is important in viewing culture to draw legitimate generalizations about a given culture or subculture without resorting to stereotyping all its members. An individual's culture serves to provide a

Figure 6.4. A Contemporary Consumer Decision-Making Model.

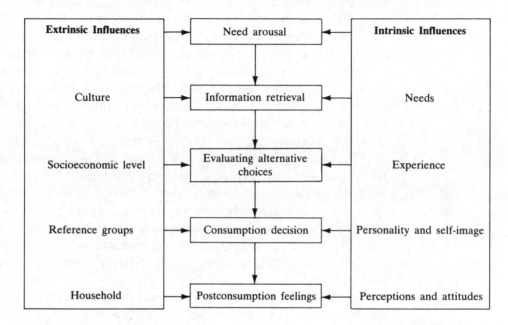

frame of reference concerning acceptable behaviors, and as such, culture is a learned set of arbitrary values. The dominant culture in the United States today stresses equality, use of resources, materialism, individualism, and youth.

In addition to the general culture of the United States, marketing must also be concerned with subcultures. Subcultures might include the Black subculture, the Jewish subculture, the youth subculture, and the Chicano subculture. One example illustrates the importance of subcultures in marketing. All of the fast-food chains are patronized by families, and parents pay the bills for the family. Much of the advertising for these chains, however, is aimed not at the parents who pay the bill but directly at the youth subculture. Research has shown that it is often the children who decide where the family will go to eat, once the adults have decided to dine out.

Second, *socioeconomic level* is a large influence in consumer decision making. Beginning in the 1950s marketing managers have attempted to correlate socioeconomic class with dining habits and patterns. Foodservice managers must identify the relative socioeconomic groups to which the operation appeals and must then appeal directly to those groups in menu offerings, decor, atmosphere, costuming, price, and level of service.

Third, *reference groups* exert tremendous influence on consumers' foodservice decisions. Every individual is influenced directly and indirectly. Marketing research has identified three types of reference groups: comparative, status, and normative. Individuals use reference groups to compare their own feelings and thoughts with others. For example, an individual may have gone to dinner at a restaurant and felt that the food and service were excellent. Before these perceptions are internalized, however, a reference group is often consulted to validate the perceptions.

Reference groups also serve a status function. For example, when an individual seeks to become a member of a group, his or her actions are likely to emulate the group members' behaviors. Finally, reference groups serve to establish norms and values that regulate the behavior of individuals. For example, consider a high school-age reference group dining out. The group norm may be that patronizing chain restaurant A is more desirable than locally owned restaurant B, yet objective analysis indicates that restaurant B's food and service are superior. The group's norms and values might still point toward the established chain restaurant.

A foodservice manager can also influence consumer behavior through the use of opinion leaders. Opinion leaders are the formal and/or informal leaders of reference groups, and their opinions normally influence opinion formation in others. Common opinion leaders are individuals who write restaurant reviews for the local newspapers and leaders within the community, such as doctors, lawyers, and politicians. Many foodservice managers have found it desirable to hold a preopening party and invite individuals who are community opinion leaders. If care is taken to assure that opinion leaders are properly impressed, the influence these individuals have on others can be substantial.

Foodservice managers often strive to create their own reference groups and opinion leaders within the operation. Frequently, repeat customers can be rewarded with complimentary samples of new menu items, or perhaps a complimentary flambé dessert. The flambé dessert creates excitement and is very likely to increase sales as individuals sitting at other tables want to become part of the excitement and often order one for their own table. The desired result is of course a snowball effect among many tables, which results in increased sales.

The fourth extrinsic influence is the *household*. A household is defined as those individuals who occupy a single living unit. There are approximately 63,000,000 households in the United States, and within every household are certain characteristics, leadership, and norms. Leadership is normally rotated among members of the household. For example, the children may decide which breakfast cereal to eat or which fast-food restaurant to patronize, while the mother and father jointly select the type of living accommodations. Foodservice market research points out that leadership is often shared. For example, the parents normally decide when the household will go out to eat, but it is the children who decide the place to go.

All extrinsic influences affect the decision-making process of a consumer whenever a choice among foodservice operations is made. The culture, socioeconomic level, reference groups, and household influences both directly and indirectly, consciously and unconsciously, the dining habits of all consumers.

Intrinsic Influences on Consumer Behavior

In addition to their extrinsic influences, consumers are influenced by personal needs, experience, personality and self-image, and perceptions and attitudes. The first intrinsic influence, needs, is very difficult to understand. Despite many years of research into consumer behavior, no one has been able to explain all consumers' needs successfully. Figure 6.5 illustrates the role of needs in consumer behavior. Simply stated, needs lead to motivation, which leads to behavioral intentions, which finally lead to behavior.

Figure 6.5. Needs Related to Consumer Behavior.

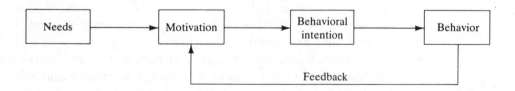

Following behavior, feedback affects and may change a consumer's motivation. Maslow identified five needs arranged in the following hierarchy: physiological needs, safety needs, love needs, esteem needs and self-actualization needs. Maslow's theory holds that individuals strive to satisfy unmet needs. As lower-order needs (physiological needs and safety) are satisfied, they no longer motivate, and as a result, the individual moves up the hierarchy while attempting to satisfy unmet needs at a higher level. When marketing a foodservice operation, efforts should be made to aim promotional efforts at several levels of need. For example, four-color photography with rich descriptions may appeal directly to the physiological need of hunger. The Perkins restaurant chain ran a series of television advertisements that featured only the food and music; the advertisements were quite successful. Another appeal to needs is the promotion of cleanliness and sanitation in appealing to the safety needs of consumers; early promotional efforts by fast-food chains emphasized this. Finally, higher-priced restaurants often emphasize service and atmosphere in appealing to the esteem needs of consumers. It is important that foodservice operators be aware of the various consumer needs and design marketing programs that address unmet needs.

McClelland[3] identified three social motives: achievement, affiliation, and power. Numerous advertising and promotional programs have been directly aimed at these motives. Such advertisements from the hospitality industry as "Taste Sheraton," "Come Sup With Us," "Have it Your Way," "We Do It All For You," "You're The Boss," and "We've Got Style" are directed at these motives.

Experience is also a major intrinsic influence on consumer behavior. As individuals confront novel situations, such as dining in a restaurant for the first time, they integrate their perceptions into an experience framework that influences future decisions. The old phrase "first impressions are important" applies directly to the foodservice industry, for if consumers are "turned off" the first time that they patronize an establishment, they are not likely to return. Foodservice managers must remember that consumers are in large part a product of their environments. Each new dining experience is integrated into a "frame of reference" against which novel situations are evaluated. This frame of reference includes beliefs, values, norms, and assumptions.

A third intrinsic influence is personality and self-image. Each individual consumer develops a unique personality and self-image over a period of time. For marketing, personality types can be grouped into various classifications: swingers, conservatives, leaders, or followers. The important thing for foodservice managers to remember is that no foodservice operation can be all things to all people. Each operation must single out a segment of the total market and then appeal directly to these consumers. These groups are known as *targeted market segments*. Many foodservice organizations experience difficulty when attempting to appeal to too wide a segment of the population or total market. The result is quite predictable; failure to satisfy any of the targeted market segments, which results in poor financial performance and often failure.

One example of this type of thinking involved a restaurant that featured a beef and seafood menu, with moderate to high prices and semiformal atmosphere. This restaurant had been fairly successful, but the owners and managers felt that more profits should and could be generated. In an attempt to broaden the targeted market, the atmosphere was made more informal, and the menu was changed to include hamburgers, snacks, sandwiches, steaks, seafood, and pizza. Thirty days after the change was made, volume had increased by 15 percent. Within three months, however, volume had fallen by 38 percent, and what had once been a profitable operation was now running in the red. In examining the performance of several foodservice organizations, one finds that it is normally those with well-defined targeted markets that are the most successful. Those attempting to be "all things to all people," however, often fail.

The final intrinsic influence is perception and attitudes. Each day, consumers are exposed to thousands of stimuli. Some of these stimuli are consciously received, resulting in a thought process, while others are simply ignored. The process by which stimuli are recognized, received, and thought about is termed *perception*. Each individual consumer perceives the world differently. Perceptions are manifested in *attitudes*. For example, some individuals' attitudes are that fast-food meals are very good because they are of high quality and low cost and offer fast and courteous service. Other individuals' attitudes are that fast-food meals are of low nutritional value and poor culinary quality and are not visually attractive. Both types of individuals hold attitudes based on their perceptions. Their perceptions may or may not be valid, but it is important for the marketing manager to remember that perceptions are the way an individual sees the world. In the mind of the individual consumer, the perceptions and resulting attitudes are correct and valid.

Understanding Consumer Decision Making

Because both extrinsic and intrinsic variables influence the decision-making processes of consumers, foodservice managers need to develop awareness of the specific influences most important to their particular targeted market segments. Once identified, this information can serve as input for the marketing information system discussed in Chapter 4 and for the systems model for developing a marketing plan discussed in Chapter 3. Figure 6.4 shows five key elements in the decision-making model: need arousal, information retrieval, evaluating alternative choices, consumption decision, and postconsumption feelings. Each of these elements is affected by extrinsic and intrinsic influences.

The decision-making process begins with need arousal. Thousands of different stimuli can trigger the awareness of a need. For example, if one feels hungry when driving down an interstate highway, this may trigger a need to seek a restaurant to satisfy the need. In another situation, the need to feel important and be treated with respect may lead someone to seek a restaurant to satisfy these needs. The need may not begin within the individual; for example, if a couple comes home after both have worked all day, and one says to the other, "Let's go out tonight; I'm too tired to cook," this manifests a joint need that only one of the two individuals may have felt. Foodservice marketing managers should recognize the wide variety of needs that consumers are attempting to satisfy when they dine out. Several of these were shown in Fig. 6.2.

Once the need is raised to a conscious level, the model holds that consumers seek to retrieve information. This information can come from a variety of sources, including reference groups and members of the immediate household, as well as the mass media in the form of advertising. If the felt need is as basic as the need to eat because of hunger, the information-retrieval process is likely to be brief; the foodservice facility selected in this case is likely to be chosen primarily because of convenience, and the number of sources of information consulted is likely to be quite small. In other situations, the number of sources consulted could be much larger. Consider the couple that wanted to celebrate their tenth wedding anniversary. The selection of the most appropriate restaurant might require that they consult several sources of information before they select an appropriate restaurant for this special celebration. The important thing for the foodservice marketing manager to remember is that consumers rely to a certain extent on the mass media for information. Advertising is therefore an effective means of communicating with consumers. Figures 6.6 and 6.7 illustrate two advertisements in which the advertiser is seeking to communicate information and, by doing so, to influence consumer behavior.

Once the consumer has gathered a sufficient amount of information, the third element in the decision-making process is to evaluate alternative choices. Consumers who ask, "At which one of several possible restaurants should I dine tonight?" go through a cognitive process in answering this question, whereby they weigh the positive and negative aspects of each alternative. They also examine the attributes of the product-service mix of

Figure 6.6. An example of an informational type of advertisement.

Courtesy: Amfac Hotels, Dallas, TX.

Figure 6.7. An example of an advertisement which uses a testimonial by outside experts to emphasize the quality of the product.

Courtesy: Saab-Scania of America.

each restaurant. Consumers consider the relative importance of each attribute of the product-service mix by asking themselves how important is each particular attribute.

Marketing managers in other industries have long recognized this cognitive process and have used it to advantage in advertising and promoting their products and services. Rather than simply discussing their products or services as if they existed in a vacuum, they make direct comparisons with the competition. This assists the consumer's cognitive process of evaluating alternatives. Of course, every advertiser makes certain that its product or service compares favorably with the competition based on the criteria selected. Figure 6.8 illustrates the automobile industry's example of this type of advertising.

Figure 6.8. An example of an advertisement which uses direct comparisons with the competition to emphasize product superiority.

Courtesy: The New Chrysler Corporation.

The fourth stage in the consumer decision-making model is the consumption decision. It is at this point that the individual actually makes the decision. All extrinsic and intrinsic variables come together to produce a decision. This decision is made based on the perceived risk associated with each alternative and the willingness of the individual to take the risk. This risk factor offers a tremendous competitive advantage for foodservice chains. When consumers step through the front door of a McDonald's, Burger King, Steak and Ale, Red Lobster, or any other nationally recognized chain, they are taking little or no risk because the product-service mix is well known to them. Independent foodservice operations must work very hard to establish themselves and thereby reduce some of the risk consumers associate with patronizing a restaurant where the product-service mix is not well known.

Following the dining experience, the final stage is postconsumption feelings. How did the actual experience compare with the perceptions prior to purchase? Was the product-service mix better or not quite up to the standards anticipated? Postconsumption feelings are based on two factors; the consumer's expectations and the actual performance by the foodservice operation. For this reason, it is very important for any foodservice operation to deliver the product-service mix promised in advertising, promotion, or personal selling. Failure to perform at or above the level anticipated by the consumer is likely to lead to negative postconsumption feelings. These negative feelings produce dissatisfaction and reduce the level of repeat patronage.

Consumer decision making is extremely complex. Marketing managers constantly strive to learn more about the way consumers reach decisions. Consumer behavior is much like all forms of human behavior; it may never be totally understood.

The Role of the Dining Environment

The dining environment assumes a very important role in management's attempt to satisfy foodservice consumers. A well-designed environment can make a guest feel more relaxed and can increase satisfaction as well as the check. A poorly-designed environment can produce the opposite effect.

Lambert[4] noted very little empirical research documenting the relationship and interaction between foodservice consumer behavior and environmental design. Several concepts, however, should be considered when designing the environment; these include personal space and territoriality.[5] Four zones make up an individual's personal space:

1. **Intimate distance.** Extending 18 inches in all directions around an individual. When someone infringes on this space, the natural response is to back away.

2. **Personal distance.**   Extending from 18 inches to 4 feet. Within this range, most normal conversation occurs.
3. **Social distance.**   Extending from 4 to 12 feet. Within this space, casual communication occurs.
4. **Public distance.**   Beyond 12 feet.

Most individuals seek to define territory and make efforts to control it. Within the dining environment, certain physical objects help to define territory. Booths are a common example, as are large rooms divided into smaller rooms to define space and territory, thereby making the guest feel more comfortable.

Foodservice customers begin to formulate opinions about a foodservice operation long before they sample the food and beverage items. While they are still outside the physical confines of the operation, opinions are being formulated about the exterior architecture and landscaping. These initial opinions are carried inside once the customer has entered. They are either dispelled or reinforced by the interior design and lighting and by other factors, such as the quality of food, beverage, and service. All internal and external factors combine to provide the foodservice customer with a total "experience." If any part of this experience is not up to the expectations of the customer, the customer may not return. As a result, customers may tell friends about their poor experiences, and negative word-of-mouth advertising will result.

Environmental Design

The design of the dining environment involves much more than interior decor and furnishings. The *environment* is really an umbrella term including many components, among them exterior design, interior design, lighting, and service personnel. All of these components form the total environment. If a guest is dissatisfied with any of these components, a poor dining experience results, and the guest is not likely to return. For example, a guest who enjoys the quality of the food and beverages and the friendly and prompt service found the lighting effect less than satisfying. What will result? The guest may not return because the entire dining experience was not totally satisfying. A foodservice operation depends on repeat business and positive word-of-mouth advertising in order to be successful. An operation cannot afford the luxury of dissatisfied customers.

The goal of any foodservice design package is to make the customer feel relaxed and comfortable. If the customer is made to feel this way, increased check averages may result. Put yourself in the customer's position whenever analyzing a foodservice environment. The following checklist has been developed to aid this process; it begins with the exterior and then moves inside the operation. When surveying the exterior, ask yourself

- Is the building easily visible?
- Are any signs or marquees in good condition?
- Is parking easy to find?
- Is the parking facility in good condition and well lighted?
- In what condition is the building's exterior?
- Does the exterior design blend with the name and overall theme?
- Are the sidewalks and entrance ramps in good condition?
- Are the entrance ways accessible to handicapped individuals?
- Is the landscaping neat and pleasant?

Then when surveying the interior, ask yourself

- Is the reception area easy to locate?
- Is the lighting transition from exterior to interior a smooth one?
- What is the appearance and condition of the floors, carpeting, wall coverings, tables, chairs, and other furnishings?
- Do the interior decor and furnishings present a unified theme?
- Is the lighting of the proper type and at the proper level of illumination?
- Are all tables or dining areas accessible to handicapped individuals?
- Are the washrooms large enough, and are they clean? Are they accessible to handicapped individuals?
- Is the heating and air conditioning on par with modern standards?[6]

A foodservice operator should keep in mind the "experience" being sold to the customer. It involves much more than food or drink. All five senses are used during a meal, and all components of the design must blend into a pleasing whole.

Color selection is of great importance in the design process because it is used to create a specific mood or feeling. Warm colors, such as reds and browns, can be used in a wide variety of foodservice operations. Cooler colors, such as blues and greens, may also be used. Color selection should be made so that each room or certain sections of larger rooms will have their own distinct touches. Such colors as red, yellow, or orange are associated with action or movement and could be used in cafeterias or fast-food operations.

When selecting materials to be used in a foodservice operation, cleanliness and sanitation are important. Of equal importance, however, is the effect they have on the customer. Well-designed materials will normally carry a higher price tag than poorly designed ones, and this extra cost will usually result in longer wear and a more solid look and feel. When making material selections consider the length of service desired. If the decor is trendy or "fad" in nature, then lower-priced materials can be used. If, however, the design is more conservative, then higher-quality and longer-lasting materials can be used.

Proper lighting can do a great deal to make the foodservice customer feel relaxed and comfortable. Different dining situations require vastly different lighting techniques to achieve this goal. Lighting may range from very bright in a cafeteria or a fast-food outlet to very subdued at a plush night club. Customers have certain expectations when they enter a foodservice establishment, and an operator should conform to these expectations in lighting selection and lighting levels. Lighting can affect both the way people look and the appearance of the food. Lighting and its effect are determined by a number of factors, including lamps (size and type), fixtures (direct or indirect), location of fixtures, controls for level of brightness, and color tones and shades.

Lamps are available in a wide range of wattages and in several types, including incandescent and fluorescent. Fixtures may be either directional or diffuse. Directional lighting fixtures are commonly associated with lower lighting and establish a more intimate atmosphere. This type of lighting places the emphasis on objects in the room (people, food, or furnishings) and creates desirable highlights on objects, such as china and glassware. It can, however, cast shadows that are particularly noticeable on people's faces. To minimize this "aging" effect, lighter tablecloths or table candles should be used. Diffuse lighting gives the impression of light, open, and airy space, much like an office. There appears to be as much light on the walls and the objects within the room. Either of these two types may be used singly or in combination to produce the desired effect.[7]

When selecting lighting fixtures and bulbs, it is desirable to allow flexibility. Lighting controls should be variable in brightness. This will allow a variety of lighting levels as demanded by different situations. The dining room may need to be bright for a working business lunch, while later in the day, the level may need to be low for a banquet. For this reason, flexibility must be designed into the system. When selecting bulbs, keep in mind the desired effect. Many bulb choices are available, and the effects range from very warm to quite cool.

The service personnel and, in some cases, the production personnel play a large role in establishing the environment of a foodservice operation. Service personnel are in constant contact with the customer and are on constant display. Production personnel have in the past been hidden in the kitchen, but many foodservice operations are being designed with open or semiopen production areas. This allows production employees to become a part of the theme or atmosphere, and greater attention must be paid to their appearance.

Foodservice consumers place high importance on the dining environment, and in some cases, they rate it as having greater importance than food quality. For this reason, more time is being spent in developing more sophisticated environments. All personnel seen by the customer become a part of the environment, and they either add to it or detract from it. Consequently, many operators now focus more attention on uniforms, or costuming. *Costuming* is a more universal word because foodservice employees are like actors and actresses; they perform for the customers. They are constantly scrutinized by the customer and are rewarded in the form of gratuities for the service person and a return visit for the operator. Costumes may be purchased in a wide variety of styles. They may, in fact, be custom designed, although this is, of course, quite expensive and time consuming. Many uniform supply companies also sell both stock and custom-designed uniforms. A foodservice operator should review catalogs published by these companies to find appropriate styles. If none are available, custom design may be the answer. The following are four of the well-known suppliers:

Career Apparel by Chatem
210 Eldridge St.
New York, New York 10002

Angelica Uniform Group
700 Rosedale Ave.
St. Louis, Missouri 63112

Barco Uniforms
493 2nd Ave.
New York, New York 10002

Bressler Industries
330 Peters Street, S.W.
Atlanta, Georgia 30302

Table-Top Architecture™

Each year, foodservice industry trade journals publish several articles concerning table-top architecture™ and make many awards each year in a variety of tableware categories. It would be beneficial for any foodservice manager to study these articles, for table-top architecture™ can have a dramatic impact on consumer behavior and perceptions, particularly in the area of perceived value. Paying more attention to plating and presentation of menu items offers several advantages, including more appetizing table-top presentation, greater perceived value for customers through control of the "look of abundance," and new menu flexibility and merchandising freshness to go with changing public tastes.[8]

Syracuse China Corporation has published two volumes entitled *The Perceived Value of Tabletop Architecture,* which present some excellent ideas for plating and presenting menu items. (Both of these volumes are available for a nominal charge from Syracuse China Corporation, 2900 Court Streeet, P.O. Box 4820, Syracuse, New York 13221.) According to this corporation, the strategy for table-top architecture involves four approaches:

1. **The standard plate.**   This features a fairly standard presentation with a garnish to add color contrast.
2. **The little less plate.**   This presentation technique uses the same basic quantity of food, but the coverage on the plate is reduced. The garnish is minimal or even omitted. This technique is very useful in situations where the impression of adequate rather than larger portions is desired.
3. **The little more plate.**   The emphasis of this approach is on coverage. Approximately the same quantity of food is placed on the plate, but it is placed in such a way as to give the impression of abundance. Frequently, garnishes are used to a much greater extent, and unusual garnishes may be used as well. This type of presentation offers a stronger visual appeal to all consumers and often commands a premium price.
4. **The dramatic plate.**   This approach goes beyond the little more plate and uses a variety of different tableware pieces to create a unique presentation. Garnishes are normally extensive. This presentation should also command a premium price.

Figures 6.9, 6.10, and 6.11 illustrate each of these presentation strategies as it applies to different meal periods. Special attention should also be given to garnishing, as this is one of the best ways to increase perceived value. Figure 6.12 provides garnishing ideas from the Syracuse China Corporation.

Figure 6.9. An example of the impact which Tabletop Architecture™ can have on perceived value.

Reprinted from *Tabletop Architecture* with permission from Syracuse China Corporation.

Round-the-Clock Feast

Call it Apfel Pfannkuchen (in German) and place on a Syracuse China Great Plate®. This can be your house specialty, a fast feast, selling big in off-hours or at mealtime.

Apple Pancake, Syrup

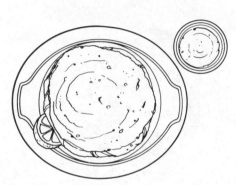

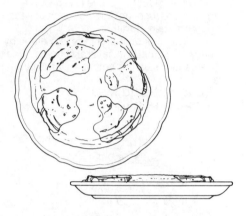

Standard

Serve whole pancake on plate. Set syrup, in Gibraltar™ Cook 'n Serve Ovenware, alongside. Garnish with orange wedge.

A Little Less

Ladle syrup over pancake.

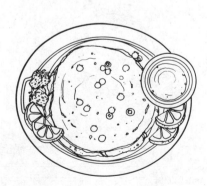

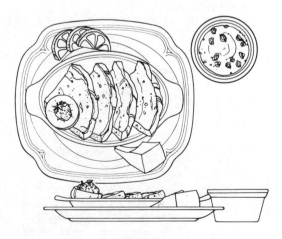

A Little More

Serve whole pancake in center of plate. Sprinkle with blueberries. Garnish each end with half orange slices; to one end add strawberries, to other end add syrup in Gibraltar Cook 'n Serve Ovenware.

Dramatic

Overlap wedges of pancake in Gibraltar Cook 'n Serve Ovenware. Garnish with peach half with strawberry in hollow. Place syrup with raisins in Gibraltar Cook 'n Serve Ovenware to side of plate. Garnish with triangle of melon and half orange slices.

Figure 6.10. Another example of Tabletop Architecture.™

Reprinted from *Tabletop Architecture* with permission from Syracuse China Corporation.

Five Ways to Frame Your Spaghetti!

Coiled or curled, spaghetti shows your chef's attention to the details of presenting this popular food.

Choose the subtly sculpted Signet® Shape or the decorative bordered Econo-Rim® or the acanthus-contoured Kent Shape, for presentations your chef can create with pride.

The Morwel medium Great Plate® with Gibraltar™ Cook 'n Serve Ovenware team up to present a fresh look for that special sauce and garden fresh garniture.

The look of abundance is created by packaging foods in several Gibraltar Cook 'n Serve items on the American large Great Plate®.

Standard
Make 3 medium meatballs; place on randomly curled spaghetti. Ladle on sauce; garnish with parsley.

Spaghetti and Meatballs in Tomato Sauce

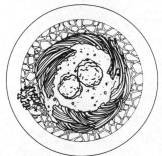

A Little More
Make 4 or 5 small meatballs. Coil spaghetti neatly in a figure 8. Add parsley sprigs and cherry pepper.

A Little Less
Use 2 large meatballs set in center of neatly coiled spaghetti. Garnish with parsley.

A Dramatic Presentation!
Heap spaghetti in Gibraltar Cook 'n Serve Ovenware. Place 3 meatballs on top. Garnish plate with endive leaves; add cucumber stick and black olive.

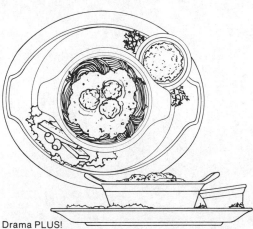

Drama PLUS!
Put spaghetti in Gibraltar Cook 'n Serve Ovenware and top with 3 meatballs. Fill ramekin with grated Parmesan cheese and set beside parsley. Garnish plate with zucchini sticks and black olives on lettuce.

Figure 6.11. Another example of Tabletop Architecture.™

Reprinted from *Tabletop Architecture* with permission from Syracuse China Corporation.

Shrimp Melba for Pride and Profit

Menu favorite built up in several great new ways has built-in customer appeal. Smart merchandising includes Gibraltar™ Cook 'n Serve Ovenware color-keyed to Syracuse China Hospitality Open Stock Dinnerware patterns to get the utmost perceived value for this higher value entree.

Shrimp Salad, Melba Toast

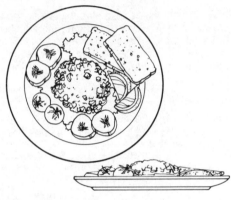

A Little Less

Bind chopped shrimp, hard-cooked egg and celery with mayonnaise; scoop onto lettuce leaf to side of plate. Garnish with lemon wedges and olives. Place toast to side.

Standard

Bind chopped shrimp and celery with mayonnaise; spoon onto lettuce leaf in center of plate. Surround with lemon wedges, cherry tomatoes and cucumber slices. Place toast to side.

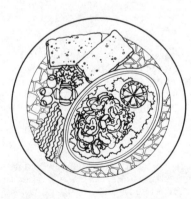

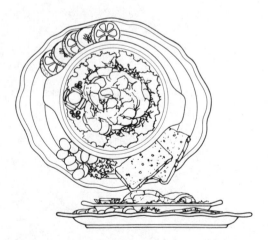

A Little More

Bind small whole shrimp and chopped celery with remoulade sauce; spoon onto lettuce in Gibraltar Cook 'n Serve Ovenware. Garnish with lemon half edged in paprika. Garnish plate with bouquet of parsley, crinkle-cut carrot sticks, radish rose and olives.

Dramatic

Dress whole large shrimp with remoulade sauce on chopped greens set on lettuce in Gibraltar Cook 'n Serve Ovenware. Garnish with capers and radish rose. Garnish plate with overlapping slices of lemon and cucumber, bouquet of parsley, bunch of grapes.

163

Figure 6.12. Garnishes can be profitable.

Reprinted from *Tabletop Architecture* with permission from Syracuse China Corporation.

Garnishes Can Be Profitable!

As operators strive to merchandise their menus to achieve new levels of customer appeal and acceptance, the garnish plays an increasingly important role. Keep entree garnishes edible and sparkling fresh . . . show patrons you care!

Garnish can be colorful.

The well-established parsley sprig is just one way to go. How about radish roses, cherry tomatoes, cherry peppers or orange slices. Try fresh mushroom slices, shoots, sprouts, marinated artichoke hearts and halves, anchovies or red peppers for their interesting colors and textures.

Garnish can be kooky!

Practically anything goes with a garnish — and garnish goes on everything! Persimmons and plums, pomegranates and pineapples, pears and peaches. Apples to zucchini — al fresco or au natural — the garnish goes on the plate, on the food, individually, in a group or a cluster.

Garnish increases value.

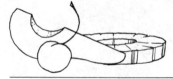

A smartly designed, well-garnished plate pays off in extra profits. Ordinary fare is elevated to specialty of the house; worked off leftovers become works of art when well garnished.

Garnish can be different.

How about popcorn as a garnish for tomato soup? One operator puts strawberries on practically everything: It's not only become a trademark, it enhances the perceived value of the dish. Chopped green onion, red or green grapes, and walnuts, pecans, and peanuts are part of a new wave of garnishes — each designed to enhance the value . . . and the profits.

Garnish can be fun.

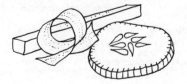

Think of where the hamburger chains would be sans garnish! Raw onion and sliced tomato are only the beginning. Today, you can get bacon, egg or guacamole toppings, fruits, vegetables — even flowers — each garnish placed in a pre-determined position on a plate to enhance the value of a basic food. Sliced or diced, whole or peeled, cut or curled, garnishes come in many shapes, colors, sizes, and textures.

Summary

This chapter has provided a broad overview of consumer behavior as it relates to the foodservice industry. Management should constantly strive to learn more about consumer behavior, for this will allow managers to serve consumers better. In this way, sales and profits can be increased, and a competitive advantage will be gained. Several foodservice industry segments differ in their product-service mixes and the consumer needs they attempt to satisfy. Segments include continental or gourmet, specialty, coffee shop, cafeteria, and fast-food.

Several techniques are commonly used to assess consumer satisfaction. These include comment cards, oral comments, the number of repeat customers, sales trends, follow-up comments, market share trends, and shopping reports. Results of consumer research studies conducted for the National Restaurant Association focus on reasons for consumer dissatisfaction and reasons for dining outside the home.

Monitoring trends for food and beverage consumption is extremely important. Only when management closely monitors such trends can the menu be kept up to date and ahead of the competition. Research information concerning wine consumption is an example of readily available information about consumer behavior.

Several traditional consumer behavior models can be helpful to management. A contemporary consumer decision-making model introduces a five-step process involving need arousal, information retrieval, evaluating alternative choices, consumption decision, and postconsumption feelings. Each of these stages in the process is influenced by extrinsic and intrinsic factors.

Finally, the role of the dining environment is an important consideration for management. Little empirical evidence is available to document the relationship between dining environment and consumer behavior suggesting that this is an area in which a good deal of further research must be done. Table-top architecture and presentation strategies do, however, offer ways in which presentation of the menu items can affect perceived value.

Questions For Review and Discussion

1. Cite and discuss examples that represent the various segments of the foodservice industry.
2. Which segments of the industry will exhibit the greatest growth in the next 10 years? Why?
3. What actions should management take to increase the level of guest satisfaction within the various segments of the foodservice industry?

4. Given the current patterns of food and beverage consumption, what trends do you foresee developing in the next 5 years? 10 years? Why?

5. Briefly review the models of consumer behavior highlighted in this chapter. What are the strengths and weaknesses of each model? How might a foodservice manager make use of these models?

6. Discuss the marketing implications of extrinsic and intrinsic influences on consumer decision making and consumer behavior. How can foodservice managers use these influences?

Notes

1. Marvin Shanken, "Wine, Beer, Spirits: Trends and Predictions," *Restaurant Hospitality,* vol. LXV, no. 3, March 1981, pp. 67–71.

2. Charles Bernstein, "Operators Must Meet Fast Changing Consumer Demands to Make it in the 1980s," *Nations Restaurant News,* vol. II, no. 20, October 24, 1977, pp. 16, 39.

3. David C. McClelland, "Toward a Theory of Motive Acquisition," *American Psychologist,* vol. 20 (1965), pp. 321–333.

4. Carolyn Lambert, "Environmental Design: The Food-Service Manager's Role," *The Cornell Hotel and Restaurant Administration Quarterly,* vol. 22, no. 1, May 1981, pp. 62–68.

5. Lambert, "Environmental Design."

6. Harry Backus, *Designing Restaurant Interiors: A Guide for Food Service Operators* (New York: Lebhar-Friedman, 1977), pp. 53–55.

7. John T. Suter, "What Lighting Can Do for You," *Food Service Marketing,* vol. 38, no. 4, p. 53.

8. *The Perceived Value of Tabletop Architecture,* vol. 1 (Syracuse, New York: Syracuse China Corporation, 1980), p. 1.

Further Reading

McKay, Edward S., *The Marketing Mystique* (American Management Association, New York: 1972).

Worchester, Robert M., and John Downham (eds.), *Consumer Market Research Handbook* (New York: Van Nostrand Reinhold, 1978).

Chapter 7

Planning and Designing the Menu

Chapter Outline

A foodservice operation's printed menu is an extremely important marketing tool, for it facilitates communication between management and consumers. If the menu is poorly designed and produced, this communication process will deteriorate. A well-designed and well-produced menu, however, will increase management's chances for success. A good menu is designed to sell.

    The chapter focuses on the following major sections:

Introduction

Menu-Planning Considerations

Selecting Menu Offerings

Producing the Printed Menu
- sources of menu-planning expertise
- the menu cover
- menu copywriting
- type style and paper stock
- menu-planning pitfalls to avoid
- wine lists and promotion

Accuracy in Menus

Cycle Menus
- cycle menu patterns
- marketing cycle menus

Evaluating Menu Effectiveness
- the importance of menu evaluation
- methods of menu evaluation

Summary

Introduction

The printed menu used by a foodservice operation affords management one of the best methods to communicate with the customer. The menu should provide more than a mere listing of the food and beverage offerings. The menu should influence the customers' selection of food and beverage items. Planning is crucial when creating menus; a successful menu does not result by chance. Careful planning and attention to design principles are needed at each step of the design process. No quick and easy formulas apply to all foodservice operations, but basic principles may be modified to fit the needs of each individual foodservice operation. The menu should complement the organization's other marketing activities. It should be designed to satisfy specific marketing objectives. A successful menu should, in fact, satisfy four major objectives.

First, the menu should further the goals of the marketing concept. Recall that the marketing concept held that the needs and wants of the consumer should be given priority. If the foodservice organization is successful in satisfying these needs and wants, then the marketing concept holds that financial success will naturally result. In short, if the consumers are happy, the operation will experience increasing volume and should succeed. It follows too that if consumers are not satisfied, volume will decrease, and the operation will not succeed. Therefore, every effort should be made to design the menu to include those food and beverage items that the targeted market segment(s) will find appealing. Establishing consumer needs and wants can be accomplished in some part through market research and analysis of internal marketing information systems and national menu census data.

Second, the menu should contribute to establishing the perceived image of the operation. For example, a menu used by an operation that appeals to young singles who desire a fun-loving atmosphere may use humorous names for menu items and cartoon drawings on the menu to establish the perceived image. A Mexican restaurant might use the drawings of a building with Mexican-style architecture on the front of its menu. The menu is one of the initial communication vehicles that the customer encounters after entering the foodservice operation. The menu's impact in the formation of a positive perceived image should not be discounted.

Third, the menu should act as a means to influence customer demand for menu items. Through menu clip-ons, menu item descriptions (copy), positioning of menu items on the menu, and special art work, the menu planner can influence customer demand. Extremely popular or profitable items are given extra attention or more prominent positioning, thereby making the customer more likely to select them. Attempting to influence customer behavior in this manner can result in a menu mix that not only increases the number of some menu items sold but can also substantially increase sales and gross profits. Experimenting with different menu mixes can result in substantially different levels of gross profitability, even without an increase in the total number of menu items sold.

Fourth, the menu is a vehicle to gain a competitive advantage. Successful operations often have selected menu items for which they are noted; these are called *signature items* and are promoted heavily on the menu, further adding to the competitive advantage. For example, Victoria Station is noted for its prime rib. Foodservice operators should attempt to create certain signature items to enhance the perceived image of the operation and to create a distinct competitive advantage.

The menu should also be used to increase repeat patronage. This can be accomplished by providing not only items that have proven to be highly popular but also a wide enough selection to prevent menu monotony. The menu can also provide a competitive advantage in appealing to new targeted market segments. By closely studying menu census data and market research data, management can identify trends and alter the menu to take advantage of changing consumer tastes. The menu might also be used to expand the market, as it does when banquet services are promoted within the regular menu. The promotional piece draws customers' attention to additional product-service offerings that they may not otherwise have considered.

Menu-Planning Considerations

Several factors should be taken into consideration during initial stages of the menu-design process. Perhaps the most obvious factor is the consumer. What are the likes and dislikes of those individuals who patronize the operation? What food items currently on the menu do they like most or the least? A detailed sales history is invaluable in menu planning. Any menu must satisfy the consumer in order to be successful; therefore, a foodservice manager must fully understand consumer behavior and must always keep the consumer in the proper perspective. The entire business should be organized so that the consumer will derive satisfaction. Managers must always strive to provide consumers with exactly what they want to buy, not just what management wishes to sell. If the consuming public is demanding fast-food items, then a prudent foodservice manager should provide these, even though a manager may, in fact, want to produce something else.

Management selects specifically targeted market segments, and the needs and wants of these market segments must always be the first consideration when planning a menu.

Once the consumer's desires are determined, another consideration arises. What is the availability and cost of the needed food and beverage products? Many food items are seasonal, and some may be difficult to obtain in a fresh state or at a reasonable price on a year-round basis. Once a foodservice manager has determined that consumers desire a certain product, then a consistent source of supply must be located.

The skills of production and service employees must also be considered. If new menu items are introduced, do the current employees possess all the talents and skills necessary to prepare and serve each new item correctly? If they do not, what training measures must be undertaken to teach them the necessary skills? Should additional employees be hired? These are important questions that a foodservice manager must ask during the initial stages of the menu-planning process.

The physical layout and design of the operation must also be considered. Is the foodservice equipment capable of producing the new menu items? Decisions regarding space limitations, equipment capacities, and layout must be made. Modifications in the layout of the kitchen and service areas may be necessary to facilitate production and serving of new menu items. In other instances, additional equipment may have to be purchased to produce and serve the new item. For example, if a foodservice manager decided to switch from American table service to a mixture of French and Russian table service, a considerable investment would have to be made in equipment.

Menus should provide consumers with the opportunity to select a nutritionally well-balanced meal. Certainly, institutional operations have a much stronger obligation to satisfy the nutritional needs of the clientele than do commercial operations. This is not to say, however, that commercial operations can ignore nutritional considerations. Every effort should be made to provide the consumer with the option of a meal that will satisfy one-third of the recommended dietary allowances.

Finally, menus must be balanced. Menus will achieve increased success if they balance several aesthetic factors. Food and beverage items must be selected so that overall the menu is a balanced variety of

- **Flavor.** Sweet, sour, spicy, hot, bland
- **Color.** Dark brown, golden brown, light green, dark green, white, red, orange
- **Texture.** Firm, soft, chewy, crisp

- **Shape.**   Cubed, solid, ground, strips, balls, sliced
- **Preparation method.**   Broiled, fried, baked, braised, boiled
- **Sauces.**   Both a variety of sauce and nonsauce items should be included.

Selecting Menu Offerings

Before the management of a foodservice establishment begins the layout and planning of a menu, managers should list potential menu items. Table 7.1 breaks down categories representing many foodservice operations. Under each category, management should list several potential menu items. Potential items can be drawn from trade journals, recipe books, and a variety of other sources.

Once this listing is complete, management should rank-order each item in each category for its customer popularity and profitability. Based on these combined priorities, knowledge of the operation, and experience, management should begin to finalize the selection of menu items to be included on the new menu.[1]

Management should also consider menu census data to select food and beverage items for the menu. Several of the industry trade journals publish menu census reports. These reports represent the findings of national research studies undertaken by respected market research firms. *Restaurants & Institutions,* for example, annually publishes a menu census. The census contains useful information relating to (1) key menu trends, such as concern for freshness, (2) trends that allow for regional differences and uniqueness, (3) best-selling items in American foodservice (Figure 7.1) and (4) menu census data broken down by type of operation.

Table 7.1. Potential Menu Item Categories.

Food	Beverages
Appetizers	Nonalcoholic
Soups	Cocktails
Salads	Beer
Entrees	Wine
Sandwiches	After-dinner drinks
Specialty items	
Desserts	

While menu census data published by *Restaurants & Institutions, Restaurant Business,* and other industry journals will not provide data specific to one operation, these reports represent excellent sources for monitoring both geographic trends (national and regional) and trends by type of operation. When these data are combined with an internally generated sales history and with managerial judgment, the result is a solid basis for decisions concerning menu item selection.

Figure 7.1. Results of *Restaurants & Institutions'* Annual Menu Census. *Restaurants & Institutions,* vol. 90, no. 7, April 1, 1982, pp. 31–70.
Reprinted with permission: *Restaurants & Institutions* magazine, a Cahners publication.

THE BEST-SELLING APPETIZERS
(by 1981 check average)

Less than $2	$2 to $5	$5 to $7.50	$7.50 to $10	More than $10
Fruit cup	Cottage cheese	Shrimp cktl.	Shrimp cktl.	Shrimp cktl.
Fresh fruit	Fresh fruit	Fruit cup	Clams	Clams
Cottage cheese	Fruit cup	Cottage cheese	Fresh fruit	Melon
Melon	Melon	Fresh fruit	Fruit cup	Oysters
Raw veg.	Grapefruit	Deep-fried veg.	Raw veg.	Crab cktl.
Grapefruit	Raw veg.	Veg. relishes	Deep-fried veg.	Fresh fruit
Veg. relishes	Veg. relishes	Clams	Oysters	Fruit cup
Deep-fried veg.	Shrimp cktl.	Oysters	Quiche	Antipasto
Egg rolls	Deep-fried veg.	Crab cktl.	Antipasto	Escargot
Quiche	Quiche	Antipasto	Potato skins	Canapés

THE BEST-SELLING SOUPS
(by 1981 check average)

Less than $2	$2 to $5	$5 to $7.50	$7.50 to $10	More than $10
Chicken	Vegetable	Vegetable	Clam chowder	Clam chowder
Chili	Chicken	Chicken	Chicken	French onion
Vegetable	Chili	Clam chowder	French onion	Vegetable
Beef-based	Beef-based	French onion	Vegetable	Chicken
Tomato	Bean	Beef-based	Beef-based	Seafood
Bean	Clam chowder	Pea	Minestrone	Minestrone
Minestrone	Tomato	Bean	Bean	Beef-based
Clam Chowder	Potato	Chili	Pea	Mushroom
Potato	Pea	Potato	Seafood	Bean
Pea	Minestrone	Minestrone	Mushroom	Pea

Fig. 7.1. *continued*

THE BEST-SELLING SALADS

(by 1981 check average)

Less than $2	$2 to $5	$5 to $7.50	$7.50 to $10	More than $10
Tossed greens	Coleslaw	Coleslaw	Tossed greens	House salad
Fruit	Tossed greens	Tossed greens	Coleslaw	Tossed greens
Potato	Potato	Potato	House salad	Sliced tomato
Coleslaw	Sliced tomato	Cottage cheese	Potato	Spinach
Gelatin	Cottage cheese	House salad	Sliced tomato	Potato
Cottage cheese	Fruit	Sliced tomato	Cottage cheese	Fruit
Sliced tomato	Macaroni	Fruit	Fruit	Coleslaw
Macaroni	Gelatin	Macaroni	Sliced cukes	Cottage cheese
Sliced cukes	Sliced cukes	Sliced cukes	Macaroni	Sliced cukes
House salad	House salad	Mixed veg.	Mixed veg.	Mixed veg.

THE BEST-SELLING SIDE DISHES/VEGETABLES

(by 1981 check average)

Less than $2	$2 to $5	$5 to $7.50	$7.50 to $10	More than $10
French fries	French fries	French fries	French fries	Mushrooms
Mashed pot.	Mashed pot.	Baked pot.	Baked pot.	Baked pot.
Green beans	Tomatoes	Mushrooms	Mushrooms	French fries
Corn	Pickles	Tomatoes	Broccoli	Broccoli
Apples	Green beans	Am. fries	Tomatoes	Tomatoes
Pickles	Am. fries	Green beans	Am. fries	Green beans
Cling peaches	Onion rings	Mashed pot.	Green beans	Zucchini
Pasta	Hash browns	Pickles	Zucchini	Carrots
Pineapple	Peas	Broccoli	Onion rings	Cauliflower
Noodles	Baked pot.	Peas	Cauliflower	Seasoned rice

THE BEST-SELLING SANDWICHES

(by 1981 check average)

Less than $2	$2 to $5	$5 to $7.50	$7.50 to $10	More than $10
Hamburger	Hamburger	Hamburger	Hamburger	Hamburger
Cheeseburger	Cheeseburger	Cheeseburger	Cheeseburger	Cheeseburger
Ham & cheese	Ham & cheese	Ham & cheese	Ham & cheese	Steak
Hot dog	Ham	Ham	Roast beef	Club
Grilled chse.	Grilled chse.	Steak	Club	Ham & cheese
Ham	Hot dog	Club	Ham	Ham
BBQ beef	BLT	BLT	Steak	Reuben
Sloppy Joe	Fish	Roast beef	BLT	Roast beef
Sub	Tuna salad	Tuna salad	Reuben	Corned beef
Tuna salad	BBQ beef	Reuben	Tuna salad	Turkey

Fig. 7.1. *continued*

THE BEST-SELLING DESSERTS

(by 1981 check average)

Less than $2	$2 to $5	$5 to $7.50	$7.50 to $10	More than $10
Cookies	Apple pie	Ice cream	Ice cream	Cheesecake
Choc. cake	Ice cream	Apple pie	Cheesecake	Ice cream
Brownies	Cherry pie	Cheesecake	Apple pie	Apple pie
Ice cream	Pumpkin pie	Pie a la mode	Choc. cake	Pastries
Choc. pudding	Choc. pie	Pumpkin pie	Pie a la mode	Fresh fruit
Apple pie	Cheesecake	Cherry pie	Sherbet	Choc. cake
Fresh fruit	Choc. cake	Choc. cake	Carrot cake	Sherbet
Canned peaches	Coc. cr. pie	Pecan pie	Fresh fruit	Pecan pie
Gelatin	Carrot cake	Choc. pie	Cherry pie	Pie a la mode
Yellow cake	Lemon pie	Carrot cake	Sundaes	Choc. pie

THE BEST-SELLING BEVERAGES

(by 1981 check average)

Less than $2	$2 to $5	$5 to $7.50	$7.50 to $10	More than $10
White milk	Coffee	Coffee	Coffee	Coffee
Coffee	Iced tea	Iced tea	Beer (reg.)	Wine
Choc. milk	White milk	Decaf. coffee	Beer (light)	Beer (reg.)
Low-fat milk	Pre/post mix	Pre/post mix	Wine	Beer (light)
Decaf. coffee	soft drinks	soft drinks	Iced tea	Iced tea
Iced tea	Decaf. coffe	Beer (reg.)	Hot tea	Hot tea
Hot tea	Hot tea	White milk	Decaf. coffee	Decaf. coffee
Lemonade	Hot chocolate	Hot tea	Pre/post mix	White milk
Hot chocolate	Diet soft dr.	Beer (light)	soft drinks	Pre/post mix
Pre/post mix	Choc. milk	Wine	White milk	soft drinks
soft drinks	Wine	Diet soft dr.	Diet soft dr.	Mineral water

THE BEST-SELLING MEAT ENTREES

(by 1981 check average)

Less than $2	$2 to $5	$5 to $7.50	$7.50 to $10	More than $10
Chili w/meat	Roast beef	Steak	Steak	Steak
Roast beef	Baked ham	Roast beef	Prime rib	Prime rib
Meatloaf	Chopped steak	Baked ham	Roast beef	Meat/seafood
Meat balls	Chili w/meat	BBQ ribs	Meat/seafood	combo
Baked ham	Sausage	Prime rib	combo	Other veal
Beef stew	Meatloaf	Pork chops	Baked ham	Veal chop
Sausage	Beef stew	Chopped steak	BBQ ribs	Roast beef
Chopped steak	Steak	Sausage	Veal chop	Lamb chop
Beef & noodles	Meat balls	Chili w/meat	Veal Parmesan	Pork chop
Sliced beef	Pork chops	Sliced beef	Other veal	BBQ ribs
w/gravy		w/gravy	Chopped steak	Veal Parmesan

Fig. 7.1. *continued*

THE BEST-SELLING SEAFOOD ENTREES

(by 1981 check average)

Less than $2	$2 to $5	$5 to $7.50	$7.50 to $10	More than $10
Tuna	Cod	Fried shrimp	Fried shrimp	Other shrimp
Cod	Fried shrimp	Other shrimp	Scallops	Scallops
Portion/sticks	Tuna	Sea. platter	Other shrimp	Fried shrimp
Fried shrimp	Portion/sticks	Scallops	Alaska king	Alaska king
Haddock	Haddock	Cod	crab	crab
Perch	Flounder	Tuna	Sea. platter	Lobster tail
Flounder	Sea. platter	Flounder	Flounder	Oysters
Other shrimp	Other shrimp	Alaska king	Clams	Clams
Sea. platter	Perch	crab	Cod	Sea. platter
Breaded portions	Scallops	Haddock	Snapper	Flounder
& sticks		Oysters	Lobster tail	Snapper

THE BEST-SELLING POULTRY ENTREES

(by 1981 check average)

Less than $2	$2 to $5	$5 to $7.50	$7.50 to $10	More than $10
Fried/broasted	Fried/broasted	Fried/broasted	Fried/broasted	Fried/broasted
chicken	chicken	chicken	chicken	chicken
Roast turkey	Roast turkey	Turkey breast	Turkey breast	Broiled chicken
Sliced turkey	Turkey breast	Roast turkey	Broiled chicken	Duck
Chicken	Chicken fillet	Chicken	Roast turkey	Chicken
w/gravy	Chicken	w/gravy	Chicken	w/gravy
Turkey breast	w/gravy	Chicken/turkey	w/gravy	Turkey breast
BBQ chicken	Chicken/turkey	salad	Roast chicken	Chicken fillet
Chicken/turkey	salad	Sliced turkey	Sliced turkey	Ch. Cordon Bleu
salad	Sliced turkey	BBQ chicken	Chicken fillet	Chicken/turkey
Roast chicken	BBQ chicken	Broiled chicken	Chicken/turkey	salad
Turkey roll	Roast chicken	Roast chicken	salad	Roast chicken
Chicken fillet	Broiled chicken	Chicken fillet	BBQ chicken	Roast turkey

THE BEST-SELLING OTHER ENTREES

(by 1981 check average)

Less than $2	$2 to $5	$5 to $7.50	$7.50 to $10	More than $10
Spaghetti	Spaghetti	Spaghetti	Omelets	Omelets
w/sauce	w/sauce	w/sauce	Spaghetti	Entree salads
Lasagna	Pancakes	Omelets	w/sauce	Quiche
Pizza	Spaghetti	Lasagna	Spaghetti w/	Spaghetti
Tacos	w/meatballs	Spaghetti w/	meatballs	w/sauce
Mac. & cheese	Mac. & cheese	meatballs	Fruit plate	Fruit plate
Spaghetti	Omelets	Pancakes	Entree salads	Lasagna
w/meatballs	Entree salads	Entree salads	Lasagna	Crepes
Ravioli	Fruit plate	Fruit plate	Quiche	Spaghetti w/
Entree salads	Pizza	Mac. & cheese	Pancakes	meatballs
Pancakes	Baked beans	Baked potato	Mac. & cheese	Eggs Benedict
Burritos	w/meat	entrees	Eggs Benedict	Cold plate
		Pizza		w/meat

Fig. 7.1. *continued*

UP-AND-COMERS, MOVERS-AND-SHAKERS: WHAT'S BEING ADDED TO AMERICA'S MENUS

The foods below may not all be among the best-sellers in their categories, but they are the foods that made the biggest percentage increases in on-menu appearance. Squid, for example, is offered on only 5% of menus, but that is nearly double its showing last year. Other foods, such as hamburgers and french fries, are on such a large percentage of menus that they have little room for growth.

Appetizers	Salads	Salad Dressings	Veg./Side dishes	Potatoes/starches
Antipasto	Avocado	Thousand island	Apples	Formed potatoes
Potato skins	Fruit	House specialty	Stir-fried veg.	Pasta (any)
Crab cocktail	Cottage cheese	Green Goddess	Fritters	Grits
Shrimp cocktail	Carrot & raisin	Italian	Fruit garnish	Noodles (any)
Escargot	Sliced cucumbers	Blue cheese	Mushrooms	White rice

Poultry	Meats	Fish/seafood	Other entrees	Sandwiches
Chick. Cordon Bleu	Meat/seafood combo	Bouillabaisse	Quiche	Vegetarian
Chicken Kiev	Steak teriyaki	Squid	Burritos	Sliced turkey
Poultry casseroles	Veal dishes	Mussels	Enchiladas	Monte Cristo
Broiled chicken	Beef Wellington	King crab	Tacos	Gyros
Rock Cornish hen	Veal chops	Pacific sole	Lasagna	Sloppy Joe

Cakes	Other desserts	Breakfast items	Juices	Beverages
Cheesecake	Fried pies	Muffins (any)	Fruit blends	Mineral water
Poundcake	Cobbler	Fresh fruit	Apple	Wine
Banana	Canned fruit	Canadian bacon	Grape	Bottled soft drinks
Carrot	Prunes	Oranges	Cranberry	Low-fat milk
Angel food	Fresh fruit	Prunes	Pineapple	Chocolate milk

Fig. 7.1. *continued*

MOST COMMON ITEMS ADDED TO MENUS DUE TO INCREASED POPULARITY

Fishing for more customers, operators at all levels of business added more fish and seafood items to meet increased demand. And the "lighter foods" trend isn't dead yet; salads, soups and sandwiches reappeared on menus in 1981.

(by 1981 check average)

Less than $2	$2 to $5	$5 to $7.50	$7.50 to $10	More than $10
Tacos/burritos/tamales	Chicken	Chicken	Other seafood	Other fish
Salads/salad bars	Chicken sandwich	Other fish	Other fish	Chicken
Chicken sandwich	Salads/salad bar	Steak/prime rib	Chicken	Other seafood
Other Mexican dishes	Other fish	Salads/salad bar	Crab/crab legs	Crab/crab legs
Pizza	Soups/chili/chowder	Shrimp	BBQ ribs	Veal dishes
Hot sandwiches	Other sandwiches	Other seafood	Shrimp	Steak/prime rib
Other sandwiches	Hot sandwiches	Chicken sandwich	Scallops	Lamb dishes
Quiche	Hamburger/cheesebgr.	Potato dishes	Soups/chili/chowder	Lobster
Soups/chili/chowder	Other Mexican dishes	Other sandwiches	Other sandwiches	Shrimp
Potato dishes	Steak/prime rib	Soups/chili/chowder	Steak/prime rib	Desserts

Fig. 7.1. *continued*

THE "BAR" CONCEPT CATCHES ON: WHO HAS WHAT

As merchandising gains importance, specialty bars are becoming more common features.

(by 1981 check average)

Feature	Less than 2	$2 to $5	$5 to $7.50	$7.50 to $10	More than $10
Salad bar	89.0%	83.5%	81.4%	80.5%	68.1%
Sandwich bar	36.0	24.2	8.5	8.0	11.0
Soup bar	21.2	23.3	20.9	13.8	11.0
Dessert bar	19.6	21.1	8.5	11.5	23.1
Full buffet promotions	10.2	17.8	30.2	25.3	27.5
Breakfast/brunch buffet	6.9	17.8	30.2	25.3	27.5
Cheese bar	3.1	1.3	3.1	6.9	5.5

CHANGES IN CUSTOMER COUNTS, REVENUES AND COSTS, 1980-1981

The good news is that customer counts increased for 50% of the industry, overall, and that operating revenues increased for 63%. The bad news is that food costs rose at 71% of the operations surveyed; labor costs were up at 74%.

(by 1981 check average)

	Less than $2	$2 to $5	$5 to $7.50	$7.50 to $10	More than $10
Customer counts:					
Increased	44.7%	54.9%	58.8%	57.4%	66.1%
Decreased	35.7	23.5	23.7	28.7	20.1
Flat	19.6	21.6	17.5	13.9	13.8
Operating revenues:					
Increased	61.6	65.4	66.9	67.2	75.7
Decreased	24.0	21.1	19.6	20.3	10.9
Flat	14.4	13.5	13.5	12.5	13.4
Food costs:					
Increased	80.2	71.0	69.9	67.3	64.8
Decreased	10.2	13.8	12.3	16.6	16.8
Flat	9.6	15.2	17.8	16.1	18.4
Labor costs:					
Increased	82.0	73.0	75.4	69.1	71.0
Decreased	8.3	12.4	12.3	11.5	12.9
Flat	9.7	14.6	12.3	19.4	16.1

Producing the Printed Menu

Sources of Menu-Planning Expertise

All foodservice managers like to consider themselves professionals in the foodservice field. Foodservice, like any other field, requires certain unique skills and expertise. Not all managers, however, possess all the necessary skills that the field demands. When planning and designing a menu, layout, copywriting, and artistic skills are needed, yet many foodservice managers do not have a great deal of talent or skill in these areas. A wise manager recognizes these shortcomings and seeks professional assistance.

A wide variety of sources is available. Some sources can complete the entire menu from initial planning to final production and printing. Others may only be able to offer expertise dealing with certain aspects of the menu. The first source of assistance is a firm engaged solely in menu layout and design. Many menu-design firms offer stock menus as well as custom-designed menus tailored to each individual operation. In developing a custom-designed menu, they will completely design and produce the concept, design, typesetting, paste-up, photography, and printing. These services are not inexpensive, but the investment in professionally designed and produced menus is normally rewarded by increased sales and by the achievement of the manager's menu objectives.

Advertising agencies may also be able to assist in menu design. Agencies maintain individuals on staff who can produce photographs and art work suitable for a foodservice menu. They also employ copywriters who may be able to add the extra flair that a menu needs to make it unique and to produce increased sales.

If a foodservice manager chooses to design a menu personally, the only outside help necessary is a top-quality printer. Most printers will be able to do the job adequately, but it is wise to work closely with a printer who has experience with menus. When selecting a printer consider the following questions: Is the printer's equipment capable of producing the size, color, and style of the menu exactly as desired? Is the printer able to provide quick service on short runs when prices or menu items change?[2]

The Menu Cover

First impressions are critically important. Therefore, the design of the cover is critical. It sets the tone, creates the mood, and establishes the image of the foodservice establishment in the mind of the consumer.

The choice of cover designs is nearly limitless, but a number of factors may limit the selection process. Cost limitations may force a manager to select a more conservative and less expensive menu cover. If cost is of great concern, then only one color should be printed on a solid-color background. This can still have a dramatic effect, yet it remains relatively inexpensive. The length of service desired for the menu is another factor that should be considered when selecting a menu cover. If a long service life is desired, heavy-weight and grease-resistant paper stock should be used.

No concrete rules dictate exactly what should be included on a menu cover, so the following are only guidelines. The name of the foodservice operation and any art work should appear on the front, while the address, phone number, hours of operation, and credit cards accepted should be included on either the front or the back cover. The cover should reflect the theme and atmosphere of the foodservice operation and should be as creative as possible. Figures 7.2–7.8 all show high-quality menu covers. Each is unique and reflects the theme and image of its foodservice operation. All feature art work that helps create an image in the consumer's mind and adds interest to the dining experience.

Menu Copywriting

The words appearing on the menu are referred to as *copy*. These words must be carefully chosen and must be designed to sell, rather than merely list, the available food items and prices. A well-written menu has a definite

Figure 7.2. The style and sophistication of this foodservice operation is shown by the drawing and type style. It is brown and black on a white background.
Courtesy: Restaurants No Limit, Inc.

Figure 7.3. This restaurant specializes in fresh fish, and this cover shows where each item on the menu originates. It is black and red on a white background.

Courtesy: Strang Management Corp.

Figure 7.4. This menu cover uses creative art work for a specific image for the foodservice operation.

Courtesy: Seaberg, *Menu Design, Merchandising and Marketing,* 3rd edition, CBI Publishing Company, Boston, MA.

Figure 7.5. This menu cover reflects the formal atmosphere of the Greenbrier Hotel. It sets the tone and establishes an expected type of dining experience.
Courtesy: The Greenbrier Hotel.

Figure 7.6. This menu cover in brown tones portrays the casual atmosphere of the restaurant.
Courtesy: The Catawba Emporium.

Figure 7.7. Menu covers can be cut in almost any shape desired. This one is cut in the shape of a lantern. It complements the theme of the restaurant, which is mining. The back cover of this menu is shown in Figure 7.8.

Courtesy: Restaurants No Limit, Inc.

Figure 7.8. The back cover of the menu shown in Fig. 7.7.

Courtesy: Restaurants No Limit, Inc.

flair that can be translated into higher check averages and increased profits. As all managers are interested in increased sales, menu copy is an excellent starting point for reaching this goal. Menu copy can be divided into three main categories: (1) listings of menu items and prices, (2) descriptive selling of menu items, and (3) copy relating to extra services or special cuisine offered by the foodservice operation.

Listing menu items and prices is the first and most basic step in developing menu copy, but it is important to consider the organization and sequencing of the items as well. In what order should the items appear on the menu? Should all the items receive equal attention? To answer the first question, one school of thought holds that the items should appear on the menu in the same order in which the customer would eat them. For example, appetizers should be followed by soups and salads, entrees, and then desserts. If a foodservice operation does not follow a rigid pattern of service, similar menu items should be grouped together. This might mean grouping sandwiches, side orders, pizzas, beverages, and complete dinners. All menu items should not receive equal attention on the menu. Not all items are equally popular with consumers, nor are they equally profitable to the operator. Therefore, items that should be given special and bolder attention are those popular with consumers, profitable for the operation, or preferably, both.

Another school of thought is that menu items should be positioned so that the most popular and profitable items are seen first by the consumer. This will initiate the dining experience in a positive manner. Figure 7.9 illustrates the eye-movement pattern typical of threefold menus. Generally speaking, a consumer looking at a single-page menu will first focus slightly

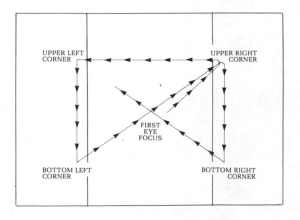

Figure 7.9. Eye movement across the threefold menu.

Source: Miller, Jack, *Menu Pricing and Strategy* (CBI Publishing, 1980), p. 1.

above the middle of the page. With a four-page menu, a consumer will focus slightly above the middle of the right-hand page when looking at the inner two pages.

Many foodservice managers merely list the menu items and the corresponding prices. The consumer's first reading of the menu copy is the "moment of truth" for any foodservice operation. The consumer is going to make a selection based on the presentation of the items on the menu. The menu should be designed with flair and should predominantly feature popular and profitable items. A menu lacking any descriptive selling of its items is dull, for if menu items and prices are merely listed, the menu looks as dull as a telephone book with names on one side and numbers on the other. Today's foodservice consumers are becoming more sophisticated and are demanding more. Consumers have been exposed to many innovative operations and are increasingly less likely to patronize operations with dull and mundane menus and presentations. The menu should not merely list; it should sell!

A wide variety of descriptions can be placed on the menu to aid in selling the items. A few examples follow:

- **Chateaubriand for Two.**   18-ounce center-cut choice steer tenderloin with Duchess potatoes, bouquetiere of fresh vegetables, and bearnaise sauce, served at tableside. (Courtesy: Restaurants No Limit, Inc., Minneapolis, MN.)
- **Don's (Now Famous) Bucket for Two.**   Consists of two Maine Lobsters, Dungeness Crab, corn—cob and all, redskin potatoes, mussels, and steamers, and we may throw in some seaweed at no extra charge. New romances may be spawned over this one. Take the lobster and the crab, for example. (Courtesy: Strang Management Corp., Cleveland, OH.)
- **Any Pork in a Storm.**   Hickory-smoked bacon, Vienna corned beef, Swiss cheese, and cole slaw served *hot* on French bread. (Courtesy: D. B. Kaplan's Delicatessen, Inc., Chicago, IL.)
- **Attila the Ham.**   Breast of turkey, Polish baked ham, shredded lettuce, tomato slices, and mayo on an onion roll. (Courtesy: D. B. Kaplan's Delicatessen, Inc., Chicago, IL.)

All menu items cannot be given such extensive description, but most items can be given some extra copy. Copy can easily be developed to show an item's preparation, ingredients used, portion size, quality of steak or meat, or any other special features. It is not difficult to add flair to a menu. The copy need not be amusing, only accurately descriptive.

The third category of menu copy is related to extra services, special cuisine, or other interesting features. A foodservice menu should never contain any blank pages. Pages that do not contain menu items should be used to promote such extra services as banquets, takeouts, or other features. Menus should be treated as advertising space. When one purchases a menu, all of it is paid for, not just the pages that carry printing, and therefore, any blank pages are a waste of money. These pages could be used to promote the operation. This copy may actively promote such profit makers as banquets, or it may reinforce the operation's image by discussing the quality of products used or by describing any special furniture or paintings the foodservice operation might own. Use the space to the greatest promotional advantage. It is better to have a patron reading about the process by which the beef is aged rather than glaring across the dining room at a waitress or reading where the silverware is manufactured. Figures 7.10 and 7.11 show menu copy used to promote extra services or cuisine or merely to enhance the operation's image.

Figure 7.10. Copy Explaining a Menu Item's History.
Courtesy: Strang Management Corp.

The Greenbrier heritage.

Heritage. It's something passed on from generation to generation. For The Greenbrier, it began over a billion years ago when the mystical waters of White Sulphur Springs sprung forth from the earth.

But, it wasn't until 1778 that people flocked to the springs to drink and bathe in its "miraculous" waters. And, as word spread about the springs and the fertile land around it, settlers came in great numbers to the beautiful Greenbrier Valley nestled in the Allegheny Mountains.

Over the following two hundred years, White Sulphur Springs has entertained kings and presidents. In rustic cottages and in grandiose suites. The years have seen belles and beaux of high society. And the battle weary soldiers of the Civil War and World War II.

But, the greatest heritage The Greenbrier has to offer is its people. The ladies and gentlemen who serve you have a heritage of their own. From generation to generation, many of their families have passed on the prestige that goes with serving at The Greenbrier.

Possibly the truest reflection of The Greenbrier heritage is the Spa. With its mineral water baths and other relaxing treatments, the Spa is a rejuvenating experience. And when it comes to service, there's nothing quite like the individual pampering you receive at The Greenbrier Spa.

Another scene of individualized service is the sophisticated Tavern Room. A warm dining experience complete with brick archways, shining pewter and silver accented by the soft glow of candlelight. Dinner service is in the continental French style and, after dinner, the Tavern Room Lounge features your favorite popular and big band music for dancing and listening (seasonal).

Or enjoy dinner dancing in an informal, country club setting. A popular rendezvous for drinks, dinner and dancing is the Golf Club. An end-of-day relaxed atmosphere prevails as the sun sets over the golf courses and mountains. Dress as sporty or dressy as you like while you enjoy the view, cocktails, dinner and music for dancing. And every afternoon at the Golf Club there's the famous Greenbrier Buffet for fabulous luncheons (spring through fall).

Wherever you dine, and whatever you do, you're always a part of The Greenbrier heritage. That of "ladies and gentlemen serving ladies and gentlemen."

Figure 7.11. Menu Copy that Sells the Consumer on the Heritage of The Greenbrier.

Reprinted courtesy of The Greenbrier Hotel.

THE
Greenbrier
WHITE SULPHUR SPRINGS
WEST VIRGINIA 24986

Type Style and Paper Stock

Through careful selection of type style and paper stock, a foodservice manager can greatly improve a menu. Type style and paper stock can be used in combination to create the desired impression. The menu is one of the few communication links with the consumer, so it must be both readable and attractive.

When selecting type style or paper stock, it is advisable to view the samples under the same environmental conditions as the consumer seeing the menu. Do not, for example, select type style or paper stock under bright fluorescent lighting if the lighting in the dining room is low-level incandescent.

Many different type styles are available in a wide range of sizes. Most printers have a wide enough selection to satisfy the needs of most foodservice operations. A few guidelines should be followed so that the final menu is both readable and attractive. Type size is measured in points, so that type ranges from 6 to 72 points. Most menus should not be printed in a type size of less than 12 points because smaller sizes are difficult to read. It is also advisable to use a different type style and size for headings than that used for the remainder of the menu copy. By doing this, the headings are bolder and stand out better. A combination of lowercase and capital letters should be used, for a menu made entirely of capital letters is more difficult to read.

The primary consideration when selecting paper stock is the length of service desired. If a menu is going to be changed weekly, it would not have to be printed on stock as heavy as one that has to be changed monthly. For menus a manager is planning to use for an extended period of time, lamination may be applied, making the menu impervious to liquids and grease. High-quality paper stock may also be protected by a leatherette cover to increase the length of service of a menu.

Menus are not inexpensive to design and produce, and the cost of the paper will represent roughly one-third the cost of printing a menu. It is, however, false economy to use a menu after its useful life is over. A consumer is easily turned off by a menu that appears dog eared or stained. Prices that have been crossed out and written in by hand only draw unnecessary attention to price increases. A menu is an important communication tool. Its appearance should be the very best that a foodservice operation can offer.

Menu-Planning Pitfalls to Avoid

Despite the best efforts of foodservice managers, many mistakes are made in menu design and production. The following are common menu pitfalls:

- **Physical size.**   Often a menu is too small to accommodate all the menu items. The result is overcrowding, which makes the menu difficult to read. On the other hand, some menus are so large that they become difficult for the guest to handle, particularly at a crowded table. Management should strive to achieve a happy medium.
- **Type size too small.**   Often the type size is too small for many people. Not everyone has 20/20 vision, and many consumers are somewhat vain and do not want to put on glasses just to read the menu.
- **Menu fails to sell.**   Many menus lack any sort of descriptive selling copy. These menus fail to communicate fully with the guest.
- **Menu items treated equally.**   Do not treat all menu items equally on a menu. A foodservice operation does not make an equal profit on all food and beverage items. To increase sales, special attention should be given to those items that are popular and/or profitable.
- **Using tacky clip-ons.**   Make certain that any menu clip-ons do not cover any part of the regular menu. It is also advisable to have the clip-on printed on the same paper stock and in the same type style as the regular menu. In this way, the clip-on will appear as an integral part of the menu, not as an afterthought.
- **Forgetting the basics.**   Be sure to include on the menu such basic information as hours of operation and credit cards accepted.[3]

Wine Lists and Promotion

Wine has two major attributes. First, it offers a chance for romance and enjoyment. Second, it can be highly profitable, especially when a substantial volume is sold. These two attributes mark wine for special attention. Many aspects of menu design apply to the design of a wine list as well. The successful selling of wine depends not only on a well-planned wine list but also on personal selling by the service personnel. Several factors should be considered when designing a wine list.

First, an idea successfully used by many foodservice organizations is to link specific wines with each individual entree on the menu. Usually, two wines are suggested as most complementary with each entree. Of the two wines suggested, one should be in the low-to-moderate price range and the other wine in the moderate-to-high price range. By suggesting wines in different price ranges, the guest has a choice without being made to feel as though the higher-priced wines are being promoted exclusively. Suggestive selling of wines to accompany each entree is highly recommended. Following the description of the entree, the suggested wines can be mentioned by name or by bin number. Another popular way to suggest wines is to list the suggested bin number in a column next to the entrees.

Second, a description of the wine on the actual wine list assists the guest, especially the novice wine drinker, in selection. Despite the ever-increasing per-capita consumption of wine in the United States, many foodservice guests are unsure of themselves when they order wine. In many cases, where the name of the wine and vintage are the only listing, the guest does not have enough information to make an informed decision. If a description of each wine were included, the guest would feel more sure of the selected wine and would not feel nearly as anxious.

Finally, the most-neglected aspect of selling wines is the service personnel. Often, they do not have the tools necessary to sell the wine properly. They need to be adequately trained not only in presenting, opening, and pouring the wine but also in how to sell the wine. Aspects of personal selling are discussed in Chapter 11.

The marketing and promotion of wine is an aspect of menu planning and design that often does not receive adequate time and attention to detail. Wine is a profitable aspect of the operation, and professionally planned wine lists are a real asset.

Accuracy in Menus

In recent years, a growing concern among consumer groups has been the operation of foodservice establishments. For a long time, little attention was given to foodservice operations, and managers were left to operate as they saw fit. Foodservice operations were, of course, subject to licensing, minimum wage, tax, and sanitation laws and codes, but the words placed on the menu were not legislated or controlled to any great extent. Consumer groups have, however, become more active in this area, and an ever-growing number of states, counties, and local municipalities are discussing and enacting legislation to prohibit deceptive or false advertising of food and beverage items on the menu.

Los Angeles County was an early national leader in adopting such legislation. An outline of these requirements follows:

- Volume must be accurate. For example, a cup of soup is less than a bowl.
- Size for such items as eggs and shrimp must meet existing requirements.
- Weight must be accurate. For example, a 10-ounce top sirloin must weigh 10 ounces before cooking.
- Grades, such as A, AA, and USDA meat grades, must not be misrepresented. For example, a steak called prime must be USDA prime, not USDA choice or any lower grade.
- Brand names must be accurate as well. Blue cheese may not be substituted for Roquefort cheese. If Jello is used on the menu, then Jello brand must be served, not another gelatine product.

- The point of origin must be exactly as stated on the menu. For example, Idaho potatoes must be used if they are named specifically on the menu; Colorado mountain trout must be from Colorado.
- The method of preparation represented on the menu must be accurate. If a menu item is represented as charbroiled, it must be exactly that and nothing else.
- Any new item represented as fresh must not be previously frozen at any time during processing or transportation.
- Merchandising terms, such as "our own special salad dressing," "chef's special sauce," or "finest quality," must not be used when the operation is unable to substantiate such statements. Commercially prepared salad dressing or sauces may not be called "house specialties."

A study undertaken under the direction of Dr. Bailus Walker, Administrator of Environmental Health Administration, in Washington, D.C., during the fall of 1977 was to determine the accuracy of menus in 141 public eating establishments. The study was conducted to evaluate the accuracy in language used to describe foods on menus. Highlights of this study include the following points:

- One hundred percent of the shrimp advertised as fresh had been previously frozen.
- Fifteen percent of the foodservice operations advertised a bakery product, implying it was freshly made or prepared on the premises when, in fact, it was a commercial product.
- Seventy percent of the fruit salads or cups advertised as fresh contained some commercially packed fruit sections with a preservative as an ingredient.
- Ninety percent of the foodservice operations listing USDA prime rib of beef were using USDA choice beef ribs.
- Eighty-five percent of the foodservice operations featuring roasts and steak cuts as USDA prime could not substantiate this grade.
- Over 95 percent of the foodservice operations surveyed purchased "ground beef," a commercially ground meat product from official USDA establishments. This product, in turn, was represented in 26 different manners on the menus, ranging from chopped sirloin to chopped tenderloin.
- In 75 percent of the foodservice operations where chicken was identified as the basic ingredient, a commercially cooked turkey product was used.
- Fifty percent of the foodservice operations were serving delicatessen products that were not kosher, as was indicated on the menu.
- Domestic blue cheese was substituted for Roquefort in 75 percent of the foodservice operations listing it on the menu.

- No beefsteak tomatoes or Idaho potatoes were available in any of the foodservice operations where these products were listed on the menu.
- Seventy-five percent of the foodservice operations stating a specific geographic origin for seafood entrees were unable to substantiate the claim.
- In more than 75 percent of the establishments where portions were prepared or sliced on the premises to meet a stated portion on the menu, a minimum of a 10- to 20-percent variance in weight favored management.[4]

This study was, of course, limited to 141 foodservice operations in the District of Columbia, and made no generalizations about the remainder of the country. Figure 7.12 is the position paper of the National Restaurant Association concerning accuracy in menus. This is a standard that all foodservice operations would do well to uphold. Compromising standards is not only unethical; it is poor marketing as well.

Several sources of assistance are available for the foodservice manager who wishes to assure that the menu is accurate. Several state restaurant associations offer services that include review of menus. If the menu is approved, the foodservice operation is able to market this approval in numerous ways, including menu stickers and table tent cards. A useful publication entitled simply "Menu Dictionary" is available from *The Cornell Hotel and Restaurant Administration Quarterly,* 327 Statler Hall, Cornell University, Ithaca, New York 14853. This booklet offers definitions and descriptions that managers would find useful when writing menu copy.

Accuracy in menus should be a major concern when a manager is writing or reviewing a menu. The following are guidelines:

- Read your menu! Check the details on the menu with what your kitchen staff actually serves. If you have made changes in purchasing or preparation but have not listed them on the menu, take immediate action to bring them into accord.
- Talk to your service personnel. Are they aware of what you serve and where it comes from? Do they describe your menu items correctly? Remember that accuracy in menus also includes the oral statements of employees as well as the printed menu. Perhaps a manager should conduct a menu review session with the entire staff.
- Evaluate consumer comments and complaints related to accuracy in menus.
- Institute a training program in handling consumer complaints. Standard operating practices should be developed for all possible situations.

Figure 7.12. National Restaurant Association Position Statement Concerning Accuracy in Menu Offerings.

Courtesy: The National Restaurant Association.

Accuracy In Menu Offerings

The food service industry has long recognized the importance of accuracy in describing its products, either on menus, and through visual or oral representation, both on ethical grounds and from the standpoint of customer satisfaction. The National Restaurant Association incorporated standards of accuracy in all representations to the public in its Standards of Business Practice, originally adopted by the Association in 1923. We reaffirm and strongly support the principles therein expressed.

"Truth in dining" or "truth in menu" laws and ordinances have been proposed in some government jurisdictions, and in a few cases adopted, in the belief that representations on restaurant menus present a unique problem in consumer protection. The National Restaurant Association believes that such legislation is unnecessary as Federal, state and many local governments have laws and regulations prohibiting false advertising and misrepresentations of products, and providing protection from fraud. In an industry such as ours, where economic survival depends upon customer satisfaction, misrepresentation is most effectively regulated by the severe sanction of customer dissatisfaction and loss of patronage.

To be equitable, the complexity of such legislation would be staggering. It is conceivable that standardized recipes for each menu listing would be required if regulatory refinement followed its logical course. The problems of enforcement, and proof if due process is observed, would be monumental, if not impossible.

The "truth in dining" movement is not confined to the proposition that restaurant menus be absolutely accurate in their representations. Legislation and ordinances have been proposed that would require the identification of a specific means of preservation, method of preparation or statement of food origin. Such requirements could unjustly imply that certain foods, processes or places of origin are unwholesome or inferior.

Government action must be confined to problems where its intervention can be effective and at a cost commensurate with the benefits to be gained.

Adopted February, 1977

One IBM Plaza/Suite 2600
Chicago, Illinois 60611
(312) 787-2525

Consumers expect and demand honest representation of food and beverages, and they have a right to get it. Accuracy-in-menu programs represent legitimate efforts by ethical business people and national and state restaurant associations.

Cycle Menus

Many managers of such institutional operations as hospitals feel that marketing does not play a part in the menu-planning and design process. Rather, their major focus is on the nutritional needs of the clients. Marketing should, however, be a major concern, in addition to nutritional concerns, because one of the biggest problems in institutional operations is menu monotony and lack of interest on the client's part. Management of institutional operations must give careful consideration to merchandising and marketing to increase client satisfaction.

Cycle Menu Patterns

Central to the menu-design process in institutions is the cycle menu. Institutional operations have developed and used many different forms of cycle menus. For example, a very short cycle of perhaps 7 days might be used in a hospital setting. A much longer cycle, perhaps 4 to 6 weeks, might be used for a university foodservice operation. This longer cycle is necessary to maintain customer interest. Table 7.2 illustrates one sample cycle pattern. Note that 18 separate daily menus have been developed, as well as 4 separate Friday and Sunday menus. These are combined into a cycle pattern that can be used for 18 weeks.

For marketing, cycle menus are most important because they can be used to reduce consumer boredom. Cycle menus should be constantly updated with new menu items to maintain consumer interest. In institutional settings, this is of critical importance. Once consumers become bored with the menu selection, it is not long before negative feelings begin to develop in other areas, such as food quality, sanitation, and price. Several excellent books are devoted solely to planning and developing cycle menus; managers with menu-planning responsibilities may wish to consult one of these sources.

Marketing Cycle Menus

In addition to producing a printed cycle menu, management should give careful consideration to the merchandising and marketing of the menu. Many managers use innovative names for menu items, ones that spark con-

Table 7.2. Cycle Menu for 18 Weeks.

Source: United States Department of Agriculture.

Week	Sunday	Monday	Tuesday	Wednesday	Thursday	Friday	Saturday
1	S–1	D–1	D–2	D–3	D–4	F–1	D–5
2	S–2	D–6	D–7	D–8	D–9	F–2	D–10
3	S–3	D–11	D–12	D–13	D–14	F–3	D–15
4	S–4	D–16	D–17	D–18	D–1	F–4	D–2
5	S–1	D–3	D–4	D–5	D–6	F–1	D–7
6	S–2	D–8	D–9	D–10	D–11	F–2	D–12
7	S–3	D–13	D–14	D–15	D–16	F–3	D–17
8	S–4	D–18	D–1	D–2	D–3	F–4	D–4
9	S–1	D–5	D–6	D–7	D–8	F–1	D–9
10	S–2	D–10	D–11	D–12	D–13	F–2	D–14
11	S–3	D–15	D–16	D–17	D–18	F–3	D–1
12	S–4	D–2	D–3	D–4	D–5	F–4	D–6
13	S–1	D–7	D–8	D–9	D–10	F–1	D–11
14	S–2	D–12	D–13	D–14	D–15	F–2	D–16
15	S–3	D–17	D–18	D–1	D–2	F–3	D–3
16	S–4	D–4	D–5	D–6	D–7	F–4	D–8
17	S–1	D–9	D–10	D–11	D–12	F–1	D–13
18	S–2	D–14	D–15	D–16	D–17	F–2	D–18

sumer interest and accurately reflect the nature of the food items. In addition, management should plan special events to maintain consumer interest. These special events should be periodically scheduled throughout the cycle (perhaps once per month). Special events might be used in a university foodservice operation to include

- Ethnic dinners (Mexican, Asian, or English)
- Special decorations and decor changes in the dining room to reflect seasonal changes

- Special entertainment in the dining room
- Special presentation of food items, such as a meat entree (steamship round of beef) carved in the dining room
- Extended hours of service offering coffee, soft drinks, and light snacks during exam week, perhaps until midnight
- Birthday cakes presented to residents on request
- Dinners offered in separate dining rooms for identified groups, such as residents of a dormitory floor, thereby promoting unity
- "Sick baskets" delivered to students who have been hospitalized because of illness or accident
- "Build your own sundae" featuring several varieties of ice cream and toppings
- Hors d'oeuvre featured in the lounge before dinner begins.

Cycle menus need not be dull. They should be designed with four objectives in mind: (1) to provide the consumer with the type of menu items desired, (2) to achieve the financial goals and objectives of the organization, (3) to provide adequately for the nutritional needs of the consumers, and (4) to maintain consumer interest and relieve monotony.

Evaluating Menu Effectiveness

The Importance of Menu Evaluation

When managers design a menu, they seek to accomplish specific objectives. With any effort, however, it is often difficult to ascertain the degree to which efforts have been successful. Some measure of evaluation must therefore be used. Performance criteria must be established prior to implementing a new menu, and actual performance must be measured against these criteria. For example, management may give special treatment to a single menu item, such as prime rib, with the objective that this entree should constitute 30 percent of all entree sales. A simple method to evaluate this objective would be to calculate the percentage of total entree sales of prime rib. In the same manner, it would be possible to determine the degree to which each objective was achieved. After the menu has been in use for some time, perhaps a month or two, the degree of success for all objectives should be analyzed.

Methods of Menu Evaluation

Numerous methods can be used to evaluate menu effectiveness. The selection of one method over another is usually a function of time and money. Many foodservice firms have purchased or leased computer systems that allow a thorough analysis. Other operations use very simplistic, yet appropriate methods.

The simplest method used to evaluate menu effectiveness is simply to count the number of times that each item is sold. In most foodservice operations today, this information is readily available from the detail tape printout and readings taken from electronic cash registers (ECRs). The ECRs use preset keys for each menu item, and so the number sold for each item is readily available. Based on this information, management can add or delete menu items or change the merchandising focus of the menu.

Another often-used approach is a comparison with menu census data. Menu census data allow management to compare sales figures and sales trends with regional and national data. These comparisons can be particularly useful in comparing an individual operation with national and regional menu trends.

Finally, computers are being used to a greater extent in evaluating menu effectiveness. Such an evaluation is based on financial performance rather than aesthetic evaluation. Usually, the evaluation of the menu is a variation of menu scoring in which the gross profitability of several menus are calculated and compared. Figure 7.13 illustrates a printout of this type of analysis. It is possible to incorporate the following as part of the analysis:

- An inflation factor that can be adjusted for increased costs for food, labor, or other expenses
- A pessimistic, moderate, and optimistic projection used in calculating the weighted average gross profit
- An analysis of unit cost, total costs, unit selling price, and total sales for each menu
- The gross profit for each particular menu mix calculated on a daily, weekly, monthly, and annual basis.

Evaluation of menu effectiveness is an important aspect of the menu-planning and design process. Management should invest the time in evaluation because the results should be increased sales and improved profitability.

Summary

This chapter is an overview of several important factors dealing with menu planning and design. The achievement of marketing objectives through the menu-design process must be considered. These objectives usually focus on the marketing concept, the enhancement of the operation's image, influ-

Figure 7.13. Gross Profitability Evaluation of Menu Performance by Computer.
(Courtesy: M. D. Olsen, Ph.D., and C. Bellas, Ph.D., Virginia Polytechnic Institute and State University.)

MENU ITEM	MIX	COST PORTION	COST TOTAL	SALES PORTION	SALES TOTAL
Rib Appetizer	99	2.050	202.95	4.50	445.50
Shrimp Appetizer	142	1.610	228.62	4.50	639.00
Mushrooms	174	0.980	170.52	2.65	461.10
Onion Rings	157	0.120	18.84	1.95	306.15
Delmonico	780	3.390	2644.20	8.95	6981.00
Filet	249	3.860	961.14	11.25	2801.25
Sirloin	301	3.410	1026.41	10.25	3085.25
Kabob	295	2.400	708.00	7.15	2109.25
Texas	93	5.140	478.02	14.25	1325.25
Sauteed Onion	37	0.130	4.81	0.75	27.75
Ribs	1391	3.200	4451.20	8.95	12449.45
Round	230	1.720	395.60	5.15	1184.50
Crab Legs	13	4.970	64.61	14.25	185.25
Liver	254	1.430	363.22	5.15	1308.10
Salad	355	0.650	230.75	3.95	1402.25
Child Salad	7	0.410	2.87	1.95	13.65
Child Prime	26	1.640	42.64	4.00	104.00
Steak & Bake	716	2.680	1918.88	8.50	6086.00
Child Hamburger	82	0.620	50.84	1.85	151.70
Flank	172	2.600	447.20	7.15	1229.80
Eggs	103	2.430	250.29	6.10	628.30
Child Buffet	60	2.640	158.40	2.95	177.00
Buffet	886	2.640	2339.04	6.45	5714.70
Ice Cream	30	0.100	3.00	0.50	15.00
Apple Pie	340	0.340	115.60	1.30	442.00
Cheesecake	114	0.770	87.78	2.10	239.40
BBQ Beans	52	0.100	5.20	0.75	39.00
Potato	0	0.200	0.0	0.85	0.0
Ranch	529	4.230	2237.67	9.95	5263.55
West	101	6.170	623.17	13.95	1408.95
Cattle	0	7.620	0.0	0.0	0.0
Fries	0	0.220	0.0	0.75	0.0
BBQ	17	1.820	30.94	4.95	84.15
Filet & Clams	329	2.900	954.10	7.95	2615.55
Skillet	32	2.190	70.08	5.95	190.40
Snapper	159	2.120	337.08	5.95	946.05
Beef Ribs	4	2.490	9.96	5.95	23.80
Teriyaki	103	2.910	299.73	7.95	818.85
Pork Chops	58	2.000	116.00	6.95	403.10
Creole	19	1.630	30.97	5.95	113.05
Chicken & Ribs	22	2.850	62.70	7.95	174.90
Prime	45	7.080	318.60	19.00	855.00
TOTAL	8576		22461.57		62448.89

Percentage Food Cost = 22461.57 / 62448.89 = 35.97 %

Gross Profit:
    Annual   479847.75
    Monthly   39987.32
    Weekly   9996.83
    Daily   1428.12

Range = 20 %

	Pessimistic	Moderate	Optimistic
Mix	7719	8576	9433
Probability	20 %	50 %	30 %

GROSS PROFIT = 40386.86 (Monthly)

encing demand by influencing the consumer's selection of menu items, and using the menu as a means to gain a competitive advantage.

Several factors that must be considered when planning a menu include consumer likes and dislikes, availability and cost of food and beverages, personnel skills and talents, physical layout of the foodservice facility, and the need for a nutritionally balanced menu. A simple technique can show how to select priorities for both profitable and popular menu items. Data from a national or regional menu census can also be used. Managers who lack the time and/or talent to produce high-quality menus should refer to sources of expertise for design assistance. The design and production aspects of the actual menu include menu cover, copywriting, type, paper stock, wine lists, and accuracy in menu. Managers should avoid common pitfalls of the menu-design process.

Selected aspects of cycle menus include both patterns and suggestions for improved marketing and promotion of cycle menus. Evaluating menu effectiveness is important, and widely used methods of evaluation are available.

The menu is of critical importance in the marketing efforts of a foodservice manager. It communicates, sells, creates the mood, and establishes the tone.

Questions For Review and Discussion

1. What factors must be considered when planning a menu? How do they affect the menu-design process?
2. How should a manager select those items to be included on the menu?
3. If you were a foodservice manager, what professional assistance would you seek when developing a new menu? Why?
4. Which of the menu covers shown in this chapter is the most effective and the least effective? How might each of these be improved?
5. How will length of service desired affect the menu cover selection?
6. What is menu copy?
7. What are the three categories of menu copy?
8. Of what value is descriptive copy?
9. Cite and discuss the guidelines established by Los Angeles County's "truth in menu" legislation. Do you feel these guidelines are fair?
10. What feelings do you have concerning accuracy-in-menu efforts? Why?
11. What role do business ethics play in menu development?
12. How do you react to the results of the Washington, D.C., survey of menu accuracy?

13. Why is it advisable to select type styles and paper stock in an environment similar to the dining room?

14. How is type size measured? What is considered to be the minimum size acceptable for a foodservice menu?

15. Of what value are cycle menus?

16. What are the most commonly used methods of menu evaluation? Briefly describe each of these methods.

Assignment

Develop the menu for one of the following foodservice facilities:

- Gourmet restaurant
- Hospital dining room
- Ethnic restaurant
- Seafood restaurant
- Coffee shop
- Family restaurant
- Steak house

Develop a menu for

- Breakfast
- Lunch
- Dinner

Develop the menu to include a minimum of

- Eight entrees
- One signature entree
- Two salads or appetizers
- Three beverages
- Two desserts (if appropriate)

Notes

1. Albin G. Seaburg, *Menu Design, Merchandising and Marketing,* 3rd ed. (Boston: CBI Publishing, 1983) pp. 3–7.

2. Seaburg, *Menu Design.*

3. Seaburg, *Menu Design.*

4. Bailus Walker Jr., Ph.D., M.P.H., "A Survey of the Accuracy of Menus in Public Eating Establishments in the District of Columbia" (paper presented before the International Society of Restaurant Associations Executives, Washington, D.C., November 17, 1977).

Further Reading

Anonymous, "Menu Design for Effective Merchandising," *The Cornell Hotel and Restaurant Administration Quarterly,* vol. 19, no. 3, November 1979).

Eckstein, Eleanor F., *Menu Planning* (Westport, Connecticut: AVI Publishing, 1978).

Kotschevar, Lendal H., *Management By Menu* (Chicago: National Institute for the Foodservice Industry, 1975).

Miller, Jack, *Menu Pricing and Strategy* (Boston: CBI Publishing, 1980).

Seaburg, Albin G., *Menu Design, Merchandising and Marketing,* 3rd edition (Boston: CBI Publishing, 1983).

Chapter 8

Menu Pricing— Strategies and Methods

Chapter Outline

Menu pricing is an important aspect of the marketing function for foodservice operations. Management should strive to maintain a high level of perceived value, and indeed many managers view this as the key element in increasing customer counts, sales, and profits. Menu pricing involves a great deal more than merely plugging food and beverage cost figures into a formula and generating a selling price.

The chapter examines the following topics:

Introduction

Menu Pricing: Theory and Strategies
- pricing objectives
- pricing approaches
- handling price changes

Marketing Factors That Affect Menu Prices
- governmental policies
- consumer's relative perception of value
- cost structure of a foodservice operation

Pricing Guidelines and Policies: Increasing Sales and Profits

Pricing Methods
- the factor-pricing method
- the prime cost pricing method
- the all costs plus profit pricing method
- the gross mark-up pricing method
- the Texas Restaurant Association pricing method
- computers in menu pricing

Summary

Introduction

Menu pricing is a function of both marketing management and cost accounting. Many foodservice operators view the establishment of menu prices solely as an outgrowth of cost accounting, but this simply is not true. Instead, the consumer and the entire marketing environment in which the foodservice establishment operates must be considered when developing menu prices for the food and beverage items included on the menu.

The establishment of menu prices is often done in a very haphazard manner. Many experienced foodservice consultants have found that foodservice managers often establish menu prices without a thorough knowledge of the cost structure of the foodservice operation and without in-depth knowledge of the marketing environment in which the foodservice establishment operates. This chapter explains the careful balance between the foodservice operation and the foodservice consumer, a balance that establishes selling prices for menu items.

Menu Pricing: Theory and Strategies

Pricing Objectives

The manner in which prices for menu items, wines, liquor, banquets, and other services are established has tremendous impact on sales, profits, market share, and perceived value. When prices are established, management must consciously decide the objectives of the price level chosen. If producing the highest possible short-term profit is desired to improve cash flow, then higher prices must be established accordingly. If, on the other hand, sales levels and profits are lower than desired, prices may be set somewhat lower to increase demand. This lower-price approach is based on the assumptions that as prices are lowered, sales volume will increase and that as prices are raised, sales volume will decrease. If a larger share of the total foodservice market is desired, prices may be lowered still further to capture a larger percentage of the market in a given area.

Establishing menu prices by clearly defining pricing objectives is a beneficial process for any foodservice organization. Consider, for example, which of the following choices is most important: (1) having a larger percentage of the total market at a lower profit margin (large market share approach) or (2) having a smaller percentage of the total market at a higher profit margin (high short-term profits approach).

Along with the traditional cost-accounting approach to pricing, management must make decisions concerning pricing philosophies. Two approaches which are commonly used are market skimming and market penetration.

Market skimming uses a relatively high initial price to produce higher profits. The word *skimming* is an important one, for that is what the established price seeks to do; it "skims" a small part of the total potential market. Market skimming can be used most effectively when the following conditions exist:

- A large potential market can be drawn from which a small percentage of individuals is willing and able to pay a higher price.
- Competition is not likely to undercut the established price for the same or a similar product-service mix.
- Management has established or can readily establish a high level of perceived value for the product-service mix, thereby helping to justify the higher cost in the consumers' decision-making process.

Market penetration operates from the opposite perspective. This approach means that the price should be set at the lowest possible level, based on fixed and variable costs. Initial profits may be small, and in fact, the initial months may not produce any profits, but by establishing the lowest possible price, the penetration approach seeks to acquire a larger and, management hopes, a loyal market share. This larger market share will generate increased sales volume and will, in time, produce larger long-term profits. Market penetration can be used most effectively when the following conditions exist:

- Targeted markets are extremely price sensitive, and any increases in prices will result in immediate and substantial reductions in volume.
- Lower prices are likely to discourage new competition from entering the market.

Neither approach is correct for all situations. Rather, management must carefully consider all the market conditions, opportunities, and pitfalls. Management must remember that one of the most common reasons cited for failure in the foodservice industry is undercapitalization. Operations are opened without sufficient financial reserves; initial cash flows are not what was anticipated, and the venture fails. This type of situation occurs all too frequently in the foodservice industry.

The manipulation of price can have a tremendous impact on the sales volume of any foodservice organization. Figure 8.1 illustrates the traditional relationship between price and sales volume. In the figure, when the

Figure 8.1. Relationship Between Price Levels and Demand. (P_1, P_2, P_3 = price levels; D_1, D_2, D_3 = demand anticipated at price levels P_1, P_2, P_3.)

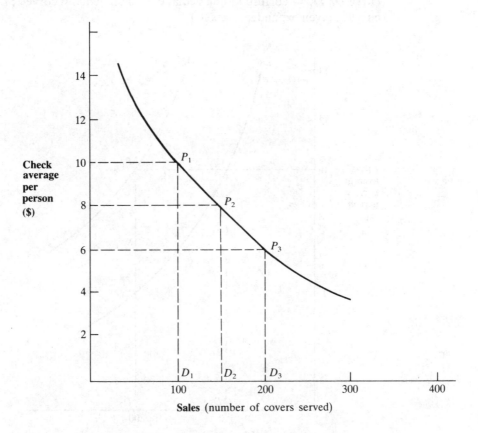

price, as measured by the average check, is established at $10 ($P_1$), the operation will serve 100 covers (D_1); at a price of $8 ($P_2$), the operation will serve 150 covers (D_2); and finally at a $6 price ($P_3$), it will serve 200 covers (D_3). Price and volume are inversely related, so that as price is decreased, volume will increase, and as price is increased, volume will decrease. If the operators in Figure 8.1 were not satisfied with the 100 covers served at a $10 check average, management might elect to lower the price to $8 and serve 150 covers, thereby generating additional revenue.

Figure 8.2 illustrates another approach, nonprice competition. In this example, if the current price is $10 ($P_1$), the corresponding demand is 100 covers (D_1). Rather than lower the price to increase the sales volume,

Figure 8.2. Nonprice Competition. (DC_1 = demand curve 1, given existing market; P_1 = current price level; D_1 = corresponding demand level on demand curve D_1; D_2 = corresponding demand level on demand curve 2; DC_2 = demand curve 2, given expanded market.)

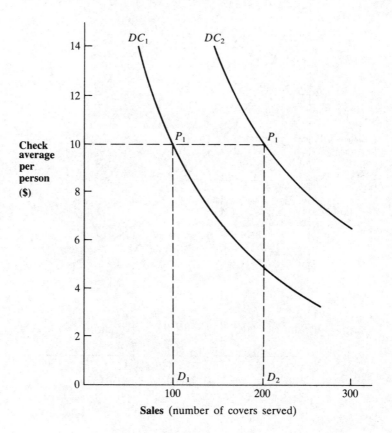

management instead chooses to shift the demand curve from the DC_1 position to the DC_2 position. How might this be accomplished? How can the demand be increased without an adjustment in price? Rather than relying solely on price as the variable that influences demand, management focuses attention on variables that can influence volume, such as marketing. By increasing the influence of such marketing activities as advertising, it is possible to shift the demand curve to a more favorable position without reducing prices.

Pricing Approaches

When management establishes menu prices, one of these three basic approaches can be used: (1) cost-oriented pricing, (2) demand-oriented or perceived-value pricing, or (3) competitively-oriented pricing. *Cost-oriented pricing,* as the name implies, is based on the costs associated with a foodservice operation. Numerous fixed and variable costs, such as food, labor, rent, insurance, and energy, may be examined as the basis for establishing menu prices. Cost-oriented pricing is the oldest pricing method and is the most widely used within the industry.

Demand-oriented or *perceived-value pricing* is pricing from the opposite perspective. Rather than thinking that a menu item costs x dollars to prepare and should therefore be sold at x dollars plus some additional amount, perceived-value pricing examines price from the consumer's viewpoint. What is the perceived value of the product or service to the consumer? How much would consumers be willing to pay for this product or service? This approach to pricing is frequently used for unusual items or highly personal service. For example, what is the perceived value of a flambé dessert prepared at tableside? What is the perceived value of banquet services, or the perceived value of atmosphere unlike any other restaurant in the area? These factors must be carefully considered when the perceived value of a product or service is determined.

The goal of this pricing method is to raise menu prices to the highest possible levels without causing the number of patrons served to decline. This obviously is not always easy to do, for the price of some items might be raised slightly and the number of patrons would fall dramatically. In other instances, larger price increases can be implemented with no reduction in demand. Economists refer to this as the *elasticity of demand.* A product or service is said to be inelastic if the price is raised or lowered and the demand for the product remains at roughly the same level as before the price was changed.

Normally, the price of food consumed away from home is thought to be elastic. This means that the propensity of any individual to purchase a meal in a foodservice establishment is directly related to the price of that meal. If the menu price were increased dramatically, the number of units sold or sales volume is likely to fall just as dramatically. Because of this phenomenon, a sort of mental perceived-value game takes place between the foodservice management and the potential consumer. The management seeks to raise the price without the consumer's becoming aware of the declining perceived-value relationship.

This pricing method boils down to the simple statement: The foodservice management simply charges "what the traffic will bear." What the traffic will bear varies tremendously depending on the situation. For example, if you were standing on a busy intersection at noon, and several foodservice establishments were within walking distance, then the price you would be willing to pay for lunch is likely to be influenced by the choices available. In fact, it might seem logical for you to go to a fast-food restaurant and buy a hamburger and a soft drink for less than two dollars. On the other hand, if you were at an amusement park and wanted to have lunch or if you were attending a sporting event and desired a meal, the only foodservice available to you may be operated by the owners or concessionaires of the facility. For this reason, the degree of competition has been reduced, and the result is that the consumer is likely to pay a higher price for the same meal. These facilities have the consumer as a "captive client," and as a result, they often raise prices far higher than would be possible if the degree of competition were higher.

Competitively-oriented pricing, as the name implies, places the emphasis on price in relation to direct competition. Some foodservice firms allow others to establish prices and then position themselves accordingly, either slightly higher or slightly lower. This method assures that the price an operation charges for an item will be within the same range as the competitive operations in the immediate geographic area. This method does, however, have several drawbacks. First, one foodservice operation may have a cost structure totally different from another operation. The first foodservice establishment might be brand new and have a mortgage with a high interest rate that must be paid each month. On the other hand, the second operation might be well established and have no mortgage payment or a much lower payment each month. For this reason, the second operation would have lower fixed operating expenses and therefore could charge a much lower menu price, even if all other expenses were equal.

Second, other expenses might also vary among different operations. Labor costs might be higher or lower depending on the skill level of the personnel, their length of service in the operation, or numerous other factors. In actuality, nearly every expense could vary considerably among different foodservice operations with the same basic product-service mix. For this reason, it is extremely risky for managers to rely on the menu prices of a direct competitor when setting their own menu prices. Each foodservice operation is unique and has its own unique cost and profit structure. This is not to say that management should not check to see the prices a competitor is charging, just to keep an eye on the competition, but it does mean that prices should never be based solely on prices at the foodservice operation across or down the street.

Handling Price Changes

Since the 1970s, handling ever-increasing prices has been a concern of all foodservice managers. The overriding concern is the impact that price increases will have on customer counts, sales volume, and profits. There is no quick and easy way to increase prices without some negative impact on consumers, but consumers have been battered by several years of rapidly escalating prices, and they have begun to accept price increases as a fact of life.

When prices are to be increased, the first thing to do is to have new menus printed. It is false economy to change the price on an existing menu, either with a stroke of a pen or with a sticker placed over the current price. No matter how well the sticker matches the existing menu, the result will look tacky. Changing prices in this manner merely draws attention to the price increase and makes the consumer that much more aware of it.

Many operators have increased prices successfully by simply repackaging the menu items. This can be done in two ways. First, menu items can be priced on an à la carte basis, with certain items priced at a lower margin than others to attract more customers. Fast-food organizations have used this approach for years. The mark-up as a percentage of selling price is much lower on a hamburger than on the french fries and soft drinks that accompany the hamburger. The check average per person will be about 2 dollars and 50 cents, yet the main meal is only 1 dollar and 25 cents and is perceived as very reasonably priced. A second method is to offer the consumer something extra at the same time the price is increased. Rather than simply raising the price of a prime rib dinner from 10 dollars and 95 cents to 11 dollars and 95 cents and then serving the same meal, many operators have found it desirable to include something extra, like Yorkshire pudding with the prime rib, and to adjust the price accordingly. For the prime rib dinner, the price might be raised to 12 dollars and 25 cents or to 12 dollars and 50 cents to include the cost of the extra item.

How should the managers of a foodservice operation respond when direct competitors adjust their prices? What impact will competitors' price changes have on sales? Management should consider several responses in response to competitors' price changes. Responses include:

- **Do nothing.** Make no overt response to the change in price. Maintain current prices and pay careful attention to daily and weekly sales figures. If a significant change in either sales (measured in dollars) or customer counts occurs, further action may be necessary.

- **Maintain the current price level and increase advertising promotion.**   The principal idea behind this strategy is to counter the competition's price reduction with an increase in the visibility of advertising and promotion. By increasing advertising, it is believed, customer counts will either remain stable or will increase. The focus of the advertising should be the nonprice aspects of the product-service mix, negating the competition's price reduction.

- **Follow the competition by reducing prices.**   In some instances, this may be the best strategy. By reducing the price, the competitive advantage enjoyed by the competition is reduced or eliminated. Lower prices are a way to increase customer counts and improve profits. One caution is noteworthy here: Competition based solely on price is seldom effective as a long-term strategy and may have a negative impact on sales and profits.

- **Increase prices and launch an increased advertising attack.**   As the competition is promoting lower prices, one very effective method to counter these efforts is to increase prices and then initiate an advertising campaign emphasizing the higher-quality aspects of the product-service mix. This strategy can be used effectively to gain a competitive advantage in a situation that may initially appear to be competitively difficult.

Marketing Factors That Affect Menu Prices

Three major factors have a significant impact on the establishment of menu prices for any foodservice operation. These factors are (1) governmental policies, (2) consumer's relative perception of value, and (3) the cost structure of a foodservice operation. Figure 8.3 illustrates the interrelationships among these factors. To establish an effective selling price for any item that appears on the menu, the manager of a foodservice establishment must possess a thorough understanding of the interrelationships among these three factors.

Governmental Policies

The government has in the last twenty years taken a much more active role in the operations of all businesses in this country. This simple fact of life applies to all businesses in the United States, not exclusively to the foodservice industry. All levels of government have exerted influence on the industry in both positive and negative ways. Every foodservice operation in this coun-

Figure 8.3. Factors That Affect Menu Prices.

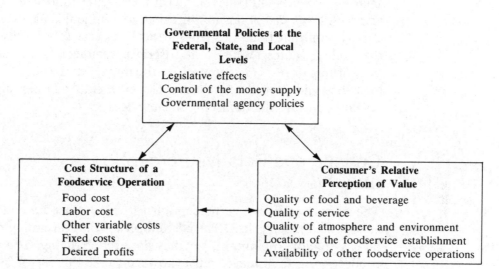

try is influenced in some manner by various governmental actions at the federal, state, and local levels. These actions have a direct impact on the menu prices that foodservice operations charge consumers who patronize them.

All the examples of the impact of the government on the foodservice industry and menu prices are too numerous to mention, but a few examples are worth illustrating. The federal and state governments directly control the wages and benefits paid to the hourly employees of the vast majority of foodservice operations in this country. When the minimum wage is raised, this has an immediate and direct impact on the menu prices that the foodservice operation charges the consuming public. In addition, most states have also mandated that the tip credit, which has been granted to the foodservice industry in the United States for many years, be reduced or eliminated completely. This also has a direct and immediate impact on menu prices.

The government also directly or indirectly influences the menu prices of foodservice establishments through the control of the money supply, which in turn affects the interest rates a foodservice owner must pay as a part of the fixed costs of operating. As the supply of money is tightened by the Federal Reserve Board, the cost of credit increases, thereby increasing the cost of operation and affecting menu prices. Various levels of government also influence menu prices through taxes on profits, wages and salaries, property, and sales along with license fees and a host of other taxes and fees. It is a fact of business life that government at all levels has become and will continue to be a "silent partner" in every foodservice operation in the United States. When a foodservice manager is in the process of establishing or revising menu prices, the impact of the government must be identified and studied very closely. Governmental action is always one important concern in establishing menu prices.

Consumer's Relative Perception of Value

The consumer's relative perception of value must be considered when establishing menu prices. The perceptions of the consuming public are not an easy factor to pinpoint, for they are ever changing. The manager of a foodservice establishment must, however, take this factor into consideration when establishing menu prices.

Perceptions of value held by the consuming public are divided into the following categories: quality of food and beverage offerings, quality of service, quality of atmosphere and environment, location of the foodservice operation, and availability of other foodservice operations.

Quality of Food and Beverage Offerings. Every consumer who patronizes a foodservice establishment forms an immediate opinion of the quality of the food and beverages served. As the perceived quality of the products increases, the price the consumer is willing to pay for those food and beverage items also increases. This results because the consumer feels that as the quality of the product increases, so too does the value; hence the price the consumer is willing to pay also increases.

Consider, for example, the perceived value of two types of restaurant meals. The first meal consists of a baked potato, a small tossed salad, a piece of Texas toast and an eight-ounce USDA good top sirloin steak. The selling price of this meal is likely to be 4 dollars and 50 cents to 4 dollars and 99 cents. Given the food quality, this price represents value to the consumer, as is evidenced by the growing demand for "family," or budget, steak houses in the last five years. On the other hand, a consumer might easily pay more than twice this price for a similar meal in another restaurant, consisting of a baked potato, a tossed salad, rolls, and an eight-ounce USDA prime top sirloin steak. This meal can also represent value to a consumer who is willing to pay a higher price for the additional quality that a USDA prime top sirloin steak offers. In the eyes of the consumer, both meals represent a good value for the price. The first meal represents a good value because the consumer is able to obtain a steak dinner for less than 5 dollars. The second meal might also represent a good value to the consumer because the beef was of the highest quality available and therefore represented value. The quality of a meal and hence the perceived value is a subjective judgment on the part of the consumer. Generally, the consumer is willing to pay a higher menu price for a meal if the foodservice operation is offering increased quality.

In addition, the individual consumer's perception of value might easily change with the time of day and an individual's attitude at a particular moment. For example, a consumer might pay approximately 2 dollars and 50 cents for lunch at a fast-food restaurant and would consider that lunch to be quality food at a fair price. The very same individual, however, might spend more than 15 dollars for dinner on the same day and would perceive that as a good value as well. Perceived quality of food and beverage items is therefore in a constant state of change; it depends on the individual and the moment for that individual.

Most foodservice corporations and chains engage in some form of market research to determine the perceived quality and value of their products in the marketplace. (See Chapter 4 for more information about market research.) These studies are critically important to these corporations, for even small shifts in perceived value can mean thousands of dollars of sales either gained or lost.

Quality of Service. The consumer has historically shown an increased willingness to pay a higher menu price in those foodservice operations offering increased personal attention and service. Consider the example in the preceding section. The budget or family steakhouse is usually designed so that the consumer passes through a cafeteria line and places an order for a main entree. The consumer then passes through the remainder of the service line and selects the accompanying items to complete the meal. At the end of the line, the consumer pays the cashier and proceeds to a table in the dining area. In contrast, the consumer expects and is willing to pay an increased menu price for the waiter or waitress service offered by the foodservice establishment serving the USDA prime top sirloin steak dinner at a price likely to exceed 12 dollars. As the quality of the service offered by the foodservice establishment increases, the consumer is willing to pay an increased menu price to cover the cost of this service.

Quality of Atmosphere and Environment.   The same example, taken one step further, points out that the higher-priced steak will usually be served in an environment offering more opulent atmosphere. Once again, the example holds true: As the level of atmosphere is raised, the consumer normally expects and is willing to pay a higher menu price.

Location of the Foodservice Operation.   The location of the foodservice operation and the resulting accessibility of the operation to the potential consumer can have a direct impact on the menu price and perceived value of the restaurant. If, for example, a foodservice operation is located some distance from a population center, that operation would need to offer a higher perceived value to induce a potential consumer to travel the extra distance necessary to reach the foodservice operation. As the cost of energy in general, and gasoline in particular, increases, this perceived value must be even greater to induce the consumer to travel the extra distance. The foodservice conveniently located near potential consumers, however, does not have to offer as high a perceived value because of its accessibility to the potential market.

Availability of Other Foodservice Operations.   As the number of different foodservice operations available to the consumer increases, the perceived value of any one of the available choices must be higher for it to achieve its desired share of the market. This point may be illustrated by a locally owned fast-food establishment that had been doing business in the same location for a number of years. Over the course of five years of operation, the establishment had produced acceptable profits in each year except the first. With each succeeding year of operation, the establishment had increased sales and seemed to be moving in a most positive direction. Then one day, construction began on a new fast-food establishment directly across the street from the established fast-food operation. This new fast-food operation was being built by one of the major fast-food companies, which have come to dominate the market in the last 20 years. Once the corporate fast-food operation opened, business at the locally owned fast-food establishment began steadily to decline, and within eight months, the establishment filed for bankruptcy.

What had happened? What had gone wrong? One of the reasons for the failure was that the perceived value by the local consumers was higher for the corporate fast-food establishment than for the locally owned establishment. The corporate establishment was able to offer a product perceived to be of a higher quality yet sold for the same price. The increased competition was more than the established operation was able to withstand. As a result, it was forced to close. In recent years, this has been a widely occurring phenomenon as more and more locally owned and operated foodservice establishments close under the pressure of the corporate giants of the foodservice industry. This trend is likely to continue well into the future and might result in the virtual extinction of the small, locally owned foodservice establishment. As far as the consumer is concerned, the corporate foodservice operations are able to offer a higher perceived value than are the small, locally owned establishments.

The ownership or management of any foodservice establishment, when planning menu prices, must examine very closely the consumers' perceptions of the quality of the food, beverages, service, atmosphere, and location as well as those of the direct and indirect competition. The consumers' perceived value is extremely difficult to understand precisely, but it is virtually certain that as the perceived value of a foodservice establishment is reduced, the volume of patrons will also decrease. Consumers will most frequently patronize those establishments that offer "the most for the money," or the highest perceived value. If consumers perceive that they are not being given enough value for the money they are spending, they will no longer patronize foodservice establishments that offer low perceived value. Consequently, the owners and managers of all foodservice operations must know their clientele in sufficient detail to understand thoroughly how their current and potential clientele perceive the value of the foodservice operation.

Cost Structure of a Foodservice Operation

The foodservice manager must be aware of the cost structure of the foodservice establishment. Calculating menu prices is a function of cost accounting, but literally, thousands of foodservice operations have established menu prices without a complete working knowledge of the costs involved in producing a given menu item. Management must consider the costs of food, labor, and other variables as well as fixed costs and the desired profits of the owner or stockholders. Each foodservice establishment will incur its own cost of operation. This is important for any manager to remember. It is useful, as a point of comparison, to refer to average or mean figures to determine how a particular foodservice compares, but one should not be tied to a strict comparison to "average" figures, for these figures may not reflect the unique and individual cost structure of a particular foodservice operation. When the time comes for a

Table 8.1. Average (Mean) Ratios of Expense Categories for Restaurants Serving Food and Beverages.

Source: Restaurant Industry Operations Report '81 for the United States (National Restaurant Association, 1981).

Cost of Merchandise Sold	1978	1980
Food	29.4%	29.6%
Beverages	7.3	7.1
Total	36.7	36.7
Controllable Expenses		
Payroll	27.0	27.5
Employee Benefits	4.3	4.8
Direct Operating Expenses	5.3	6.5
Music and Entertainment	0.8	0.9
Advertising and Promotion	2.8	1.9
Utilities	2.7	2.5
Administrative and General	5.6	5.4
Repairs and Maintenance	1.8	1.7
Occupation Costs		
Rent, Property Taxes, and Insurance	5.6	4.8
Interest	1.0	0.9
Depreciation	2.5	2.3
Other Additions and Deductions	(0.1)	(0.4)
Net Income Before Income Tax	4.0	4.5
	100.0%	100.0%

foodservice manager to establish menu prices, the unique cost figures for the individual foodservice operation must be considered on their own merits.

For example, a well-established foodservice operation may be able to charge a lower price than another foodservice operation charges for a particular item because the fixed costs for the mortgage might be lower than for a newer operation with higher fixed costs. The newer operation's adjusting prices to be closer to the older establishment might seem to be the recommended course of action when a manager is considering only the competition, but in the long run, it might be the easiest route to bankruptcy.

Many factors play a part in the decision to raise, lower, or adjust the menu price of an item or combination of items. First, the policies of governmental agencies and legislation passed at the federal, state, and local levels have a tremendous impact on the manner in which a foodservice manager operates. Second, the value perceptions of the consuming public concerning the quality of the entire foodservice operation can have an impact on the prices the foodservice operation is able to charge. Finally, the unique cost structure for each and every foodservice operation will determine, to a large extent, the prices the operation must charge to remain solvent and to produce the level of profitability that the owners demand.

Pricing Guidelines and Policies: Increasing Sales and Profits

If the menu price determined by the foodservice manager must strike a very fine balance between the consumer's need for value and the owners' need for maximum return on investment, menu prices must be determined to induce new patronage by individuals who have not before patronized the foodservice operation. At the same time, prices should be developed so that the new prices will not drive away any of the current patrons. Therefore, one of the major goals of any pricing method should be to maintain the current clientele while adding to the total volume of the foodservice operation by inducing first-time patronage.

Prices should be established with the maximum long-term profits of the firm in mind. It would be easy to set prices at a level that would produce very high rates of return for a brief period of time, but after a few days or perhaps a few weeks, the consumer would realize that the perceived value of dining at that particular foodservice establishment was declining. When this happened, the total volume and profitability of the foodservice operation would be likely to fall significantly. Therefore, it is the wise manager who decides to focus attention on long-term, rather than short-term profits. This pricing philosophy is most likely to enjoy the greatest long-term success. It is like the story of the hare and the tortoise, in which the slow but sure tortoise had eventually covered more ground than the speedier hare.

Many foodservice managers are tempted to reduce the price of an item in the hope that more patrons will purchase that item and the result will be increased gross sales figures. This is a trap for the unwary manager. Simply stated, for the foodservice operation to enjoy increased gross revenue, many more patrons need to be served, and increased volume unto itself is no guarantee of increased gross sales. Fig. 8.4 illustrates one example in which the gross revenue from a reduced price is lower by 2.7 percent, even though more patrons (20 percent) were served.

Figure 8.4. Marginal Revenue.

	Menu Price		**Covers Served**		**Gross Sales**
Beef Stew	$4.50	×	100	=	$450.00
Beef Stew Special	$3.65	×	120	=	$438.00
				Total =	$12.00 (loss)

The term *marginal revenue* refers to the difference between the gross sales at the old price and the gross sales at the revised, or "special," price. The goal of management should be to produce positive marginal revenue, or an increased total gross sales figure. In Fig. 8.4, however, the opposite was the result. Even though the manager was able to serve 20 percent more patrons, the resulting gross sales figures were less than before the menu price had been changed. This reduction in gross sales is compounded by the two major expense items, for food and labor will have to increase for the operation to serve the additional 20 patrons. Therefore, the reduction in gross sales is even more dramatic when it is coupled with the resulting increase in expense. When both of these factors are combined, the obvious result is reduced profits, or increased losses, despite the fact that 20 percent more covers were served.

The caution for the foodservice manager is this: Reduce prices as a means to increase volume only after all other marketing and merchandising avenues have been exhausted. A creative foodservice manager should be able to devise hundreds of creative marketing techniques that will result in increased gross sales. Almost any foodservice manager can produce increased volume when the food and beverages are sold at a loss. It is the truly professional foodservice manager who can produce both increased volume and increased profits while holding costs below projected figures.

Finally, the establishment of menu prices is not something to be left to chance. Prices should be established after careful analysis of the costs of operation and the competitive environment in which the foodservice establishment operates. For example, one restaurant established menu prices by preparing new items and then asking members of the management team what they thought the particular items were worth. This is, of course, a most unusual pricing method, and one that should not be emulated. The result of this method of pricing was a food cost in excess of 50% and a very large loss for the owners of the foodservice operation. Through careful market research and professional pricing methods, the operation was able to reduce food costs to 38% and consequently to increase profits dramatically.

Menu prices should be established with the following general guidelines:

- Menu prices must strike a fine balance between the consumer's need for value and the owners' need for profits.
- Menu prices should be established with maximum long-term profits, not short-term profits, in mind.
- As a method to increase the number of covers sold, projected marginal revenues should be studied closely before menu prices are reduced.
- Menu prices should be established in a logical manner, using a professionally tested method.

Pricing Methods

The pricing methods outlined here represent most of the common pricing methods in use in the foodservice industry today. Although some of these methods have not yet enjoyed widespread use in the industry, this is not to say that they are unsatisfactory methods. Each pricing method offers both advantages and drawbacks.

The basis of professional foodservice management is a thorough knowledge of the costs of operation of a foodservice establishment. The only way that a manager can thoroughly know the costs involved in purchase, storage, and production of food and beverage items is through standard recipes and recipe cost worksheets that detail the costs of producing the standard recipe item. Figures 8.5 and 8.6 illustrate these two important management tools.

Figure 8.5. Standard Recipe for Roast Ribs of Beef.

Source: LeRoi A. Folsom, *The Professional Chef,* (Boston: CBI Publishing, 1974).

Roast Ribs of Beef

YIELD: 50 portions	EACH PORTION: 8 oz. beef (bone-in)	
INGREDIENTS	*QUANTITY*	*METHOD*
Ribs of Beef, oven ready	2 (about 20 lb. ea., bone in)	1. Place ribs in roast pan fat side up. Insert meat thermometer. Roast in oven at 350°F. 2 hr. Add mirepoix; season. Cook until thermometer reads 140°F. for rare or 150°F. for medium rare, about 2½ to 3 hr.
Mirepoix:		
Onions, medium cut	1 lb.	
Celery, medium cut	8 oz.	
Carrots, medium cut	8 oz.	2. Remove to clean pan and hold in warm place. Let stand ½ hr. before serving. Stand roast in carving position on a tray that will hold meat juices until time to serve.
Salt	to taste	
Pepper	to taste	
Brown Beef Stock) OR Consomme) hot	½ gal.	3. Pour fat off roast pan and deglaze with hot beef stock or consomme. Simmer vegetables lightly, keeping au jus as clear as possible. Strain and adjust seasoning and skim fat. Make gravy.

Figure 8.6. Recipe Cost Worksheet for Ribs of Beef Recipe.

Yield or Number of Portions to be Prepared: __50__

Cooking Time: __2-2½ Hrs.__ Date: __2-1-83__

Cooking Temp: __350°__ Prepared by: __R.D.R.__

Ingredients	Amount			Unit	Unit count	Cost per unit	Total constituent cost
	Weight		Measure, count				
	A.P.	E.P.					
USDA Choice #109 Rib	40#	25#		#	40#	$2.89	$115.60
Onions	1#2oz	1#		#	1#2oz	.28	.315
Celery	9oz	8oz		#	.75#	.35	.263
Carrots	9oz	8oz		#	.75#	.30	.225
Salt		totaste				—	.02
Pepper		totaste				—	.02
Brown stock			½ gal	gal	.5	.25	.125

Total Cost __$116.58__

Direct Labor Hours to Prepare: __2.0__

Average Cost of Direct Labor per Hour: __$4.15__

Total Direct Labor Cost: __$8.30__

Estimated Cost per Portion __$2.33__

This menu item, the roast rib of beef, is used as an illustration of a standardized recipe and recipe cost worksheet. When the roast rib of beef is combined with a tossed salad and dressing, vegetable, and rolls and butter, the total raw food cost of this dinner will be $3.51. (Note that this cost is not intended to represent current market costs of food.)

The Factor-Pricing Method

The factor method of menu pricing is one of the most popular methods currently used in the foodservice industry. It uses the raw cost of the food as the sole determining factor in establishing the menu price. Steps in factor pricing are as follows:

Step	Example
1. Establish a desired food cost percentage. This percentage must be determined by managers or owners and depends on many factors, including other expenses and desired profits. Typically, the desired food cost percentage falls within the range of 30 to 45 percent of gross sales.	35%
2. Divide this food cost percentage into 100 to obtain the multiplier.	100/35 = 2.86.
3. Multiply the raw food cost of the menu item by the multiplier to determine the selling price of the item.	$3.51 x 2.86 = $10.04.

The major advantage of the factor method is that it is simple and straightforward. Because it bases the menu price of an item solely on the raw food costs, it has a major disadvantage. As the cost of labor and other expenses have increased, it may no longer be profitable for a foodservice operation to establish menu prices based solely on the cost of the food. Instead, it may prove to be advantageous to take into consideration the costs of other variable and fixed expenses, such as labor, utilities, and occupancy.

In addition, this pricing method may conceal menu items that are being sold at a loss. Consider the following example:

	Raw Cost	x	Factor	=	Selling Price	Profit Margin
Roast beef dinner	3.51	x	2.86	=	$10.04	$6.53
Beef stew Bordelaise dinner	1.75	x	2.86	=	$5.01	$3.26

The profit margins for the steak dinner and beef stew Bordelaise dinner are $6.53 and $3.26, respectively. Will these two margins contribute to the payment of the following expenses: labor, rent, insurance, heat, light, and power? Will they both generate a profit? If, for example, a manager has determined that to meet expenses and break even, the operation must generate a profit margin of $4.00 per entree, the result would then be a $2.53 profit on the prime rib dinner and a loss of 74¢ on the beef stew Bordelaise. When using the factor method, an operator would be wise to look closely at each item's profit margin to assure that a profit will be realized on each and every item sold.

The Prime Cost Pricing Method

The prime cost method of pricing was developed by Harry Pope of St. Louis and has been used successfully for several years. This method takes into account the two major expenses of any foodservice operation: food and labor. The prime cost of a menu item is the cost of food and labor, as in the equation

$$\text{Prime Cost} = \text{Raw Cost of Food} + \text{Labor Cost.}$$

The prime cost method necessitates that the manager establish a targeted prime cost percentage for all menu items in much the same manner that a manager establishes a targeted food cost percentage when using the factor method of pricing. The prime cost method is illustrated as follows:

Steps	Example
1. Determine the raw food cost.	$3.51 for a roast rib of beef dinner $2.43 for a stuffed flounder dinner
2. Determine the direct labor cost.	$2.35 labor for production and service
3. Add together the cost of food and the cost of labor.	$5.86 for roast rib of beef $4.83 for stuffed flounder

Steps	Example
4. Determine the desired prime cost percentage	55%
5. Divide the desired prime cost percentage into 100 to determine the multiplier.	100/55 = 1.82.
6. Multiply the prime cost by the multiplier derived in Step 5 to determine the menu price.	Roast rib of beef, $5.86 x 1.82 = $10.67. Stuffed flounder, $4.83 x 1.82 = $8.79.

The prime cost method represents an advance in menu-pricing methods. It is not, however, without its own drawbacks. First, no allowance is made for the other expenses a foodservice operation incurs in the production and service of a menu item. In addition, no allowance is made for the profit toward which most managers strive. It is instead assumed that if the prime cost percentage does not exceed a predetermined percentage of gross sales, the operation will achieve the desired level of profitability.

The All Costs Plus Profit Pricing Method

This method of menu pricing overcomes some of the drawbacks of both the factor method and the prime cost method. The all costs plus profit method of menu pricing takes into account the raw cost of the food or beverage item, the labor costs involved in producing and serving the item, and all the variable and fixed expenses that the restaurant must pay to stay in business. In addition, the owner or manager of the operation must also predetermine the percentage of profit desired for each menu item. The steps involved in this method are as follows:

Step	Example	
1. Determine the raw food cost of the item or entree.	Roast rib of beef dinner,	$3.51
	Stuffed flounder dinner,	$2.43
2. Determine the production labor costs involved in preparing this item or entree.	Roast rib of beef dinner,	$1.62
	Stuffed flounder dinner,	$2.43

Step	Example
3. Determine the cost of service labor by dividing the total labor cost expense for service by the number of covers served.	$1125.00/1500 = 0.75.
4. Determine the cost per cover for all other expenses.	$1738.75/1500 = $1.16.
5. Determine the desired percentage of profit.	15%

A number of methods can be used in determining the production costs involved when producing a menu item. First, a time and motion study can be undertaken to yield precise results concerning the actual time and costs incurred when producing a particular menu item. This, however, may not be feasible for the average foodservice manager because of the time involved in completing such a study. Second, the foodservice manager can determine an average production labor cost for all items by dividing the number of meals prepared into the actual labor expense in dollars. For example, 2000 dollars/1800 covers = 1 dollar and 11 cents per cover. This method does not take into account that some items are labor intensive while others require very little preparation. If this method were used, items prepared from scratch would incur the same labor costs per unit as the convenience items.

A third method is to assign relative labor costs per unit to the various menu items. For example, a foodservice manager might divide the menu items into three categories: low, medium, and high labor costs. The criteria for each category must be determined by the individual manager, but low-cost items might require less than 5 minutes to prepare: medium-cost items might require 5 to 10 minutes to prepare; and items requiring over 10 minutes of preparation time would be high-cost items. Once criteria are established, the manager then assigns each menu item to the appropriate category. At the end of the week, or perhaps as much as one month of observation, the operator simply totals the number of meals served and then subtotals the number of menu items in each category. For example, out of 1500 meals served, the breakdown might be as follows: low labor cost—380 meals, medium labor cost—835 meals, high labor cost—285 meals. During this same time, total expense for production was $2358.50.

Assuming that it takes twice as long to prepare a medium-cost meal and three times as long to prepare a high-cost meal the following equation would be used to determine the cost of one unit of labor.

$$380x + 2(835x) + 3(285x) = \$2358.50$$
$$380x + 1670x + 855x = \$2358.50$$
$$2905x = \$2358.50$$
$$x = 2358.50/2905$$
$$x = 0.81$$

Therefore, a low-cost item would require $0.81 of labor to prepare; a medium-cost item would require $1.62; and a high-cost item would require $2.43 to prepare.

A formula for the all costs plus profit method is as follows:

$$\frac{\text{Raw food cost} + \text{Production labor cost/item} + \text{Service labor cost/cover} + \text{Other expenses cost/cover}}{100 - \text{Desired profit percentage}} = \text{Menu selling price.}$$

The selling price of the roast rib of beef dinner would therefore be calculated as follows:

$$\frac{\$3.51 + \$1.62 + \$0.75 + \$1.16}{0.85} = \$8.28.$$

The stuffed flounder dinner would be priced with this formula:

$$\frac{\$2.43 + \$2.43 + \$0.75 + \$1.16}{0.85} = \$7.96.$$

The first advantage of the all costs plus profit method of pricing is that profit is built into the selling price. It is not left to chance or to the skills of management; instead, it is a planned part of the price-planning picture. Second, all other expenses are taken into consideration when a selling price for a food item is established, and unlike either the factor method or the prime cost method, the selling price is based on the broad range of expense items unique to each individual foodservice establishment. Third, the selling price of higher-cost entrees is reduced by using this method. This makes these items more desirable to the potential consumer, and therefore sales of these items should increase.

The all costs plus profit method of pricing also has its drawbacks. First, it is much more complicated to calculate menu selling prices using this method. Second, this method will raise the lower-cost menu items slightly, possibly making these items less attractive to potential consumers. Third, it may be difficult for a manager to determine the precise costs necessary when this method is used. Finally, it may also prove difficult for an owner or manager to predetermine the desired profit percentage.

The Gross Mark-up Pricing Method

This pricing method is useful in situations where the foodservice manager is dealing with a specific clientele and a group of menu items for which the price range is not widely distributed. This method deals with actual dollars and cents of mark-up and gross profit, rather than with the percentages that other methods often use. The formula is rather simple: The cost of the raw food item is simply added to a gross mark-up amount that the foodservice manager has determined is necessary to cover the other costs of doing business while providing the desired level of profitability.

Suppose, for example, that a foodservice operation had budgeted a total of $750,000 in annual sales with projected food costs of 35% or $285,000. In addition, the projected annual consumer count is 100,000 covers. Given these figures, one can use the formula

$$\text{Gross mark-up} = \frac{\text{Gross sales} - \text{Cost of food sold}}{\text{Projected number of covers served}}$$

and make this calculation:

$$\frac{\$750,000 - 285,000}{100,000} = \$4.65.$$

Once the gross mark-up figure is determined, it is simply added to the cost of the raw food product or entree to determine the menu price for that particular menu item. For example,

	Cost of raw food	+	Gross mark-up	
Roast rib of beef dinner	$3.51	+	4.65	= $8.16
Stuffed flounder dinner	$2.43	+	4.65	= $7.08

The advantages of this method are as follows. First, the selling price of high-cost items is likely to be reduced somewhat, thereby making these items more desirable to the potential consumer. This will also make it easier for the manager to promote these items, for the stigma of a high price tag has been removed. Second, the method is easy to use, especially for an established foodservice operation.

    The drawbacks to this system are first that the system is adaptable only to operations with a menu that is not subject to fluctuation or change. Second, this method is best suited to an operation that is well established and can accurately project the gross sales, cost of food sold, and number of covers served, for if these figures are inaccurate, the entire pricing system will be in jeopardy, and the operation might easily suffer financial losses due to miscalculations of the menu selling prices.

The Texas Restaurant Association Pricing Method

This method was developed and first used in the state of Texas; hence the name. This method begins with an accounting of all expense items except food cost, and a determination of the desired profit percentage of the owners. Once these figures are determined, the optimal, or ideal, food cost percentage is determined. At this point, the menu price is determined using the factor method but based on the ideal or optimal food cost percentage. The steps involved in this method are as follows:

Step	Example
1. Total all operating costs in dollars, excluding food and labor for a period of at least two to three months. (Here the period is one year.)	$111,500
2. Convert this figure to a percentage of gross sales for the same time period.	$111,500/$500,000 = 22.3%
3. Determine the labor cost as a percentage of gross sales.	$135,500/$500,000 = 27.19%.
4. Determine a desired profit percentage.	15%
5. Add the percentages established in Steps 1 through 4.	22.3 27.1 <u>15.0</u> 64.4%

Step	Example
6. Subtract this figure from 100. The answer represents the ideal, or optimal, food cost percentage.	$100 - 64.4\% = 35.6\%$
7. Divide the optimal food cost percentage into 100 to determine a multiplier.	$100/35.6 = 2.81.$
8. Multiply the raw food cost of the menu item by the multiplier to determine the selling price of the item.	Roast rib of beef dinner, $\$3.51 \times 2.81 = \$9.86.$ Stuffed flounder dinner, $\$2.43 \times 2.81 = \$6.83.$

This desired profit percentage may vary somewhat from item to item. Desired profit depends on the risk of spoilage and the volume of sales for the item. Figure 8.7 shows the recommended profit percentages for a number of categories. The exact profit percentage must be determined by each foodservice manager, depending on local market conditions.

Figure 8.7. Recommended Profit Percentages for Menu Items.

Entrees	10–25%	Á la carte	10–40%
Appetizers	20–50%	Vegetables	25–50%

Table 8.2 illustrates the menu prices and profit margins generated for the two menu items, roast rib of beef and stuffed flounder. It should be noted that each method generates a different menu price and profit margin. For this reason, no one method is considered correct for all situations.

Computers in Menu Pricing

In recent years, computers have become much more widely used in the foodservice industry. While performing a variety of functions, computers can be of particular value in menu pricing. With a computer, a record of inventory items and prices can be maintained and updated as necessary, and

Table 8.2. Comparison of Menu Prices Using Different Methods

	Roast Rib of Beef Dinner		Stuffed Flounder Dinner	
	Menu Price	*Profit Margin*	*Menu Price*	*Profit Margin*
Factor Method	$10.04	$6.53	$6.95	$4.52
Prime Cost Method	$10.67	$7.16	$8.79	$6.36
All Cost Plus Profit Method	$ 8.28	$4.77	$7.96	$5.53
The Gross Mark-up Method	$ 8.16	$4.65	$7.08	$4.65
Texas Restaurant Association Method	$ 9.86	$6.35	$6.83	$4.40

this file can then be used to precost a particular menu item or an entire menu. The precost figures are then combined into a variety of menu mixes to determine the particular menu mix that will produce the largest gross profit.

Figure 8.8 illustrates a computer printout for this type of menu pricing. Such programs are useful because additional variables can easily be included in the menu-pricing process. For example, an inflation factor can be adjusted for increased costs for food, labor or other expenses, or a weighted average for pessimistic, optimistic, and moderate customer count projections can be incorporated. As computers become more economically feasible for many foodservice operations, the use of this resource in the menu-planning process should not be discounted.

Summary

Menu pricing is by no means an easy task. Many variables must be considered as management attempts to strike an often-delicate balance between consumer demand and the price level.

This chapter focused on selected pricing theory and objectives, along with the pricing strategies of market skimming and market penetration. Price and nonprice competition, including cost-oriented, demand-oriented or perceived-value, and competitively-oriented pricing, and their relationship to sales volume are also important considerations.

Figure 8.8. Menu Pricing with a Computer.

(Courtesy M. D. Olsen, Ph.D., and C. Bellas, Ph.D., Virginia Polytechnic Institute and State University, Blacksburg, VA 24061.)

DINNER

		COST		SALES	
MENU ITEM	MIX	PORTION	TOTAL	PORTION	TOTAL
Chicken Cordon Bleu	159	2.860	454.74	6.95	1105.05
BBQ Ribs & Chicken	185	4.224	781.44	8.95	1655.75
Steak-Ka-Bob	194	4.433	860.00	8.95	1736.30
Rib Eye	198	4.565	903.87	8.95	1772.10
Prime Rib-1 inch	189	4.829	912.68	9.95	1880.55
Prime Rib-English	155	3.102	480.81	7.95	1232.25
Stuffed Shrimp	211	5.346	1128.01	9.95	2099.45
Stuffed Flounder	185	3.718	687.83	7.95	1470.75
Shrimp Scampi	206	5.830	1200.98	10.95	2255.70
Scallops In Wine	159	3.267	519.45	7.95	1264.05
Seafood Thermidor	142	2.926	415.49	7.95	1128.90
Rainbow Trout	185	3.773	698.00	7.95	1470.75
Gulf Red Snapper	194	4.950	960.30	9.95	1930.30
Crab Cakes	194	3.927	761.84	7.95	1542.30
Seafood Combination	198	6.061	1200.08	11.95	2366.10
	2754		11965.50		24910.30

Percentage Food Cost = 11965.50 / 24910.27 = 48.03 %

Gross Profit:
   Annual   155337.19
   Monthly   12944.77
   Weekly   3236.19
   Daily   462.31

Range = 20 %

	Pessimistic	Moderate	Optimistic
Mix	2479	2754	3029
Probability	20 %	50 %	30 %

GROSS PROFIT = 13074.03 (Monthly)

Among the variables that affect menu prices are governmental policies, the consumer's relative perception of value, and the cost structure of the foodservice operation. Management must carefully weigh the influence of each of these variables when establishing prices for the entire product-service mix. Management should not rely too heavily on a single variable.

Finally, several cost structure pricing methods, including the factor method, the prime cost method, the all costs plus profit, the gross mark-up method, the Texas Restaurant Association method, and the computer in menu pricing, together provide the foodservice manager with many different pricing methods from which to choose.

Questions For Review and Discussion

1. What are the major marketing factors that affect menu prices?
2. Why do profit percentages vary so greatly among companies in the foodservice industry?
3. What methods can a foodservice manager use to induce more patronage without lowering menu prices?
4. Of what value is a standardized recipe?
5. Discuss the term *consumers' perception of relative value*. How does this affect a manager when menu prices are established?

Problem

Given the following information, calculate the menu prices of each item using the following pricing methods:

1. The factor method
2. The prime cost method
3. The all costs plus profit method
4. The gross mark-up method
5. The Texas Restaurant Association method

Information given: Raw food costs and relative labor costs

	Food costs	Production labor cost
Chicken Kiev dinner	$2.45	$2.25
Sirloin steak dinner	$3.84	$1.50
Broiled scrod Mornay dinner	$2.81	$2.25
Broiled pork chop dinner	$3.29	$1.50

Desired food cost	37%
Total labor cost percentage	24%
Desired prime cost	60%
Projected annual sales	$1,250,000
Projected annual cost of food sold	$462,500
Projected annual number of covers served	104,150
Total of all expenses except food and labor	15% or $1.80/cover
Service cost per cover	$0.68

Chapter 9

Advertising and Promotion: An Overview

Chapter Outline

As the marketing environment in which foodservice organizations function becomes more competitive, the importance of advertising and promotion increases. This chapter focuses on advertising and lays the foundation for the final two chapters. Emphasis here is on defining commonly used terminology, advertising budgets, positioning and strategy, and planning and evaluating advertising campaigns.

The chapter covers the following topics:

Introduction
- functions of advertising
- criticisms of advertising

Definitions of Advertising Terms
- advertising and promotion
- national and local advertising
- cooperative advertising
- advertising throughout the life cycle

Establishing Advertising Budgets
- functions of advertising budgets
- advantages and disadvantages of advertising budgets
- budgeting methods
- a budgeting system

Advertising Positioning and Strategy
- developing strategy
- developing a central appeal
- keys to successful advertising

Planning and Evaluating Advertising Campaigns
- types of advertising campaigns
- campaign checkpoints
- an advertising planning model
- evaluating an advertising campaign

Summary

Introduction

Functions of Advertising

The terms *advertising* and *promotion* evoke many different responses from foodservice managers. Some smile, remembering a successful promotional effort of the past. Others simply view advertising as a waste of time. They claim that advertising and promotion are something that should be used to sell automobiles or laundry detergent, but not foodservice operations. These individuals usually champion word-of-mouth advertising, claiming that good food and service will produce satisfied consumers, who in turn will produce more consumers. While this argument has some truth to it, those managers who fail to engage in a significant advertising program may be missing a unique opportunity to increase both customer counts and total sales. Advertising is not something to be limited to the chain operations, such as McDonald's and Wendy's, nor is it only something a manager does when business is poor and needs a shot in the arm.

Advertising and promotion are marketing functions that need to be managed as all other functions. They demand management's time and attention if they are to be successful, for advertising must be planned, implemented, coordinated, and evaluated with care if it is to achieve increased sales. What can advertising and promotion do? First, advertising and promotion present information to the consumer. They tell about new products, new services, new decor, and other items of potential interest. Second, they reinforce consumer behavior by communicating with those individuals who have patronized a particular foodservice operation in the past. Exposing these consumers to a continuous flow of advertising is likely to induce repeat patronage by reinforcing their positive dining experiences.

Third, advertising induces first-time patronage. If consumers are exposed to a continual flow of advertising, their curiosity is aroused and often results in patronage. If a first-time consumer is rewarded with a pleasant experience, a repeat consumer has been found. At least a portion of the advertising must be directed toward individuals who have not already patronized the operation. Some managers believe that the key to success is to build a steady group of repeat consumers, and while this is a good aspect of a promotional strategy, other efforts must be aimed at those who have not previously been guests. Fourth, advertising enhances the image of foodservice operations. Advertising does not always seek to promote a specific product or service; it can instead seek to create and reinforce an image for the consuming public. Words and phrases often contribute to this image building; for example, the McDonald's "We Do It All For You" and

Sheraton's "We've Got Style" both seek to maintain a specific image that has been created in the mind of the consumer.

Still, a significant number of foodservice owners and managers do not believe in advertising. Some will argue that the only good form of advertising is word of mouth; "Let our patrons speak good words about us, and we'll succeed," they claim. Unfortunately for these individuals, this point of view does not always hold true. Many independent operations are simply being squeezed by larger national and regional chain advertising, while many managers withdraw from all advertising, rationalizing that they cannot compete with the big chains. The result is the all-too-often predictable bankruptcy!

Advertising and promotion are necessarily a vital part of the marketing program of all types of foodservice operations. But just what should advertising do? What should it accomplish? Generally speaking, advertising should set out to accomplish three goals: (1) establish awareness in the minds of consumers, (2) establish positive value in the minds of consumers, and (3) promote repeat patronage and brand loyalty among consumers.

Awareness must be created among those consumers who have not heard of a particular foodservice establishment. This awareness should create sufficient interest so that patronage results. Next, to induce both first-time and repeat patronage, a positive perceived value must be established and reinforced in the minds of consumers. All consumers have a limited amount of resources chasing after unlimited wants; hence only those products and services offering a high level of perceived value will be rewarded with patronage. A foodservice operation might have the very best food and service in a given market segment, but if it offers a low perceived value, the number of consumers served is likely to be small. Finally, advertising should strive to promote brand loyalty and repeat patronage among the highest percentage of consumers possible. Very few foodservice operations, except perhaps those in tourist areas, can survive on one-time patronage only. Repeat business must be encouraged and promoted. Even better than repeat patronage is brand loyalty, wherein consumers begin to prefer one foodservice operation over and above the direct competition. This is, of course, a very lofty goal, but one that is attainable.

Criticisms of Advertising

Many critics of advertising raise questions about whether a foodservice operation should advertise. Several typical questions and responses follow.

Doesn't a lot of advertising contain misleading information?   Advertising is indeed a powerful force in the marketplace, and occasionally, it may be used by a dishonest manager to deceive. This type of logic would hold, however, that because one apple in a box was rotten, the entire box should be thrown out.

The government has gone to great lengths to protect the consumer. Many other groups, including the Better Business Bureau and the National Advertising Review Council, strive to limit the amount of false and misleading advertising. Also, it simply is not in the long-term interests of any foodservice operation to deceive its consumers. Advertising seeks to induce first-time and repeat patronage by promising consumers specific products and services. Failure to deliver as promised hurts the advertiser's credibility and sales.

Doesn't advertising result in a vicious spending circle among competitors? Some believe that if two foodservice operations (A and B) are in direct competition, A's spending more on advertising means that B will increase expenditures to counteract the efforts of A. A in turn will increase expenditures to regain the advantage over B, and so on. This simply is not the case. It is not the dollar amount spent but the effectiveness of the advertising that counts. Consumer advocates who claim that this circular relationship results in increased prices and should therefore be limited would also limit research and development and test marketing, because these costs are also passed on to the consumer.

Why should the consumer have to pay for advertising? Doesn't this result in higher prices?   Yes, the consumer pays for advertising. Consumers bear the cost of raw materials, labor, and all other variable and fixed expenses in producing a food or beverage product. Consumers do not, however, necessarily pay a higher price as a result of advertising. Very often, advertising features lower prices in the form of specials, coupons, and the like.

Economy of scale is also possible through advertising. All foodservice operations have certain fixed expenses that must be paid whether zero, one, or one thousand consumers are served. As more consumers are served, the cost per consumer for fixed costs is reduced and these reductions can actually lower, rather than raise, prices. Increased volume also allows a manager to purchase all supplies in larger quantities, often lowering the price further. Yes, the consumer does pay for advertising, but this price is not necessarily higher.

Doesn't advertising give the larger chains an unfair advantage?   Yes, large chains do have very definite advantages over smaller firms, simply because of a broader financial base and depth of resources. This is a part of business life and should not be tampered with. Mere size does not necessarily mean monopoly, as there are many thousands of small, independent foodservice establishments in operation. Several years ago, some people believed that McDonald's was beginning to establish a virtual monopoly in the fast-food segment of the industry. These people held that McDonald's would drive the independent operations out of business and would then consume many of the smaller regional chains. Much to the surprise of these people, along came Wendy's, which moved from small stature to a position as number three behind McDonald's and Burger King in a few short years. Large chains do enjoy certain advertising advantages, but these advantages hardly create a monopolistic marketplace.

Doesn't advertising make consumers purchase things they do not want or cannot afford? In some cases, yes. Advertising seeks to persuade consumers to purchase specific food and beverage products from the advertiser. No one is forcing consumers to purchase these products and services. Some would argue that an expensive dining experience is unnecessary when a simple diet will adequately satisfy dietary requirements. Most dining out is an acquired taste, and once acquired, it needs to be satisfied just as other needs do. Consumers are the ones who make the final decision concerning how their limited resources will be allocated. Advertising simply makes them aware of choices and attempts to encourage patronage.

Definitions of Advertising Terms

Advertising and Promotion

The American Marketing Association defined advertising as ''Any paid form of nonpersonal presentation and promotion of ideas, goods, or services by an identified sponsor.'' This definition is uniformly accepted throughout the business community. It can be broken down into four component parts:

1. **Paid form.** Any advertising is paid for and controlled by the individual or group that is the sponsor. Because someone is paying for the space (newspaper, outdoor) or time (radio, television), this individual or group has complete control over what is said, printed, or shown. Any promotion that is not paid for is called *publicity*. Because the individual or group is not paying for the time or space, those involved do not have complete control and hence are at the mercy of the writer or producer. A common form of publicity is a review of a food-

service establishment in a dining or food section of a local newspaper. Publicity can obviously be either favorable or unfavorable.

2. **Nonpersonal.**   Advertising is done through the mass media without personal contact or interaction between the seller and the potential buyer. Advertising relies strictly on nonpersonal promotion of goods, services, or ideas.

3. **Promotion related to ideas, goods, or services.**   Advertising need not be restricted to the promotion of a tangible physical product or good. It may try to influence individuals to change their ways of thinking or their behavior. The National Restaurant Association's "We're Glad You're Here" promotional campaign was a successful attempt to make people feel good about dining out without specifically advertising any one foodservice operation.

4. **Identified sponsor.**   All advertising has an identified sponsor.

Promotion is a broader-based term denoting efforts undertaken to induce patronage. It includes personal selling that is face-to-face communication between the seller and the prospective buyer as well as other efforts designed to increase sales. Simply stated, advertising is a form of promotion, but all forms of promotion are not necessarily advertising.

National and Local Advertising

Advertising can be divided into two broad categories, national and local. National consumer advertising is aimed at a national audience by using network television and radio or national print media, such as magazines. This form of advertising normally promotes the general name of the chain, not individual locations or stores.

Local advertising is used not only by the major foodservice chains but also by second-tier chains, regional chains, and independent operations. Local advertising using television, radio, print, and other media is used extensively in the foodservice industry. This is the level where the action really lies, and to coin a phrase, the battle of foodservice market shares is won or lost in the trenches of local advertising.

Cooperative Advertising

A simple fact of business life for many managers is that specific advertising media are too expensive for the organization to use. For many managers, cooperative advertising is an excellent alternative. Cooperative advertising, as the name implies, involves having two or more parties work together as sponsors of an advertisement that provides benefit to all parties involved.

For example, a group of foodservice operations located in a given geographic area may join together and promote dining in the area without promoting any one operation specifically. By joining together and sharing the expenses, managers are able to advertise in more expensive media and reach new audiences. Cooperative advertising is an area of tremendous promise because it allows a manager to expand the advertising media selection. Caution should be exercised, however, to assure that all cooperative advertisers are represented fairly and equally. Herein lies the major drawback of cooperative advertising.

Cooperative advertising is often favored by national advertisers as a way to improve relations with local store owners. For example, if a national foodservice chain wanted to place a series of advertisements in local newspapers or on a local radio station, it would pay what is known as the ''national rate,'' or the highest rate for the advertising space or time. If, however, a local store owner placed orders for the same amount of space or time, the store owner would pay the local rate, which is lower than the national rate. Cooperative efforts between the national chain and the local store owner benefit both parties. The two split the cost of the advertising, with each normally paying 50 percent of the cost. The local store owner is then able to purchase a good deal more advertising than would have been possible without the assistance of the national chain. The national chain, on the other hand, is able to purchase the space through the local store owner at the local advertising rate. Thus, the national chain is able to purchase the same amount of advertising space at a reduced cost, and the local store owner pays 50 percent of the reduced cost. In this way, the national chain is able to get more advertising time and space for the same dollar investment and can also build improved relations with the local store owner because they worked together.

Advertising and Promotion Throughout the Life Cycle

As discussed in Chapter 2, all foodservice operations progress through a distinct life cycle (Figure 9.1). As an operation moves through the stages of the life cycle, different advertising approaches must be used, as the following correspondence indicates:

Life Cycle Stage	**Advertising and Promotion Stage**
Introduction	Introductory stage
Conservative expansion	

Life Cycle Stage	Advertising and Promotion Stage
Rapid expansion	Expansion stage
Plateaued maturity	Stabilization stage
Decline or regeneration	Introductory, expansion or stabilization stage (depending on the trends of the business)

Figure 9.1. The Life Cycle of Foodservice Organizations. (Stage I = introduction; stage II = conservative expansion; stage III = rapid expansion; stage IV = plateaued maturity; stage V = decline or regeneration.)

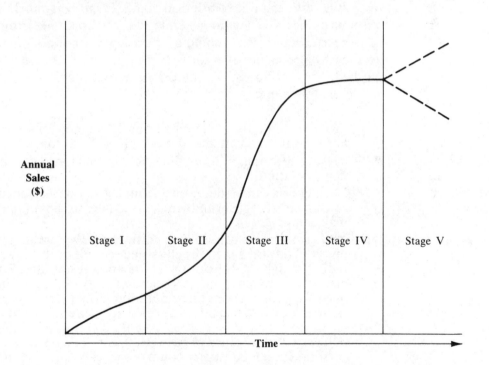

Introductory Stage.   Rarely does a new foodservice open without creating some interest in the local community. The goal of all foodservice managers should be to capitalize on this natural curiosity and make it work to the advantage of the new foodservice establishment. Two broad-based philosophies are often used. One promotes solely the quality and desirability of the one foodservice; the other involves direct comparisons with major competitors (*comparative advertising*), indicating that the products and services offered by the advertiser are superior to those offered by the competition. Both of these philosophies have been implemented with success by many different types of operations. One brief word of caution deserves mention, however: If a direct comparison to other operations is made, every effort must be made to deliver the products and services as promised. Failure to do so will result in a marked drop in credibility and effectiveness of subsequent advertising. Once deceived, the consumer is wary! The principal goal during this phase is to build volume within the operation. Every effort must be made to reach potential consumers and encourage first-time patronage. All potentially targeted segments should be identified and specific strategies developed to reach these markets.

It is very desirable to bring all management personnel with marketing responsibilities together to generate ideas for possible promotion. These idea-generating sessions should produce a wealth of potential promotions, leading to a schedule of what is to be done and when it is to be accomplished. The list of possible promotional ideas is endless; a few examples include the following:

- Signs can announce "Coming Soon" for a new foodservice operation and perhaps indicate the number of weeks until the grand opening.
- Press releases can indicate the wheres, whats, whens, and whys of the new operation.
- Mailing lists can be developed from a guest book signed by first-time consumers. This list can then be used later as a mailing list for direct-mail campaigns.
- Numerous media can, of course, be used. One rather novel approach involved advertising in the classified section of the newspaper and on radio for high-quality personnel for a new restaurant. The results were not only surprising, but very successful. Hundreds of individuals applied for jobs, making the restaurant "the place" to work. In addition, the advertisements described in some detail the atmosphere, menu, and image of the restaurant, thereby informing the general public of the existence of the restaurant. The result was high-quality personnel, high consumer counts, and very satisfied management.
- Community opinion leaders, such as doctors, lawyers, and restaurant reviewers, can be invited to opening-week parties and the like, all designed to enhance the image of the foodservice operation. The goal, of course, is to present a positive image and influence those who refer to these leaders.
- Numerous door prizes, contests, and raffles can be used to encourage patronage. The American consumer seems infinitely willing to take a chance on getting something for nothing or something for next to nothing. Consider the success of Las Vegas and Atlantic City gam-

bling. This approach is simply an application of psychologist B. F. Skinner's variable-interval reinforcement schedule. Individuals will continue to take chances, even though the probability of winning is very small.

- Handbills or flyers represent an inexpensive, yet effective method of introductory promotion. These can, of course, be used as direct-mail pieces, or they may be distributed by other means. One new restaurant located near a large shopping mall and several office complexes distributed handbills offering a variety of discounts and freebees at these locations. In addition, they invited the secretaries of the high-ranking management personnel to a complimentary lunch and formed a secretaries' club that provided incentives and rewards to those secretaries who provided the restaurant with the largest number of reservations. The results were predictable; very high volume and all parties involved satisfied.

The list of potential introductory advertising and promotional ideas is endless. Each management group must determine a sound strategy for the introductory stage of advertising and promotion.

Expansion Stage.   The expansion stage of advertising is based on name recognition and awareness of many consumers. If the introductory stage has been successful, a solid core of consumers has been established. With this core, expansion advertising must take two approaches: (1) to reinforce and remind those consumers who have patronized the foodservice establishment and induce repeat patronage, and (2) to reach those consumers who have not patronized the operation, thereby expanding volume with a significant number of first-time consumers.

The expansion stage marks a well-established image within the marketplace. During this stage, the mention of the name of the foodservice establishment brings a distinct image to the consumer's mind. Expansion advertising should therefore seek to reinforce the most positive aspects of this image. Most foodservice operators successfully reach the expansion stage of advertising, and are seeking to retain current consumers and draw new ones. The strategies used include comparative advertising, stressing the special advantages offered by the product-service mix of the operation.

One promotional technique that has grown in popularity has been the use of coupons. These are normally distributed in one of three manners: through a variety of print media, by direct mail, or by service personnel at the time the bill is paid. Coupon promotions are generally most effective in increasing consumer counts. A word of caution, however: If a large number of foodservice operations in a given geographic area offer coupon discounts, the consumer can become conditioned to coupons as a way of life, and the result is that they will only patronize foodservice operations that offer such discounts. The situation could deteriorate into one in which all foodservice establishments lose, as was often the case in the bygone days of "gasoline wars" among competing stations.

Stabilization Stage. Only the largest and most successful foodservice organizations achieve this stage of the advertising life cycle. The firms that achieve this level are very well established and have the tremendous advantage of nearly universal name recognition and reinforcement. The best example is McDonald's; a McDonald's advertisement need not even mention the product or service in order to be successful. Simply by saying, "McDonald's, We Do It All For You," the advertisement serves to reinforce the image and quality of the organization in the minds of the consuming public.

Regeneration Stage. The goal of any firm that reaches this stage of its life cycle and the stabilization stage of the advertising life cycle is to use its competitive advantage to launch new products and services that will further strengthen the organization. By adding to the product-service mix, the firm can attract new consumers and will further strengthen its market standing. McDonald's again serves as an excellent example, as it has repeatedly used its number-one position in the fast-food segment to launch new products and services, most notably a variety of breakfasts, such new hamburgers as the Quarter-Pounder™, such other sandwiches as McChicken™ and McRib™, and such dessert items as sundaes. All of these products contribute to the wealth of the organization and serve to broaden the market appeal. All have, of course, been test-marketed prior to being introduced into the system. They serve as examples of ways an organization can market new products and services from a position of strength and, as a result, become stronger still. Granted, no foodservice organization enjoys the strength of McDonald's, but the same concept can be applied on a smaller scale at the regional or local level.

Establishing Advertising Budgets

Functions of Advertising Budgets

Budgets should predict and monitor revenues and expenses. Major expenses, such as labor or food, are tangible and more easily predicted and monitored. Advertising is also an expense that must be carefully planned, monitored, and controlled. As compared to major expense items, advertising may not seem like a large percentage, but because advertising is not tangible, careful planning and control must be implemented.

Many foodservice managers do not budget advertising expenditures. Instead, the advertising function is handled in a "seat of the pants" manner with funds allocated solely on the basis of managerial whims. Some managers advertise when business volume is slow, thereby hoping to increase volume. Others attempt to reduce expenses by cutting back on advertising when a decline in volume occurs. Both approaches are subject to error because they are based on whim rather than on a rational decision-making and budgeting process.

Advertising budgets serve several useful functions; (1) to provide a detailed projection of future expenditures, (2) to provide both short- and long-range planning guides for management, and (3) to provide a method of monitoring and controlling advertising expenses by comparing actual expenses against projections.

Advantages and Disadvantages of Advertising Budgets

Numerous executives debate the pros and cons of budgeting advertising expenses. These are summarized as follows.

Advantages of Advertising Budgets

- Developing budgets forces management to look into the future. Although both the past and the current conditions certainly need to be considered, the future is the key. All management personnel must develop the ability to project future trends, revenues, and expenses. Failure to do so can easily lead to management by crisis.
- Budgets serve as reference points. Advertising budget projections need not be solid figures cast in stone. Budgeted figures and media plans are, of course, subject to modification if the marketing situation changes dramatically. The budget, however, is important as a point of reference, a goal, and a standard against which actual performance can be compared.
- When advertising budgets are developed, all management personnel with marketing responsibilities should be involved in their preparation. This involvement fosters improved communication among individuals. In addition, as all managers have input into the development of the plan, support for the plan increases as each manager "owns a piece" of the plan. Once individuals identify with the budget as it is developed, this will increase their personal motivation to see that it is implemented successfully.

Disadvantages of Advertising Budgets

- Time is money. To prepare an advertising budget properly, a considerable amount of management time is necessary. The old phrase "time is money" was never more true. As the highest-paid management personnel engage in planning the advertising budget, the cost to the organization can be considerable. This represents time that some say could be spent more profitably performing other functions. The question to raise is, "How much is it worth to the organization to have well-developed budgets and plans?"
- What events will shape the future? Certainly, the future is always going to be somewhat uncertain, but astute managers should be able to foresee trends and adapt to take full competitive advantage of these trends. Foodservice operations often fail because management does not foresee changes and, as a result, is unable to adapt in a timely manner. Successful management must develop a proactive rather than a reactive posture; it must foresee change before it occurs and adapt to allow the operation to benefit from the change. A reactive posture means that management simply awaits changes and tries to adapt as best it can. Continual adaptation can easily result in management without direction and management by crisis. Clearly, proactive is superior to reactive management as an advertising and marketing strategy.

Budgeting Methods

Advertising budgets are normally either fixed or contingency. *Fixed budgets,* by definition, are those based on a given prediction of sales volume and expected advertising activity. Projected expenditures are normally held firm, even if the assumptions on which the budget was based prove to be incorrect. *Contingency budgets,* on the other hand, are developed based on several sets of assumptions. This development means that if situation A happens, then implement plan A, if situation B occurs, then implement plan B, and so on. This type of budget draws its name from its basis on a number of contingencies, or plans developed to be appropriate for several possible outcomes.

The development of weighted projected annual revenue figure or a similar approach is used in the development of a contingency approach to an advertising budget. (Refer to Tables 3.2 and 3.3 to refresh your memory.) Recall that three different budgets are developed based on optimistic, moderate, and pessimistic levels of sales. Based on actual sales trends, the advertising budget developed for that contingency is then implemented.

There are perhaps 20 to 30 methods to use in developing an appropriation for advertising. All of these methods are, however, variations on three basic methods: (1) the percentage of sales method, (2) the desired objective method, and (3) the competitive method.

The percentage of sales method has found very wide use in the food-service industry. The method offers relative simplicity; sales are forecast, and a given percentage of this forecast is allocated to advertising. Within the foodservice industry, the amount of money spent for advertising is typically between one and six percent of gross sales. This method offers several advantages:

- It is very simple and straightforward.
- Some managers prefer to view all expenses as a percentage of sales, including advertising.
- It works well if sales can be forecasted accurately and market conditions are stable.

There are drawbacks as well:

- This method holds that if sales decline, so too will advertising expenditures. This is not a valid argument; instead, advertising should be increased.
- Increased advertising should result in increased sales, yet this method holds that an increase in sales results in an increase in the advertising budget.

The desired objective method involves the development of an advertising budget based on well-defined objectives. Management must plan precisely what it wishes to accomplish through advertising. Based on these objectives, management must then decide what type and what amount of advertising will be necessary to achieve the objectives. Many factors must be considered, including projected sales, previous advertising, financial position of the firm, and competition within the marketplace. Advantages to this method include the following:

- Rather than simply allocating a fixed percentage of sales for each budget period, management must critically evaluate advertising expenditures.
- Advertising efforts are tied to specific measurable objectives, thereby making evaluation easier.
- Several variable factors, such as competition within the marketplace, are considered.

Two major disadvantages, however, must be considered:

- It is difficult to determine the precise mix of advertising that will accomplish the objectives satisfactorily.

- Engaging in this type of budget preparation is very time consuming, especially when one considers that advertising and promotion represent only one line item on an income statement.

The competitive method for establishing an advertising budget involves direct comparison with the advertising efforts of major competitors. Based on the type and amount of advertising done by the competition, management then establishes a budget that will roughly match the activities of the major competition. Advantages include the following:

- A relative level of equilibrium is established with regard to the competition.
- The method is simple and straightforward, especially if an industry average is used.

Disadvantages of the competitive method include the following:

- Relative advertising budgets and media decisions made by one firm usually are not applicable to other firms. How can management be assured that the competition's advertising is appropriate for its operation?
- Basing future advertising plans on the past performance of others is shortsighted in that it does not focus attention on the future.

A Budgeting System

Those exposed to the budget-preparation process for the first time are often overwhelmed. Images of smoke-filled rooms and political in-fighting sometimes develop until the process has been experienced and understood. Figure 9.2 illustrates the budget system in a manner that encapsulates the process in an easily understood format. Initially, upper management must determine future objectives. At the same time, the desired future performance for advertising is projected by taking into consideration: trends, future influential factors, past performance, and input from subordinates. A preliminary budget is prepared and is then compared with the short- and long-range objectives of upper management. If the budget appears to satisfy the objectives, it is adopted, and controls are established. If the budget fails to meet the objectives, then the objectives and/or the budget must be revised to bring the two into harmony.

Figure 9.2. The Budgeting System.

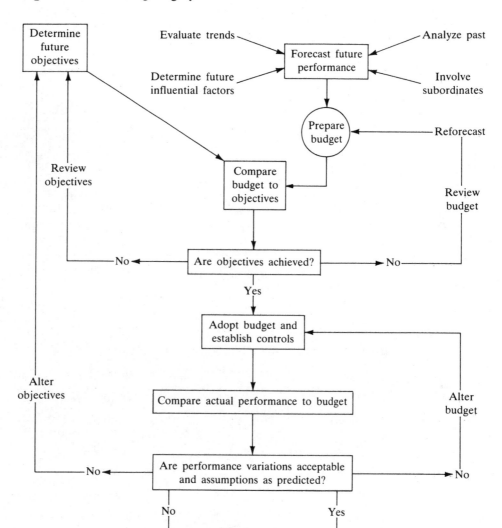

Once the budget is implemented, a simple control process is used. If the advertising performs as planned, the monitoring process continues. If, however, evaluation shows that the advertising is not successful, several avenues can be taken:

- The advertising can be changed to increase the probability of satisfying evaluation standards.
- The budget can be modified based on changing market conditions.
- The short- and long-range objectives can be changed based on new available information.

Table 9.1 provides information concerning the advertising budgets for some of the large foodservice chains. These figures serve as interesting comparisons.

Table 9.1. Advertising Budgets Within the Foodservice Industry.

Source: "Institutions 400", *Institutions,* vol. 87, no. 2, 1980, p. 44. *Courtesy: Restaurants & Institutions* magazine.

Chain	1979 Spending	1980 Budget
McDonald's	$170,000,000	$200,000,000
Burger King	59,992,500	80,000,000
Kentucky Fried Chicken	55,000,000	70,000,000
Wendy's	40,000,000	65,000,000
Marriott Corp.	35,000,000	40,000,000*
Hardee's	30,000,000	35,000,000*
Pizza Hut	25,000,000	30,000,000
Long John Silver's	16,000,000	18,000,000
Arby's	15,000,000	17,000,000
Bonanza	14,700,000	16,500,000
Ponderosa	14,000,000	16,000,000
Red Lobster	13,000,000	15,000,000
Dairy Queen	12,500,000	14,500,000
Sambo's	9,000,000	9,250,000
Denny's	8,800,000	10,000,000*
Dunkin' Donuts	8,000,000	10,000,000
Arthur Treacher's	6,500,000	7,500,000

Table 9.1. Advertising Budgets Within the Foodservice Industry (*continued*).

Chain	1979 Spending	1980 Budget
Burger Chef	6,000,000	8,000,000
Taco Bell	5,000,000	5,500,000
A & W	4,500,000	5,000,000
Burger Queen	4,200,000	5,400,000
Jack in the Box	4,000,000	3,500,000*
Collins	4,000,000	4,800,000
Shakey's	4,000,000	4,500,000
Mr. Steak	3,800,000	4,500,000
Big Boy	3,300,000	4,000,000
Intl. House of Pancakes	3,000,000	3,500,000
Famous Recipe Fried Chicken	2,500,000	3,500,000
Shoney's South	2,450,000	2,700,000
Pioneer Take Out	2,200,000	2,800,000
Tastee Freez	2,000,000	2,500,000
Popeye's Fried Chicken	—	2,000,000
Godfather	1,805,000	4,000,000
Victoria Station	1,723,173	1,500,000

Institutions' estimate.

A Rolling Advertising Budget

One of the drawbacks to a traditional annually prepared budget is the amount of preparation time. Many personnel hours are required to solicit input from subordinates and combine it in a finished and workable budget. For this reason, a rolling budget may be implemented. A rolling budget begins with an established 12-month budget. At the end of the first month (January, for example), actual figures are compared with budgeted figures, and based on this and other input, a budget is formulated for January of the next year. At the end of the next month (February), actual figures are compared with those budgeted, and a budget for the following February is formulated. In this way, the budget is prepared in a piecemeal fashion, yet each month is examined while the results are still fresh in everyone's mind. By formulating a budget in this manner, a manager always has a budget projection for a full 12 months in advance. By considering each month separately, management avoids rushing to complete a full 12-month budget in a short period of time.

Advertising is not an expense to be taken lightly. It must be carefully planned, and its results should be monitored. With careful planning, a modest investment in advertising can produce satisfactory results. Without careful planning, a large investment may produce dismal results. The amount of money spent is not nearly as important as the way it is spent. Whatever method is used to establish an advertising budget, the level of advertising activity is important. Management should be aware of a distinct relationship between the number of advertising exposures and the consumers' purchasing response. This relationship is shown in Figure 9.3.

With a relatively small number of advertising exposures, the impact on consumer purchasing behavior will be minimal. A very low level of advertising activity will not have an impact on consumers because they are exposed to many other advertisements each day, and any advertising needs to overcome the "noise" or "clutter" in the advertising media. Raising the level of advertising to reach a threshold point, the point at which consumers become aware of the advertisements, begins to affect the purchasing response. For example, if a single consumer is exposed to a radio advertisement once, the effect of this single exposure will be minimal. If this same consumer is exposed to the advertisement five times, however, the threshold point may be reached, and the combined frequency of exposures will begin favorably to affect purchasing behavior.

Once the threshold point is reached, any increases in the level of advertising exposure will also result in a favorable response in consumer purchasing, although this relationship is subject to the law of diminishing returns. Beyond the saturation point, any increases in the total number of advertising exposures will not result in similar increases in consumer purchases. In fact, if the total number of advertising exposures is increased further, to the supersaturation point, consumers will actually turn against the advertiser and reduce the level of patronage. The precise levels at which the threshold, saturation, and supersaturation points occur will vary from organization to organization. Only through experimentation with different levels of advertising can the optimal level of advertising exposures be established and maintained.

Figure 9.3. Relationship Between Consumer Purchasing Behavior and the Total Number of Advertising Exposures.

Credit: Reprinted from "Technological Innovation, Entrepreneurship, and Strategy," by James Brian Quinn, *Sloan Management Review,* Spring 1979, vol. 20, no. 3, pp. 19–30, by permission of the publisher. © 1979 by the Sloan Management Review Association. All rights reserved.

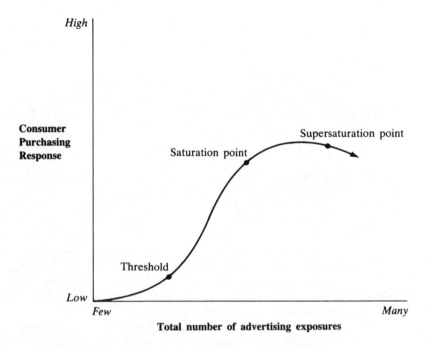

Advertising Positioning and Strategy

The language of advertising often sounds like the language of war. Campaigns are launched, and advertisements are aimed at targeted markets. Advertising need not be anything like war, but successful advertising is the result of carefully planned strategy.

A manager must first decide how to position the produce-service mix. *Positioning* is the manner in which the consumer views the product-service mix, and each foodservice operation is positioned differently. For example, several years ago, McDonald's consumers viewed the franchise as a quick-service, standard foodservice operation. Burger King's consumers viewed this franchise as more flexible, a result of the "Have It Your Way" positioning. Before any advertising decisions are made or strategy is plotted, the operation's position must be determined.

Developing Strategy

Successful advertising does not result from haphazard planning and execution. A single advertisement may be very good, but successful operations produce consistently superior advertising. One of the keys to successful advertising is repetition. Long-term advertising success does not result from an occasional advertisement. An operation must strive constantly to place its name in front of consumers, and it must also position itself in the proper manner.

Advertising succeeds when good strategy is developed. Strategy is not a magic formula mixed up in a smoke-filled room. It does not require a secret formula. Strategy development revolves around five key points:

1. Objectives—What should the advertising do? What goals does management want to achieve? For example, a new foodservice operation may set recognition among local residents as an objective, while another foodservice operation might seek to increase sales on slow nights, such as Mondays and Tuesdays. For this operation, most of the money would concentrate on promotions designed to increase volume on these nights.

2. Targeted audience—Who is the customer or potential customer? Advertising is not a success when used in a shotgun manner. Successful advertising addresses a specifically targeted market and talks directly to that market. Many advertising programs fail because they attempt to appeal to too broad a targeted market.

3. Key consumer benefit—Consumers can be skeptical and often need a benefit, or a reason to buy, before they are persuaded. This is the pitch to the consumer. What key ideas or benefits should be promoted? Why should the consumer come to this operation instead of another? True differences between foodservice operations are rare, but a list of products and services the operation offers should stress those different from or superior to those offered by other foodservice facilities.

4. Support—To have a successful advertising campaign, the key benefit must be supported in some manner. Consumers today are somewhat skeptical of advertising claims; who can blame them? Included in any advertisement should be a reason for the consumer to believe in the benefit. Consumer testimonials or test results showing superiority are often used for this purpose.

5. Tone and manner—The advertising strategy must have a "personality." This personality should blend with the image and positioning of the foodservice operation. McDonald's has been extremely successful with Ronald McDonald when advertising to children. This figure makes McDonald's seem like a fun place to be. Another national chain, Red Lobster, has featured service personnel in advertisements emphasizing quick and friendly service. The tone and manner selected should blend with the overall theme that management is trying to

create and should show the potential customer the nature of the operation.[1]

Developing a Central Appeal

Developing a central advertising appeal is not an easy process. Considerable time and thought must be devoted to the creative process before a viable appeal is found. Several rules of thumb exist for the development of this appeal:

- A central appeal must offer some value to the consumer. If the central appeal does not speak directly to the needs of the primary targeted market, the chances for success are greatly reduced. A well-developed marketing information system should provide specific data about the marketplace, enabling management to be in tune with the values of consumers.
- The appeal must be distinctive. All advertising must compete not only with all other foodservice advertising but also with all consumer advertising, with everything from automobiles to washing machines. For the advertising to be effective, the appeal must offer something that separates it from everything else. Distinctive appeals include the "roadrunner" theme of Hardee's advertising as well as the Arby's "Don't Worry Mom, I'm Eating Right," and Long John Silver's "Put a smile on your taste."
- The appeal must be believable. Claims made for the product-service mix must be backed up if the appeal is to have credibility. Because some consumers are more skeptical than others, the appeal should be believable to those who might at first have doubts. The Arby's appeal about eating right can be made more credible by supplying consumers with a nutritional analysis of the various meals available, showing that the food is nutritionally adequate.
- The appeal should be simple. Consumers are confronted each day with thousands of advertising stimuli, and if one is to be recalled, it must be simple and straightforward. Effective and simple appeals include "We Do It All For You," "Square Meal, Square Deal," "The Burgers Are Better At Burger King," and "You, You're The One."

Keys to Successful Advertising

To be successful, advertising needs to be approached in a systematic manner. H. Victor Grohmann, Chairman of Needham and Grohmann, Inc., offers several suggestions for how to improve advertising efficiency.[2]

- **Time.**   Advertising should not be considered a necessary evil. Sales and operations are equally important and require time for an advertising program to generate satisfactory results.
- **Budgets.**   These should be developed for the needs of each operation. It makes little sense to base an advertising budget on figures and percentages that represent the national average. Generally, a manager must have the courage to spend enough to produce successful results.
- **Study.**   A manager needs to analyze the operation and determine the operation's advantages as compared to the competition. Disadvantages also need to be identified so that they might be minimized or eliminated completely. This evaluation must be done constantly so that any changes in the competitive situation are noted and adjustments made quickly.
- **Analysis of market segments.**   Each year, many people change jobs and move, and as people change jobs, their lifestyles change too. No market segment is constant; all are always changing. For this reason, management must know the patrons of the foodservice operation. By doing this, management can modify the operation to meet changing consumer demands.
- **Media.**   Media must be selected very carefully to be effective. Media used must match the intended targeted markets. Each type of media offers advantages and drawbacks, which are discussed in Chapter 11.
- **Formulation of a plan.**   Advertising cannot be successful if it is approached in a haphazard manner. It is important that continuity be established among all forms of advertising so that advertising gains momentum. Continuity can be established through the consistent use of logos, distinctive type styles, music, or any creative touches to make the advertising stand out from other advertisements. Managers should not be afraid of advertising and should draw up plans designed to produce results. Nothing is worse than spending too little money on advertising so advertising expenditures should not be cut. To be successful, advertising must be used regularly, not intermittently. Successful advertising is based on repetition.

Planning and Evaluating Advertising Campaigns

Single advertisements may be creative or humorous and may convey a message, but by themselves, they are not able to achieve the necessary degree of advertising effectiveness. Many foodservice advertisers purchase print advertising or a few radio spots only at certain times of the year, particularly when business is slow. This type of advertising is not likely to be as effective as it could be, because continuity between the advertisements is lost. Such advertisements are not packaged as a campaign but are instead a hit-and-miss approach. An *advertising campaign* includes all forms of advertising held together by a single message or overall theme. A campaign is the overall plan or strategy that guides the development of all forms of advertising.

Campaign planning is initiated by considering the competitive situation, currently targeted markets, potentially targeted markets, and market positioning. An astute manager should always be aware of the advertising activities of major competitors. This, of course, is not to say that the competition should dictate advertising activities, but awareness of competitors' activities may indicate trends. For example, is the competition pushing food quality, service quality, drive-through service, atmosphere, or something else? Awareness of the efforts of direct competition may allow a manager to counter the competition's benefits and gain a competitive advantage.

Both the currently targeted markets and the potential new markets must also be evaluated. How can management best reinforce the current markets to promote repeat patronage? What type of message will reach these markets most effectively? In addition, what new markets should be explored? What is the best type of message to use to overcome uncertainty and resistance and thereby promote first-time patronage? Can these two messages be combined, or are they best kept separate? The market positioning must also be considered. How is the operation perceived by repeat consumers and by potential consumers? Is this the same perception that management wishes to project?

Types of Advertising Campaigns

Advertising campaigns come in all patterns and sizes, depending on the resources and needs of the individual foodservice organization. Generally, campaigns are organized geographically as national, regional, or local campaigns. Each is self-explanatory and will differ in sophistication and media selection. Local campaign planners often feel that they are at a distinct disadvantage because they have smaller advertising budgets and less marketing expertise. This need not be a disadvantage; instead, it is often just the opposite. The use of local radio spots and local print and/or television advertising allows the advertiser to speak directly with the local clientele. Often the local advertiser has a much clearer understanding of the targeted market and is thereby able to achieve a competitive advantage over regional and national advertisers.

Campaign Checkpoints

When developing the theme for a campaign, Roman and Maas suggest that the advertiser consider four checkpoints:[3]

1. **Maintain visual similarity.** This similarity applies to the visual media. Most common of all approaches is the use of a well-defined logo or the same layout, type style, or set in all advertisements. Are advertisements easily recognized without looking at the name? If not, perhaps the visual similarity needs further attention. In national fast-food advertising, visual similarity is maintained by the McDonald's golden arches and the Hardee's roadrunner.

2. **Maintain verbal similarity.** Phrases and statements are repeated in all advertisements, reinforcing the advertiser's image and message. In the hospitality industry, a well-known form of verbal similarity is Holiday Inn's, "The Best Surprise Is No Surprise."

3. **Maintain similarity of sound.** With the increased use of television and radio advertising, maintaining similarity of sound is also important. The use of the same announcer and/or the same musical logo can aid in maintaining this similarity. Almost everyone could hum or sing the McDonald's song, indicating superior similarity of sound.

4. **Similarity of attitude.** Projecting consistent attitude and positioning is critical to the success of an advertising campaign. All media advertisements should project a consistency of attitude in order to establish continuity.

An Advertising-Planning Model

For many managers, one of the most difficult aspects involved in managing the advertising and promotional function is the detail of planning, implementing, and evaluating an advertising campaign. Figure 9.4 illustrates an advertising-planning model. This visual format makes it easier to conceptualize all aspects of the process and should provide a novice planner with a structured framework from which to work. The model contains five components: input from the marketing information system, organizational objectives, planning and strategy formulation, implementation, and evaluation of advertising effectiveness.

The first component, input from the marketing information system, includes information from three separate areas. First, relevant information concerning consumer behavior should be reviewed and analyzed. What are the trends in consumer behavior? How are dining habits changing? What foodservice themes are "hot," and what themes are "not so hot"? Input concerning the product-service mix is also important. What are the sales

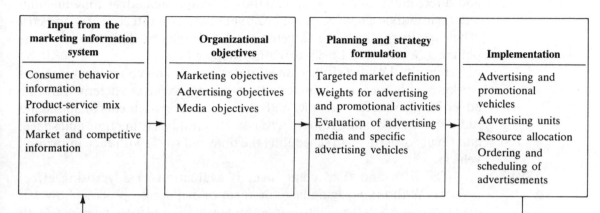

Figure 9.4. An Advertising-Planning Model.

Input from the marketing information system	Organizational objectives	Planning and strategy formulation	Implementation
Consumer behavior information Product-service mix information Market and competitive information	Marketing objectives Advertising objectives Media objectives	Targeted market definition Weights for advertising and promotional activities Evaluation of advertising media and specific advertising vehicles	Advertising and promotional vehicles Advertising units Resource allocation Ordering and scheduling of advertisements

Evaluation of advertising effectiveness

trends for all the menu food and beverage items? Information concerning the activities of direct and indirect competition is also of value in planning the advertising campaign. The use of this type of marketing information is discussed in Chapter 4.

The second component, organizational objectives, should be established in three separate areas: marketing, advertising, and media. Marketing objectives focus on such things as market share, producing a specified percentage increase in sales volume or a specified percentage increase in repeat patronage. Advertising objectives focus on such topics as increasing consumer awareness and drawing consumers away from the competition with advertisements demonstrating the superiority of the organization's product-service mix. Media objectives focus on the selection of the individual media to achieve the marketing and advertising objectives. For example, an objective might read, "to plan media selections so as to have 90 percent of the targeted market segments exposed to at least two of the advertisements."

The third component, planning and strategy formulation, involves the formal definition of the specifically targeted markets. Given the limited resources available, it is virtually impossible to reach the saturation point with all targeted market segments. Therefore, what specifically targeted market segments are most important? Weights should be established for all of the desired advertising and promotional activities. For example, what proportion of the resources available should be allocated for radio, print, and direct mail, and all other activities. Finally, each advertising medium and their individual vehicles are evaluated based on effectiveness and cost efficiency in reaching the targeted market segments. This aspect of the planning process will be discussed in Chapter 11.

Fourth, the advertising plan is implemented. This component includes working with each of the selected advertising vehicles, determining the advertising units (for example, half-page print advertisements or 30-second radio spots), allocating resources to pay for the advertising time and space, and finally ordering and scheduling the time and space with each individual vehicle.

The fifth and final component is evaluation of advertising effectiveness. Without engaging in some form of evaluation process, how will management know to what degree the advertising efforts have met with success? Three important reasons explain why some form of evaluation procedure should be undertaken. They are

1. **To come to understand the consumer.**   This involves learning what consumers want, why they want it, and how best to serve these wants.
2. **To avoid costly mistakes.**   By testing advertising effectiveness, errors that might have gone undetected are noted, and adjustments can be made. In this way, both the effectiveness and cost efficiency of advertising is increased.
3. **To add structure.**   Rather than viewing advertising as a business expense for which the impact is impossible to measure, the impact of advertising can be measured. If sales increase by 10 percent, what is the reason for this increase? What types of advertising and promotion have had the greatest impact on sales?[4]

Evaluating an Advertising Campaign

Several years ago, the president of a large retail chain was discussing his firm's advertising efforts with a group of business people. When one person posed a question about evaluating advertising, the president responded, "I suspect that half our advertising is wasted. The only problem is that I don't know which half." This story may bring a smile to one's face, but it is often an accurate assessment of the situation. Large foodservice organizations engaged in national campaigns normally have the resources to evaluate advertising effectively. Smaller advertisers and local advertisers often are not able to evaluate advertising effectiveness.

Advertising effectiveness can be measured for both its short- and its long-term impact. Short-term measurements are usually given most attention because they reflect directly the income statement and the financial position of the organization. In addition, managers' tenure and bonuses are normally based on short-term performance. The long-term effects of advertising, however, should not be overlooked. Long-term effects are reflected by repeat patronage, brand loyalty, and an asset called "good will." It is difficult, however, to measure the long-term residual effects of advertising with a reasonable margin for error. In the last several years, econometric techniques have advanced to the point where measuring advertising effectiveness is more precise. Although this section does not explore these techniques, an interested reader may refer to the *Journal of Marketing Research* for further information.

Advertising can be evaluated subjectively by the management of a foodservice operation, either alone or in conjunction with an advertising agency. Experienced management plays a key role in this type of evaluation. If management has successfully directed advertising campaigns, subjective evaluation may indeed be adequate. This is especially true of agency executives, as they often have a wealth of experience that allows them to gauge quite accurately the overall effectiveness of advertising efforts.

It is also wise to maintain a file of all advertisements. These can then be available for easy reference and reviewed periodically for "winners" and "losers." Subjective evaluation does have a place in the overall evaluation of advertising effectiveness. The experience and expertise of agency personnel and foodservice managers should not be discounted. These resources are best used in combination with objective methods.

It is almost impossible to measure advertising effectiveness objectively unless well-defined objectives have been formulated prior to initiating a campaign. How would management know whether they were successful if they were not able to compare actual performance with specific objectives? As stressed in Chapter 3, clearly defined, quantifiable objectives are very important. Variances between actual performance and objectives are noted and corrective action taken. In the event that the advertising proves more successful than expected, this too should be evaluated so that the success might be repeated.

Objective testing of advertising is time consuming and expensive. Not all operations can afford or will want this type of testing. Testing is invaluable if undertaken with care and cost effective if used occasionally. Following is a brief review of commonly used techniques, although not all are suitable for all types of operations:

1. **Copy testing.**   This involves pretesting the copy of an advertisement prior to running it in the media. Several advertisements are normally

shown to a group of consumers, and questions are asked of the group. Typical questions include, "Which advertisement would interest you most?" "Which advertisement is most convincing?" "Which advertisement is most likely to cause you to patronize the foodservice establishment?" These questions can be asked of an entire group assembled to review a series of advertisements, or personal interviews can be conducted.

2. **Inquiry and sales.**   Direct-mail advertising lends itself to the inquiry and sales method. This involves keeping a tally of each inquiry and sale. For example, if a series of advertisements were run to promote banquet business, how many people phoned or contacted the operation? How many of these inquiries were converted into sales? From these tallies, it is easy to compute a cost per inquiry and a cost per sale for this type of advertising.

3. **Coupons and split runs.**   Coupons can be tallied to evaluate the effectiveness of one promotion against others. For example, did the sundae special sell more than the special french fries promotion? Coupons are used extensively by the foodservice industry because they allow for easy evaluation. Coupons can be carried one step further and used to compare one medium against another. For example, suppose that management had a choice among three print media in which to place advertisements. Which one will reach the targeted market most effectively? The same advertisements and coupons could be run in the three media with each coupon coded so that a tally could be made of the number of coupons from medium A, B, and C. In this way, a relative ranking of effectiveness is possible.

4. **Sales tests.**   The level of gross sales or sales of specific items can be monitored following a specific period of advertising aimed at increasing the sales in general or increasing sales of specific items. It is often difficult to take into account all the variables that affect sales both positively and negatively and thereby establish a cause and effect relationship.

5. **Consumer testing of awareness, recall, and attitude.**   Through assembled groups, telephone surveys, direct-mail surveys, and personal interviews, consumers can be tested to determine their relative awareness concerning a specific foodservice operation. Have they heard of the operation? Do they patronize it? If so, how frequently? Do they recall seeing any advertisements? Which ones do they recall? When shown certain advertisements, do they recall seeing them? (This is known as *aided recall*.)

Summary

The advertising and promotion function, as applied to foodservice marketing, provides a broad-based overview of a process that includes promotion, national and local advertising, and cooperative advertising.

An advertising life cycle can be defined to correspond with the foodservice life cycle discussed in Chapter 2. It consists of three major stages: introduction, expansion, and stabilization. Each stage calls for a unique approach to advertising and promotion with goals appropriate for the life cycle position of the organization. The introductory stage seeks to arouse curiosity and promote first-time patronage. The expansion stage is based on name recognition and promotes not only first-time patronage but also repeat patronage. Finally, the stabilization stage, if an operation is able to reach it, is based on almost universal name recognition and a very positive image in the marketplace. This stage is one in which the organization is able to advertise from a position of market strength.

Numerous types of advertising include word-of-mouth advertising, which is helpful and often effective, but to reach the highest level of success, management must engage in various different advertising efforts. Generally, advertising seeks to satisfy three goals: (1) to establish awareness in the minds of consumers, (2) to establish a positive perceived value in the minds of consumers, and (3) to promote repeat patronage and brand loyalty among consumers.

The development of advertising budgets includes functions, advantages and disadvantages to budgeting, types of advertising budgets, methods for developing advertising budgets, the budgeting system, and rolling advertising budgets. Advertising budgets perform several functions: to provide a detailed projection of future expenditures, to provide both short- and long-range planning guidelines for management, and to provide a method of monitoring and controlling advertising expenses by comparing actual expenses against projections. Advertising budgets are usually either fixed or contingency, and they are developed using three major methods: (1) the percentage of sales method, (2) the desired objective method, and (3) the competitive method.

A budgeting system provides an easily understood presentation of budget development. Advertising positioning and strategy includes formation of an objective, a targeted audience, key consumer benefits, support for the benefits, and an appropriate tone or manner. The development of an advertising appeal includes six keys to successful advertising.

Finally, planning and evaluating advertising involve noting campaign checkpoints. A five-component advertising planning model includes input from the marketing information system, organizational objectives, planning and strategy formulation, implementation, and evaluation of advertising effectiveness.

Questions For Review and Discussion

1. How are advertising and promotion integrated with other marketing functions?
2. What are the major advantages and drawbacks to advertising?
3. Define the following: (1) advertising, (2) promotion, (3) national advertising, (4) local advertising, and (5) cooperative advertising.
4. Cite and discuss in some detail the advertising life cycle. How is this life cycle integrated with the organizational life cycle?
5. Develop a planned and rational argument both for and against foodservice advertising.
6. What are the three major goals of advertising?
7. How would you respond to the charges raised by advertising critics?
8. Of what value are advertising budgets?
9. Cite and discuss the methods of developing an advertising budget.
10. What is a rolling advertising budget? How is one developed?
11. What is meant by positioning?
12. How might advertising strategy be developed?
13. Critique the six keys to successful advertising.
14. What is an advertising campaign?
15. What factors should be considered when planning a campaign?
16. Cite and discuss the major campaign checkpoints.
17. Do you believe that advertising is wasteful? Why or why not?
18. How might advertising be made more effective?
19. What techniques are used to evaluate advertising effectiveness?

Notes

1. Kenneth Roman and Jane Maas, *How To Advertise* (New York: St. Martin's Press, 1976), pp. 1-3.

2. H. Victor Grohmann, "Ten Keys to Successful Advertising," *Cornell Hotel and Restaurant Administration Quarterly,* vol. 17, no. 2, August 1975, pp. 3-7.

3. Roman and Maas, *How to Advertise,* pp. 1-3.

4. C. H. Sandage, V. Fryburger, and K. Rotzoll, *Advertising Theory and Practice* (Homewood, Illinois; Richard D. Irwin, 1979), pp. 533-536.

Chapter 10

Advertising and Promotion—Personal Selling and Internal Promotion

Chapter Outline

This chapter focuses on the aspects of promotion and selling that do not make use of the paid mass media. Many foodservice organizations focus on the more visible and glamorous mass media, such as television, radio, and print advertising, yet internal promotion and personal selling are equally important.

This chapter is divided into the following sections:

Introduction

Personal Selling
- defining the function
- techniques for successful personal selling
- telephone selling

Internal Selling and Promotion
- missed selling opportunities
- training customer-contact employees
- incentive programs for customer-contact employees
- tools of the trade—gimmicks, contests, and displays
- entertainment

Publicity and Public Relations

Summary

Introduction

The foodservice industry is a people-oriented business. Foodservice operations promote hospitality, yet hospitality cannot be purchased, cannot be traded, and does not appear on the menu. Hospitality is intangible, yet it is absolutely necessary for success. When service personnel project the "spirit of hospitality," the results can be dramatic—increased sales, increased profits, increased consumer satisfaction, and, yes, increased employee satisfaction and motivation. Foodservice operations also sell atmosphere, convenience, entertainment, escape, and social contact. All of these are related to the spirit of hospitality and are equally intangible. All deserve consideration as promotable items.

Personal selling plays an important role in the promotion of a foodservice operation. It may, for example, take the form of sales calls on club or association officers to solicit banquet and meeting business. Personal selling also takes place at the counter of a fast-food operation when the smiling service person asks, "Would you like a fruit pie to go along with your fries and burgers?" These personal selling efforts should be supported by internal promotion and public relations activities. When combined, personal selling, internal promotion, publicity, and public relations can provide the necessary force for a successful operation.

Personal Selling

Many foodservice operations do not engage in any form of personal selling involving sales calls. Dining rooms or parts of dining rooms are available for banquets and meetings, yet they are often underused. Management simply waits for a prospective client to come in and ask about booking a banquet or a meeting function. Prospective clients have been known to ask timidly, "Could you accommodate the monthly meeting of the XYZ club?" Management is usually very willing to cater such functions, but prospective customers often are not made aware of these available services, and no effort is made to solicit this type of business. Management should not wait for business to come and ask; it should go out and ask for business! No one needs to be timid or shy about asking for business; it will not hurt a professional image. If foodservice establishments do not solicit, the hotels and motels attract all the group business. Management must go out and solicit banquet business for a foodservice establishment.

Defining the Function

What is personal selling? Selling is an interpersonal process whereby the seller ascertains, activates, and satisfies the needs and wants of the buyer so that both the seller and the buyer benefit. Selling need not be one-sided. It can satisfy both parties, the buyer and the seller. Prospective clients for banquet services, for example, can derive benefits, for the burden of planning, organizing, and directing all of the various aspects of a banquet function is taken away from the client. For most clients, this is a tremendous relief, as they no longer are directly responsible for the event. Of course, the foodservice operation also benefits, through increased sales and profits.

Why should a foodservice operation engage in personal selling? First, it allows the operation to be presented in an interpersonal manner with a prospective client. The sales presentation need not be supported by expensive visual aids. Sales calls and presentations can be as simple as having a foodservice manager or an appropriate representative schedule an appointment with the president of a local club or visit a local business and ask for its business. These sales calls give the foodservice operation exposure and provide the prospective clients with another choice when arranging group meetings and banquet functions. Second, sales calls allow for two-way communication between the foodservice operation's representative and prospects. Prospects are able to ask questions, and the representative has the opportunity to present the foodservice operation more adequately than is possible through advertising. The representative can personally demonstrate how the operation will be able to satisfy the specific needs of the prospect.

Personal sales calls can be both time consuming and expensive. Large operations will need to hire an individual or several individuals to act as sales representatives. In this case, the organization and activities of these individuals will closely resemble those used by hotel sales offices. Most foodservice operations however, will not need full-time sales personnel. Instead, a member of the management team can readily assume this responsibility on a part-time basis. It is important that the representative be given adequate time to devote to personal selling. Often, if the sales responsibilities are merely assigned to someone without a reduction in other job responsibilities, the results are very disappointing.

Sales calls should be made on prospective clients as well as previous clients. Previous clients should receive follow-up calls to cultivate a continuing business relationship. If the previous experiences left the client feeling unhappy, this is all the more reason to follow-up with a sales call. Perhaps the situation can be corrected and negative word-of-mouth advertising prevented. Often the mere attention to the client's needs and a sincere effort to improve will be enough to convince the client the foodservice organization should be given some business. There is nothing better than a satisfied client and nothing worse than an unhappy one.

What makes a good salesperson? What are the qualities most likely to lead to success? Successful selling is a learned behavior achieved through practice, practice, and still more practice. Successful salespeople are not born; they are made. The following list includes several qualities that most successful salespeople possess:

- **Spirit of hospitality.**   Individuals who engage in sales calls should project hospitality. How could anyone successfully sell a foodservice operation without showing courtesy, tact, and a concern for people? If the individual making the sales call does not treat the prospect with hospitality, how is the prospect to expect anything better at a meeting or banquet?

- **Appearance.**   The appearance of the salesperson should reflect positively on the foodservice operation and should be approximately the same style as that of the prospective client. It is not wise to appear too flashy; conservative dress is the accepted rule.

- **Knowledge of the foodservice operation.**   A salesperson should be totally familiar with all aspects of the facility, including banquet menus, sizes of groups that can be accommodated, dates and times available, audiovisual equipment available, function room set-ups, and any special services available. A sales representative must be prepared to field any question that the prospect might pose. An important role of the salesperson is to know the product service-mix thoroughly.

- **Determination.**   Normally, many sales calls are made before a booking is obtained and a contract is signed. A sales representative must possess the determination to continue to make sales calls even after several prospects have said no. This requires ambition and a willingness to keep trying. Just because prospects say no does not mean that next time they will not respond positively.

- **Above-average common sense and personality.**   All individuals working in a sales capacity are likely to encounter difficult prospective clients from time to time. A successful salesperson has the ability to take a difficult sales presentation and turn it into a positive one. Having above-average common sense, or what many refer to as "horse sense," as well as the personality to persevere will carry the salesperson through these difficult situations.

Techniques for Successful Personal Selling

Three basic types of sales calls are follow-up calls, initiating calls, and blitz calls. *Follow-up calls* are those arranged with representatives of groups and organizations that have previously been clients of the foodservice operation. Their main purpose is to remind the client of the operation's willingness to be of service and to solicit repeat business. *Initiating calls* are those made on people who have not been clients in the past yet represent solid prospects. The purpose of these calls is to create awareness of the product-service mix and to encourage a site visit so that the prospective client might see first hand what the facility has to offer. Few bookings are made at the time of initiating calls, but it is the first step in cultivating a better relationship. A *sales blitz* saturates an area by making many times the normal number of sales calls and distributing literature describing the product-service mix. A successful blitz reaches as many potential clients as possible. Sales blitzes often use a varied approach involving not only personal sales calls but also telephone selling as well as other forms of advertising using the mass media.

Successful salespeople generally focus on four components of successful selling; these are (1) prospecting and qualifying, (2) planning and delivering sales presentations, (3) overcoming objections, and (4) closing the sale.

Prospecting and Qualifying.   Identifying prospective clients is a critical activity if the sales efforts are to be successful. Generally 20 to 30 percent of all sales calls are scheduled with prospective clients, those who have not previously booked a banquet or a meeting function with the foodservice operation. No foodservice organization can rely totally on repeat business; rather, the organization must commit itself to seeking and cultivating new business, allowing the organization to expand its market.

In the process of identifying and qualifying prospects, foodservice sales representives should determine whether prospective clients represent good prospects before they invest a good deal of time. The following questions are helpful in determining whether a prospect is a good one:

– Does the prospect have needs and wants that can be satisfied by the product-service mix of the foodservice organization? If the needs and wants of the prospect differ substantially from the product-service mix of the foodservice operation and personal selling is undertaken anyway, a sales representative is likely to be wasting both his or her own time, as well as the time of the prospective client.

- Does the prospect have the ability to pay? It is important to determine whether the prospect has income or credit reserves to pay for a function. Many foodservice operators can recount stories of lavish functions for which they have never been paid because the client was either unwilling or unable to pay. This is a particularly important question to consider when dealing with individuals rather than with corporations.
- Does the prospect have the authority to sign a contract and commit the organization for a banquet or meeting function? While not a total waste of time, it is terribly frustrating for sales representatives to cultivate prospective sales only to find that the individuals with whom they have been dealing do not have the authority to sign a contract and commit the organization for a function.
- Is the prospect readily accessible? It is important that the sales representative be readily able to schedule an appointment with the prospect. It may be difficult to schedule a sales presentation with such individuals as presidents of companies, and hence they may prove to be poor prospects.

Locating suitable prospects is a task confronting all sales representatives. What methods can be used to obtain leads that will result in good prospects? The following list represents a few potential sources:

- **Inquiries.**   Often individuals visit or call the foodservice operation and request information concerning banquets and/or meeting rooms. These individuals and the groups they represent are ready-made prospects.
- **Names given by existing clients.**   This approach is called the "endless chain." Simply ask each of the existing clients to supply the names of one or more individuals, groups, or companies that might be prospective clients. The resulting list is then qualified to determine the most attractive prospects, and personal selling begins. It is important to follow-up with a thank you letter to the individual who supplied the name of the prospect, especially when the lead results in a banquet contract. The mutual contact also serves as a means of introduction with the new prospect.
- **Centers of influence.**   Every community has its own leaders and influential people. These individuals make excellent prospects because they tend to be active in the community; they are "joiners." Additionally, it is an excellent idea for the sales representative and other members of the management staff to belong to community and civic organizations. In this way, they can establish personal relationships with these community leaders.
- **Develop lists.**   Often lists of prospects are simply developed from such sources as the telephone directory, chamber of commerce, and local clubs and organizations. These lists should then be qualified to identify the most likely prospects.

- **Direct-mail prospecting.**   Lists can also be used to initiate direct-mail prospecting. Promotional material is mailed to a list of prospects, and the sales representative can either follow up with a telephone call seeking for an appointment or wait for an inquiry.
- **Cold calls.**   Finally, personal sales calls without prior arrangements or appointments can be made. These are called "cold calls." The sales representative simply visits the prospect's office and asks to see the prospect. Rarely does this type of call result in a signed banquet contract, but it does open some doors for future contact with the prospect. Cold calls can, however, be quite time consuming and, as a result, very expensive.

Planning and Delivering Sales Presentations.   Soon after qualifying a prospect as a good candidate for the product-service mix of the foodservice operation, a sales representative should make contact with the prospect and schedule an appointment. Sales representatives should be assertive and honest. They should tell the prospect who is calling, the foodservice organization represented, and the reason for the call. It may also help to "break the ice" to mention a common associate or a common interest, but sales representatives should be honest and up front. They should not attempt to schedule the appointment under false pretenses, as this will only hurt in the long run.

The overall goal of any personal selling activity is, of course, to promote purchase on the part of the prospect. Rarely, however, does this occur without a well-planned sales presentation. The AIDA approach is one that has long been used in training sales personnel. It stands for *A*wareness, *I*nterest, *D*esire, and *A*ction. To sell the prospect successfully, the sales representative must help move the prospect through each of the four steps of the AIDA model.

Before making the sales call, a sales representative should develop an outline of the presentation. What points should be stressed? How should they be presented so that the foodservice operation is perceived positively? What should the sales call accomplish? It is not advisable to prepare a canned sales pitch that is merely replayed for each new prospect. Instead, a sales representative should be natural and straightforward, not waste words, and get right to the point. A sales presentation should begin by telling the prospect who is calling, who is represented, and why this foodservice operation wants and deserves this prospect's business. It may be best to use a checklist of points to be covered, for it is better to refer to a list than appear unorganized during the presentation.

It is also important to be aware of the nature of the prospect. Some individuals have time to sit and talk; others are too busy. A sales representative should be able to vary the presentation to suit the needs of the prospect. Every effort should be made to make the prospect comfortable by establishing rapport. Every effort should also be made to emphasize the strong selling points of the foodservice operation's product-service mix, while linking these strengths to the needs of the prospect. For example, some foodservice establishments have specialized to such an extent in wedding receptions that they can make even the most nervous bride feel at ease. Such a solid history is a real selling point.

An acquired skill that sales representatives can develop is the art of listening. Often sales representatives feel that they must do all the talking if a sale is to be made. Nothing could be further from the truth. Selling also requires concentrating on what the prospect is saying and on the nonverbal behavior. A good sales representative allows the prospect to ask questions uninterrupted and does not try to anticipate questions and jump in with a canned response before the prospect has finished asking the question. Listening is a learned skill, one that is critical to successful selling. Selling means focusing attention on prospects and learning to hear what they are really saying.

Overcoming Objections.   No matter how good a sales representative may be, sooner or later (and probably sooner) a prospect will object during the sales call. For the sales call to be successful, of course, these objections must be overcome. A simple, yet effective approach directs the sales representative to use these three steps:

1. Listen; allow the prospect to explain the objections fully.
2. Reflect or rephrase the prospect's feelings to assure the prospect that you fully understand the objection.
3. Acknowledge or perhaps even agree with the prospect, then present evidence that supports the foodservice operation's position.

Closing the Sale.   Despite otherwise successful sales efforts, many sales representatives fail to get a firm commitment from the prospect. They simply fail to close the sale. Closure can be as simple as, "Which of the banquet menus I've shown you would you like for your October 15th managers' meeting?" Closure involves summarizing the major selling points and striving for agreement on the part of the prospect. Simply stated, closure involves asking for business. A sales representative should not be shy but should simply ask for business.

Telephone Selling

Many foodservice establishments use the telephone as another effective means of soliciting group business. Telephones can be used to qualify prospects before personal sales calls are made. This can save a lot of time and money by allowing sales representatives to make personal sales calls only on those who represent viable prospects. Telephone sales calls are conducted much like personal sales calls.

Telephone sales calls must be handled carefully. Used properly, the telephone is an inexpensive and effective sales tool. Used improperly, the results can be disastrous. All individuals who use the telephone need to be properly trained in telephone etiquette and telephone sales. This training is simply common sense, yet each day millions of dollars of potential business are lost because of poor telephone etiquette and sales techniques. Almost all local telephone companies are able to offer training for those who will use the telephone as a tool. This training can then be followed with printed material. Although it is common sense, people sometimes just need to be reminded. As the Bell System keeps reminding us in its national advertising, use phone power!

A wealth of potential group business is available. It just takes a little planning and some extra work on the telephone and in the field. A sales representative should not forget but should ask for business in a straightforward and sincere manner. Many of the strategies and ideas discussed here apply not only to personal selling by sales representatives but also to the sales efforts undertaken by service personnel within the foodservice.

Internal Selling and Promotion

When the consumer comes through the front door of a foodservice operation, all the attention of management and the service employees should be focused on satisfying the consumer. Foodservice is not like the retail business; consumers do not come into foodservices to browse; they come in to buy. Yet all too often, the service employees show about as much enthusiasm for selling as for changing a flat tire. Instead of performing as professional salespeople, they often serve as little more than order takers. They saunter up to the table with pad in hand and ask unsmilingly, "Ya ready to order?" When asked such a simple question as how an item is prepared, the answer is often, "I don't know; I'll ask the chef." When they bring items to the table, they often ask, "Who had the roast beef?" while the plate is passed from one guest to the next. Sound familiar?

Missed Selling Opportunities

Lack of professional selling on the part of service employees results in lower sales, less satisfied consumers, and often a failing operation. All this is simply a matter of missed opportunities. For example, in an actual situation, four friends were having dinner at a table cloth restaurant. They were seated by the host, following a greeting of "Do you have reservations?" After about three minutes a waitress (call her Sally) appeared at the table, said "Hello," filled the water glasses, and presented each guest with a closed menu. She then asked, "Would anyone like anything from the bar?" Each guest placed an order, and in a few minutes, Sally returned with the drinks. When the drinks were about half finished, she returned asking, "You ready to order?" Each guest placed an order, and Sally took the orders without speaking except to ask, "What kind of dressing?" and "What kind of potato?" Sally failed to try to solicit another round of drinks. She failed to sell the group the specialties of the house or any à la carte items, such as mushrooms to accompany the entree. Sally did not suggestively sell anyone in the group a higher priced, more desirable entree or other item. She failed to present a wine list or suggest a wine with dinner, even though the guests may have wanted wine. Simply stated, Sally failed to do her job properly.

Figure 10.1 illustrates the financial impact of these missed opportunities. Potential sales were lost because the waitress was an order taker, not a salesperson. The total potential sales missed amounted to approximately $32 for the party of four. Although a foodservice operation is not likely to get all $32 from every table, $16 or $8, or even $1 of increased sales is certainly worth the extra effort. For the waitress, the potential extra gratuity was $4.80. The actual result of the evening was a total bill of $54.80

Figure 10.1. Missed Opportunities for a Table of Four.

Extra drink sale	4@ $2.00	=	$ 8.00
Trading up or à la carte sale	4@ $1.25	=	$ 5.00
Wine sale	1@ $11.00	=	$11.00
Dessert/after-dinner drinks	4@ $2.00	=	$ 8.00
	Potential sales lost =		$32.00
	Potential Gratuity lost @ 15%		$ 4.80

plus sales tax and gratuity. If an operation were able to recover only half of the missed opportunities, gross sales would increase by more than 30 percent. How many people like Sally work in the average foodservice operation?

Think about this situation for a moment. Whose fault is it? Why was it that Sally did not do a better job of suggestive selling? Of course, the blame must fall on management because management failed to provide Sally with proper training and supervision necessary to make her and every other service employee a salesperson rather than an order taker.

Training Guest-Contact Employees

How is it best to train service employees? What could have been done to prevent the situation just described? Three basic aspects of training with which management must be concerned are cognitive, psychomotor, and affective. These are defined as follows:

- **Cognitive.** This refers to learned or memorized job knowledge, such as how a specific menu item is prepared or what type of wine would best accompany a given menu item.
- **Psychomotor.** These are learned skills that involve the physical use of the body. Examples include preparing a Caesar salad or opening and pouring a bottle of wine.
- **Affective.** These are more difficult to teach because they involve the formation of attitudes, beliefs, and perceptions. These in turn affect motivation and the overt behavior that the guest is able to observe. Even if the cognitive and psychomotor skills are perfect, poor affective training can lead to dissatisfied guests. Many foodservice managers focus most of their attention on the psychomotor and cognitive aspects of training, which are important, but the affective should not be overlooked. It is important that a service employee's attitude be molded through training as well. The National Restaurant Association's "Project Hospitality" has sought to foster the development of affective skills. When employees come in contact with guests, they represent the operation. They cannot make this representation a good one unless their attitudes are positive. They must be trained to project the spirit of hospitality, which must begin with management and filter down through the organization.

A simple approach to training is best. First, the training should be planned carefully. A trainer should take the training responsibility seriously and should have complete competence in all three aspects included in training. An outline should be prepared to detail the subject matter covered in the training session. Nothing creates a more negative impression in the mind of a trainee than a disorganized trainer. Remember that the goal is to develop competence, and projecting incompetence in training is not the way to begin.

Second, the trainer should plan to cover only what the trainee can learn in each training session. Time should be set aside for training, instead of being done "as we go." For service personnel, individuals should be thoroughly trained before performing their particular jobs without supervision. It is also desirable to cover the material in several short training sessions rather than one long session. Trainees will remember things better, and the training will be more successful.

Third, the trainer should show and explain for the trainees specifically what it is they should be able to do; they should then be allowed to practice. For example, suggestions as to how to sell wine, sell extra drinks suggestively, or sell more expensive menu and à la carte items are important. The service personnel should practice the procedures and selling aspects of service in a role-playing format. Following these sessions, observers should critique the sessions and offer comments. These sessions can be very useful to both new and experienced employees if the role-playing situations include such things as handling guest complaints and questions.

Fourth, it is important that all trainees be provided with feedback. All new employees want to know how they are doing. Follow-up procedures frequently assure that a new employee is performing in the proper manner. It is important that the new employee be corrected in a constructive manner; a manager should always praise publically but correct privately!

Training service personnel is of critical importance if internal selling is to be successful. An employee must be aided in developing job knowledge (cognitive aspects), physical ability (psychomotor aspects), and a positive attitude (affective aspects).

Incentive Programs for Guest-Contact Employees

Service personnel have difficult jobs, ones in which they must meet and deal with guests constantly. If service personnel are to perform well, they must be motivated. Motivating these individuals will take every bit of managerial skill available. One method used successfully by many operations is the incentive program. Incentive programs involve a reward, either large or small, for satisfactory and superior job performance. Incentives are given for a wide variety of accomplishments, including highest sales per month, most bottles of wine sold, highest check average, most dessert items sold, and most guest compliments. Incentive programs are usually operated for a specific period of time (a week or a month), and the reward is usually based on an objective measure, such as the number of items sold. The reward need not be money; it can be almost anything from recognition to a weekend for two at a hotel or time off at Christmas. Motivating the service personnel does not necessarily mean money or things of material value have to be used as the reward.

Tools of the Trade— Gimmicks, Contests, and Displays

Service personnel cannot be expected to increase sales without management support. A wide variety of internal promotion methods include table tent cards, banners, food and beverage displays, management contact with guests, and posters. The possibilities are limited only by management's imagination and available resources.

One of the best ways to generate new ideas is to become a regular reader of the industry trade journals. These publications are filled with ideas that other operations are using to increase sales and profits. Rarely is an idea totally new, and someone else's idea can be modified and made to work for a particular organization. Several professional journals are listed here:

Restaurant Business
633 Third Ave.
New York, New York 10017

Restaurant Hospitality
P.O. Box 91368
Cleveland, Ohio 44101

Food Service Marketing
2132 Fordhem Ave.
Madison, Wisconsin 53704

Restaurants & Institutions
1350 E. Touhy Avenue
Des Plaines, Illinois 60018

Nation's Restaurant News
425 Park Ave.
New York, New York 10022

Restaurant Design
633 Third Ave.
New York, New York 10017

Every foodservice operation should engage in a number of forms of internal promotion. The possibilities are endless; the following ideas should serve as a start. Many restaurant managers have installed a wheel of chance in their lounges. Printed on the wheel are drink prices, ranging from normal prices down to as low as 50 percent off. A free drink is sometimes one of the markings on the wheel. During certain hours of operation, the bartender spins the wheel every 15 minutes to establish drink-selling prices.

This creates involvement on the part of the lounge patrons and adds the element of uncertainty to the lounge atmosphere.

Table-top promotions have long been a popular way to increase sales. Table tent cards are an inexpensive way to promote a special "entree of the week," a "wine of the month," or any number of items. Tent cards should be neat and fresh and changed frequently. Banners placed on the exterior of the building have been used successfully, especially by fast-food operations. These banners have been used to promote specials and to alert consumers about new menu items.

A simple, yet effective promotion is to post a copy of the menu outside the foodservice operation. Often, those passing by will stop to look at the menu and, as a result, will patronize the operation. This is particularly true if the menu is professionally put together and unique in some aspect.

Contests are also quite popular. Of course, the most visible contests are those conducted by the giants of the fast-food segment. While not every operation can match their number and value of prizes, there is no reason that contests could not be used to increase both first-time and repeat patronage.

Entertainment

Entertainment can generate increased sales and more satisfied patrons. Entertainment during the last several years has taken many forms. These have included large-screen television, various forms of disco, and other forms of media entertainment. Live entertainment, however, has long been regarded as the most powerful form.

Live entertainment is not the proper approach for all foodservice operations, but it should at least be considered. Several questions should be asked, including

- What impact will entertainment have on volume, both in sales dollars and number of customers?
- Is the physical layout of the facility suitable for live entertainment?
- How will the costs associated with live entertainment, such as payment to performers and increased advertising, be covered?

First, the impact that entertainment will have on sales volume should be analyzed closely. The breakeven point should be calculated. Different methods to cover the costs of entertainment are feasible; these include charging higher prices to offset the increased costs, instituting a cover charge or a cover charge and a minimum purchase, and covering costs through increased sales.

Second, the physical layout of the facility must be examined closely. Is the configuration of the facility suitable for live entertainment and perhaps for dancing? Many operators have discovered that their facilities were simply too small for live entertainment, but many have made this discovery after having made the commitment to live entertainment.

When selecting entertainment of any type, the marketing concept should be a paramount concern. Management should focus on the needs and wants of the customers and attempt to satisfy the customers rather than themselves. If the customers want rock music, yet the management prefers jazz, there should be no question as to which type of entertainment is selected.

Publicity and Public Relations

A well-planned publicity and public relations program can offer foodservice operations more benefits than advertising can offer. Publicity and public relations encompass all efforts undertaken in an effort to generate a favorable perceived image of the organization within the community. They can take many forms, including newspaper stories and releases, subsidizing a little league team, supplying food to flood victims, joining a local civic group, or hundreds of other approaches. Developing news releases is the most common form.

Newspapers, especially smaller ones, are anxious to print stories of local human interest. Sometimes they do not have the personnel available to research and write the stories, and so they rely to a certain extent on news releases they receive. Releases should contain information related to who, what, when, where, and how the story took place. All information should be accurate and brief. One or two pages is a good length. The most important information should be placed in the opening sentences or paragraph, as most readers will not read the entire piece. Photographs with captions are also very useful because they often tell a story more effectively than a printed story. The newspaper editor will use the release to write the story, making whatever changes are deemed appropriate. The foodservice manager does not have any control over the editing process, but many successful managers have received free publicity that they could not have afforded to purchase if they were buying advertising space.

Publicity and public relations programs are limited only by the imagination of the management. Other ideas include grand opening activities that may involve a press dinner, news releases starting three months prior to opening, or signs on the construction site announcing the opening date; honoring civic leaders with special dinners or allowing civic groups and charities to hold meetings in the facility at reduced or free rates; or sponsoring a free party for the best repeat customers.

Summary

This chapter has focused on the major aspects of personal selling and internal promotion. Personal selling has become an activity that most foodservice organizations can no longer ignore. Active personal selling is an excellent way to increase sales and profits. Techniques for successful personal selling include prospecting and qualifying, planning and delivering sales presentations, overcoming objections, and closing the sale. Telephone selling is a useful form of personal selling.

Internal selling and promotion is a combination of professional selling on the part of service personnel and efforts by management to promote through table tent cards, banners, and other means. Alone, none of these will achieve success; they must be mixed together.

Training is critical to the development of an effective service staff. Service personnel cannot be expected to learn to sell by themselves; management must offer assistance. Training should be focused on three aspects: cognitive, psychomotor, and affective. Each is important, and when integrated, the result will be a valued and effective employee. Training techniques include the need to plan the training program, divide the training into several short time segments, show and explain the tasks to the employee, allow the employer to demonstrate the tasks to the employee, allow the employer to demonstrate the task, practice it, and provide adequate feedback following the training sessions.

Incentive programs are an effective method of motivating service personnel. They must be planned carefully and used with care. Other aspects of motivation must be considered.

Tools of the trade, such as gimmicks and contests, are an important aspect of internal selling and promotion. These types of activities allow the foodservice operator to gain a slight competitive advantage over major competitors. The long-term effects may not be great, but the short-term increases in market share and profitability can be dramatic.

Entertainment should also be considered as a means to increase both the number of customers and total sales. Several aspects of entertainment should be considered by the foodservice organization.

Finally, publicity and public relations must also be considered in any promotional program. Efforts should be undertaken to generate news releases and other means by which positive publicity can be generated.

Questions For Review and Discussion

1. What personal qualities that you possess should help you be a successful salesperson? What qualities would you have to develop?
2. Should a foodservice operation engage in personal selling? Why or why not?
3. What methods or techniques are most likely to lead to successful personal selling?
4. What information should a news release contain? What type of situation or information would make a good news release?
5. What are the aspects of a successful training program? Discuss each of those aspects.
6. Do you believe that most foodservice personnel receive adequate training? Justify your answer.
7. Cite and discuss the four aspects of personal selling.
8. What should a foodservice manager consider when selecting entertainment?

Assignments

1. Develop an instrument that could be used to evaluate the service personnel of a foodservice operation. Visit several local operations and use the instrument to evaluate the performance of the service personnel. If you were managing each of these operations, what action would you recommend?
2. Using an actual restaurant as an example, carefully plan a training program for each new service person. Be sure to include content, training methods, time schedule, people involved, cost, and expected outcomes. Prepare a proposal suitable for presentation to the unit manager.
3. Select an event or happening at a local foodservice establishment and write a news release.

Further Reading

Coffman, C. Dewitt, *Hospitality For Sale* (East Lansing, Michigan: The Educational Institute of American Hotel and Motel Association, 1980).

Dahmer, Sondra, and Kurt Kahl. *The Waiter and Waitress Training Manual,* Second Edition (Boston: CBI Publishing, 1982).

Goodman, Raymond, Jr., *The Management of Service for the Restaurant Manager* (Dubuque, Iowa: Wm. C. Brown, 1979).

Nykiel, Ronald A. *Marketing in the Hospitality Industry* (Boston: CBI Publishing, 1983).

Chapter 11

Advertising and Promotion— External Advertising Media

Chapter Outline

This chapter examines the most visible of all advertising and promotion, the external advertising media. Each of the media and the techniques that apply to it are discussed individually to demonstrate an appreciation for its strengths and weaknesses.

The chapter is divided into the following sections:

Introduction

Relations with an Advertising Agency
- advantages and disadvantages in working with an agency
- selecting an advertising agency
- agency compensation

Media Selection
- factors affecting media selection
- developing media plans
- media scheduling

Print Advertising
- techniques for successful print advertising
- developing copy for print advertising
- print advertising terms

Radio Advertising
- techniques for successful radio advertising
- selecting radio spots
- producing radio commercials
- radio advertising terms

Television Advertising
- techniques for successful television advertising
- types of television commercials
- classes of television advertising
- television advertising terms

Direct-Mail Advertising
- techniques for successful direct-mail advertising
- mailing lists

Outdoor Advertising
- techniques for successful outdoor advertising
- types of outdoor advertising
- outdoor advertising terms

Supplemental Advertising Media

Summary

Introduction

No one questions that advertising and promotion are extremely powerful forces in the foodservice industry. They must be managed with care and used to the maximum advantage of the organization. External advertising constitutes a major area of marketing effort for most commercial operations, as numerous media are employed in an effort to communicate with selected targeted markets. The success of these advertising efforts rests to a large degree on the media and the manner in which they are used. Many times, advertisers spend large amounts of money without achieving the desired results. In other cases, advertisers spend only a relatively small amount, yet the results are dramatic. It is useful to remember that it is not how much, but how, advertising dollars are invested! The word *investment* is what advertising is—an investment. Dollars allocated to advertising are expected to generate increased sales; a positive return on an investment is expected.

External advertising is important because it can make the difference between success and failure. Management must ask three simple questions in initial advertising planning:

1. To whom should the advertising be directed? Specifically, what targeted markets have been identified as primary and secondary markets? Which individuals represent opinion leaders and reference group leaders?
2. Where do these people live? Once the targeted markets are identified, it is imperative to determine where these individuals live and work. In many cases, this will be as easy as determining the leaders of the business community in a small town. In other instances, determining where these individuals live and work will prove quite difficult. Suppose, for example, that a table cloth restaurant operated in the

suburbs of a major city. Where should the restaurant advertise? How should the targeted markets be reached? Where do these people live and work? These questions may not have self-evident answers, and a considerable amount of research and discussion may be necessary before the answers are determined.

3. What media should be used? This is like the proverbial 64-dollar question. Would it be best to use print advertising? Perhaps radio or television should play a major role? What about outdoor or supplemental advertising? Should directories, such as the yellow pages, be considered?

Relations with an Advertising Agency

Advantages and Disadvantages in Working with an Agency

Should a foodservice organization use the services of an advertising agency? With the exception of small foodservice operations, which because of their size, do not devote a large amount of money to external advertising, all operations should consider the use of an agency. The final decision is certainly for each organization to make, but agencies offer several advantages. First, an agency can increase the effectiveness of advertising; its work is more professional, and its use of media is better. Second, agencies can be especially helpful, if not necessary, in overcoming the special production requirements of radio and television advertising. Third, using an advertising agency is like maintaining several part-time specialists, copywriters, artists, and layout professionals, on staff. Fourth, agencies are able to maintain closer contacts with media representatives than can a single advertiser. Finally, some advertising agencies are able to offer consultative services related to such advertising and marketing projects as test marketing.

Management must, however, consider the negative aspects of using an agency. First and foremost is, of course, the question of money. "There is no such thing as a free lunch," and top-quality professional assistance will cost money. Furthermore, if the foodservice operation has access to adequate free-lance talent and assistance, the services of an agency may not be required.

Managers have to make decisions about how advertising will be handled. These decisions should be based on the following factors: the amount of available time to devote to advertising, the sizes of the targeted markets, the media to be used, management's knowledge of and experience in advertising, and the amount of money to be spent on advertising. Advertising agencies are able to provide a wide variety of professional services, including campaign planning, market research, media selection and production, public relations, and campaign evaluations.

Selecting an Advertising Agency

What types of advertising agencies exist? How are advertising agencies organized? Agencies come in all shapes and sizes, from one-person operations to large agencies employing hundreds of individuals. Generally, a small advertiser should avoid the very large agencies because these often are not able to give the personal attention that the small advertiser needs and wants. Agencies that push out advertising in huge quantities may lack creativity and may resort to a production-line approach.

Figure 11.1 illustrates the typical organization of a large advertising agency. Most foodservice advertisers have little contact with the agency beyond the account executive and perhaps the creative staff. The relationship between the account executive and the client is critical and should be of primary concern when selecting an agency. A manager should remember that this individual will be in charge of the account and that the management of the foodservice operation will need to work closely with the account executive. The account executive and hence the agency should be selected with the same careful screening that any other member of the

Figure 11.1. Typical Advertising Agency Organizational Chart.

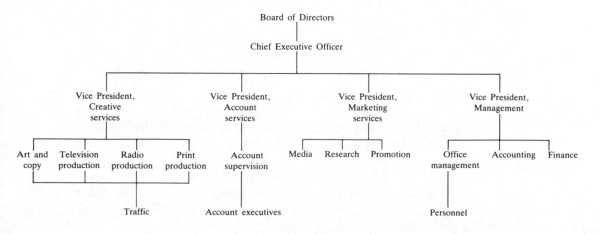

management team would receive. The management of the foodservice operation must establish a positive working environment with the account executive if the relationship is to be successful.

Therefore, if the agency-client relationship is so important, just how should a foodservice manager go about selecting an agency? Numerous techniques can, of course, be used, but a rational, well-planned approach is best. Entering into an agency-client relationship is not a move to be taken lightly, but it can be based on a rational process. A few recommendations follow.

First, make a list of the needs that an agency must satisfy. It is also wise to make a list of the major problems or symptoms unique to the character of this foodservice operation. Begin a list of questions in selecting an agency, such as ''What is the reputation of the agency?'' ''What experience does the agency have with foodservice accounts?'' ''How much depth of talent does the agency have?'' Other needs and criteria should be listed, but these will depend on the needs of an individual foodservice organization.

Second, make a list of prospective agencies. This will involve checking the track records of several agencies as well as informing them of the organization's interest. Some managers prefer to use an agency questionnaire to gather preliminary data from prospective agencies. An example of such a questionnaire is shown in Figure 11.2. Using this type of questionnaire offers both pros and cons. It allows management to gather information from a variety of agencies and then use that information in initial screening. It does, however, occasionally ''turn off'' an agency, making the agency feel that the prospective client is asking for too much information before the agency-client relationship has been established.

Third, after a list of prospective agencies has been developed, it must be narrowed to a few viable agencies. At this point management should be prepared to meet with agency representatives, review samples of their work, listen to ideas, and evaluate the agency against the organization's needs and criteria.

Agency Compensation

How are advertising agencies compensated? Typically, agencies receive payment in four ways: (1) commissions from media, (2) fees paid by client, (3) service charges for creative and production work, and (4) charges for advertising for which a commission is not paid.

Commissions of 15 percent are normally paid to the agency by the media. For example, if an advertisement costs 700 dollars, the agency

Figure 11.2. Advertising Agency Questionnaire.

Source: Harvey R. Cook, *Selecting Advertising Media: A Guide for Small Business,* 2nd ed. (U.S. Small Business Administration, Small Business Management Series, no. 34), 1977, p. 93.

1. _____
             Name   *Phone*

   _____
    Street and number   *City*   *State*   *Zip*

2. Proprietorship _____ Partnership _____ Incorporated _____

3. Who has control? _____

4. Media recognition? _____

5. How long have you been in business? _____

6. Billings: Now _____ two years ago _____ five years ago _____

7. Present accounts (Attach list showing name and address, type of business, and number of years with your agency.)

8. Three largest active accounts:

Name	Percentage of your total billings
_____	_____
_____	_____
_____	_____

9. Percentage of total billings you place with each medium:

Newspapers _____	Consumer	Directories _____
Business	magazines _____	Direct mail _____
papers _____	Radio _____	Other _____
Farm papers _____	Television _____	(Explain)
Business	Outdoor _____	
magazines _____		

10. Accounts lost during last five years. (Attach list showing name, type of business, dates with your agency, and reason for termination.)

11. Number of full-time salaried employees:
    Executive and professional _____
    Clerical   _____

12. Account executive who would be assigned: _____
    Experience and other qualifications: _____
    _____
    _____

would collect 700 dollars from the client but would pay the media 700 less 105 dollars (15 percent), or a total of 595 dollars. Agencies often do not generate sufficient revenue from small advertisers to cover production and creative costs, and therefore they charge other fees. Such fees are often monthly retainers and hourly charges for creative work. Charges are also levied for such production work as photography and typesetting. These are usually billed at a rate of cost plus 17.65 percent. Finally, charges are made for advertising on which commissions are not paid, such as direct-mail and local newspaper advertising.

Establishing a positive agency client relationship is of critical importance. Management should be willing to work closely with the agency and be honest and open in communication. A manager should be critical of the agency's work but should not nit pick each advertisement. Attention should instead be focused on the broader overall strategy. Taking an active interest in the relationship is a very positive step in making the relationship a good one.

Media Selection

Selection of media is one of the most critical decisions facing management. The product-service mix must be positioned in such a way that maximum effectiveness in each medium is achieved. Consideration must also be given to the types of media to be used and the allocation of resources among the selected media. Finally, contracts must be arranged with each medium, a time-consuming process if managers do this themselves.

Factors Affecting Media Selection

First and foremost when selecting media is the nature of the targeted market. A medium should be selected based on its ability to reach the maximum number of potential consumers, at the lowest cost per thousand consumers (C.P.M.).

Second, the objectives of the overall campaign must be considered. Is the advertiser seeking maximum impact, or is continuity with previous and future advertising more important? For example, if a well-established restaurant had used a refined and sophisticated approach in newspaper and magazine advertising, it would not make sense for it to advertise on an AM rock radio station, for it would break up the continuity among advertisements in different media.

Third, consideration must be given to the amount of coverage desired. The relative costs of the various media must be weighed when decisions are made. The sizes and frequency of advertisements should be analyzed carefully.

Fourth, the activities of the direct competition should be reviewed and trends identified. This is not to say that media should be selected based on a "monkey see, monkey do" philosophy, but it is sound management to keep close tabs on the advertising efforts of major competitors.

Developing Media Plans

The development of media plans involves planning the media to use, and determining when specific media will be used and how a specific combination of media will allow the organization to achieve its advertising objectives. Media plans must involve answers to these questions: (1) What specifically targeted markets are to be reached, (2) When does management want to reach these targeted markets, (3) Where do these targeted markets live and work, (4) What ways are best to reach these targeted markets, and (5) Why?

It is important clearly to identify those individuals the advertising should reach. Demographics are perhaps the easiest way to define markets. For example, all advertising might be aimed at men and women between ages 25 and 35 with annual incomes above 15,000 dollars. Advertising might be slanted toward women such that a 60-to-40 ratio of female-to-male exposures is achieved.

When is the best time to reach these targeted markets? Are there specific times of the year when management wants to concentrate advertising, such as the fall in preparation for Christmas banquet business or the winter months to increase business? What time of the day does management want to reach the targeted markets? The worst time to try to convince people that they should dine in a restaurant is, of course, right after they have eaten.

Where do these individuals live and work? If management truly wants to make maximum use of advertising expenditures, this information will prove useful. How best to reach targeted markets? This is the question that separates successful advertising from the less than successful. Specifically, which media will be most effective?

Finally the question why: A solid rationale for each decision is essential. Decisions based on intuition or "gut feelings" may be huge successes, but in the long-term, objective decisions are usually superior. Management must review the plan with some degree of skepticism, constantly questioning why a certain course of action is best for the organization.

Media Scheduling

Each foodservice operation must tailor the scheduling of media to fit its individual needs. Generally speaking, however, there are three approaches to scheduling, as shown in Figure 11.3. *Continuous advertising* involves keeping the amount of advertising relatively constant over time. This type is appropriate for those foodservice operations with very stable volumes. *Flighting media scheduling* involves a schedule set up in spurts and stops. Periods of blitz advertising are used with no advertising between blitzes. *Pulsing advertising* balances the previous two approaches in that it provides a constant low-level flow of advertising with intermittent periods of blitz advertising. Ideally, high levels of continuous advertising are normally thought to be superior, but economic considerations may necessitate the adoption of either flighting or pulsing media scheduling.

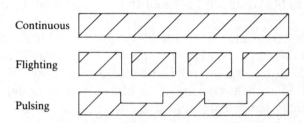

Figure 11.3. Approaches to Media Scheduling.

Print Advertising

Print advertising includes both newspapers and magazines. Print advertising is used more frequently by foodservice advertisers than other media because it offers several advantages. The specific advantages of newspaper advertising are

- **Ease of scheduling.**   If a manager decides to run an advertisement on one day's notice, it can normally be scheduled in the next day's newspaper.
- **Relatively low cost.**   When placing local advertisements in a newspaper, the cost is usually low.
- **Flexibility of advertising copy.**   Copy can easily be changed, allowing advertisements to be tailored to fit ever-changing market conditions.
- **Broad appeal.**   Newspapers reach all demographic segments in a geographic area.

- **Coupons.**   Newspapers allow for the use of coupons, which can increase volume and are also valuable in evaluating advertising effectiveness.

Drawbacks to newspaper advertising include

- **Short life span of the advertisement.**   Newspapers are read one day and found in the trash can the next day.
- **Difficulty of pinpointing the targeted market.**   This causes a good deal of wasted circulation and raises the cost per thousand potential consumers.
- **Competition within the newspaper.**   It is easy to have an advertisement buried amid other advertisements, decreasing readership and effectiveness.
- **Poor reproduction of photographs.**   Newspaper production and printing does not reproduce photographs with clarity. Drawings are usually a better choice.

Magazines offer these advertising advantages:

- **Superior reproduction of art work and photographs.**   Color photographs reproduce particularly well.
- **Longer life span of advertisement.**   Through pass-along readership, magazine advertisements are seen by more people and have a longer life span than that of newspapers and other media.
- **Audience selectivity.**   Some magazines are aimed at the general population, but through the use of regional and metropolitan editions as well as selective market magazines, advertisers can pinpoint specifically targeted markets.

Drawbacks to magazine advertising include

- **Lack of timeliness.** Magazine publishers require advertisers to adhere to closing dates far in advance of the distribution date. This does not allow for immediate changes of layout and copy if market conditions change rapidly.
- **High production costs.**   Costs associated with magazine advertising are generally substantially higher than newspapers.
- **Magazines not suited for local market.**   Magazines are generally either regional or national in scope and are often of limited value to local foodservice operators. Their maximum advantage is derived by regional and national chains. City magazines do, however, overcome this drawback.

Techniques For Successful Print Advertising

As with all types of advertising, no hard and fast rules exist; only guidelines can aid in management decisions. The following guidelines, developed over time, are generally accepted within the advertising community.

First, every effort should be made to attract the consumer's attention with the headline. Many print advertisements are ineffective because a large percentage of consumers skim through the pages and never read the entire advertisement. The headline must therefore get the attention of the reader and deliver the message. Figure 11.4 illustrates print advertising of independent as well as chain operations.

Second, print advertising is more effective if visual components, such as art work and photographs, are used. Although photographs do not generally reproduce well in newspapers, simple drawings can be used very effectively to increase readership. Photographs and art work are both effective in magazines.

Third, every effort should be made to keep the layout and copy simple and straightforward. Print readers are less likely to read an advertisement that looks crowded and contains many ideas. Instead, the advertisement

Figure 11.4. A Sample Newspaper Advertisement.

Courtesy: Marriott Corp. and Blacksburg Marriott Inn.

should have one or perhaps two points and no more. Print advertising is one place where "less is more," and this means more effectiveness.

Fourth, print advertising lends itself to the use of coupons. Coupons serve to increase volume and can be very valuable in assessing the effectiveness of print advertising media. Coupons should be designed so that they are really mini advertisements that can be clipped out and will convey the message without the rest of the advertisement. Placement of coupons is important both within the advertisement and on the page on which the advertisement appears. They should be placed at the edge of the advertisement, and the advertisement at the edge of the page to make it easier to clip them out. Simple things like coupon placement can increase advertising effectiveness dramatically.

Finally, when a given print advertisement has been effective, management should not hesitate to repeat it. The advertisement may seem old hat to the management of the foodservice operation, but many potential consumers have not seen the advertisement or do not recall it. Therefore, what has proven successful in the past should be repeated.

Developing Copy
for Print Advertising

For some individuals, developing advertising copy is simple and easy; for others it is painful and frustrating. This section offers a few ideas and clues to make the task easier. Copywriting does not require the brains of a genius or the writing skills of a Pulitzer Prize winner. It simply requires looking closely at the consumer and the foodservice product-service mix.

The first step is to take a close look at the product-service mix. What does the establishment offer that is appealing to the potential consumer? It is important to avoid generalizations, such as "good food" or "fine atmosphere." These phrases may be true, but what will they do for the consumer? Those items that could separate the operation from others and give it a real competitive edge should be listed. Emphasis should be placed on the tangible aspects of the product-service mix, such as the decor or service personnel. This will help the consumer remember the advertisement.

Second, it is important to talk directly with the potential consumer and discuss the benefits of the foodservice operation. What is the operation going to do for the consumer? What specific benefits are offered? What specific needs are satisfied? For example, one table cloth restaurant appealing to the business community advertised a "lightning lunch" and featured six entrees that could be served immediately. This claim was backed up with the guarantee that, if the guest was not served and presented with the check within 30 minutes, lunch was free. The advertising was successful because it satisfied a need of the business community for fast, yet courteous service.

Third, the consumer benefits should be listed in priority order. Perhaps it is best to develop two or three advertisements around the top three benefits and translate these consumer benefits into headlines. Headlines can take many forms. For example:

Type of Headline	Example
Direct-promise headline	You'll love our 42-item salad bar.
News headline	Grand Opening—July 1st
Curiosity headline	Who says you can't get something for nothing?
Selective headline	To all single women
Emotional headline	Mother's Day—What have you done lately for your mom?

Once the headline is developed, the copy for the remainder of the advertisement is written. It should reflect and support the headline and should be brief. This is not to say that long copy cannot be successful. Instead, each word, each sentence, and each paragraph must say exactly what the copywriter wants it to. All the words must count and must drive home and support the benefits to the consumer. Writing, rewriting, and further editing are the key elements in developing copy that sells. Copy should be clear; nothing is worse than vague advertising copy. When a vague phrase such as "fine food" is used, it is meaningless to the consumer. Copy should instead explain what this food will do for consumers and how it will make them feel.

Print Advertising Terms

Following are terms commonly used in print media, although some apply to other media as well:

- **Agate line.**   A measurement by which newspaper and some magazine advertising space is sold, regardless of the actual type size used. There are 14 agate lines to the inch. Therefore, if a manager wanted advertising space two columns wide and three inches deep, the firm would be charged for 84 agate lines.
- **Base rate.**   The lowest rate for advertising in print media. This rate is for run of paper (R.O.P.) and means that the medium, at its discretion, puts advertisements wherever there is space.

- **Bleed.**   An advertisement that extends into all or part of the margin of a page. Rates for bleeds vary with the medium used. Most media usually charge extra for bleeds.
- **Circulation.**   The number of copies distributed. Primary circulation includes those who subscribe, while secondary circulation includes those who read pass-along copies. It is very difficult to measure secondary circulation.
- **Controlled circulation.**   For business publications, this is now usually called qualified circulation. It is nonpaid. For suburban newspapers, it means delivery of nonpaid copies to people in a specific area, regardless of whether they are subscribers.
- **Cooperative advertising rates.**   Rates, falling between national and local rates, often offered by media to groups of smaller retailers pooling their cooperative advertising allowances.
- **C.P.M. (Cost per thousand).**   The C.P.M. formula is the oldest means for comparing media rates. For print the cost per 1,000 units of circulation is calculated on the basis of the one-time rate for one black and white page.
- **Frequency.**   The number of times the same audience—listeners, readers, or viewers—is reached. It is expressed as an average, as some people may see or hear an advertisement only once, while others see it a dozen times. Frequency can be increased by advertising more often in the media used currently, adding more vehicles in a medium currently used, as in using two newspapers instead of one, and expanding into other media, such as radio as well as in newspapers.
- **Milline formula.**   This is used to compare the costs of advertising in different newspapers. It is customary to use the cost per line per million circulation, called the *milline rate*. (Line rate × 1,000,000/ Circulation = Milline rate.) The reason for multiplying by 1,000,000 is that the larger figures are easier to compare. If the rates compared are quoted in column inches, this rate can be used in the formula instead of the line rate. The same rate base—line or column inch—must be used for all newspapers compared.
- **Reach.**   The number or percentage of people exposed to a specific publication. The reach is usually measured throughout publication of a number of issues. It is the net unduplicated audience.
- **Volume rate.**   Also called a bulk rate, a volume rate may be for total space, time used, or total dollars expended during a contract period, usually 12 months. As more advertising is done, unit costs decrease. Newspapers generally quote their rates in agate lines or column inches. Rates get progressively lower as the number of lines increases.

Radio Advertising

Radio advertising finds extensive use in the foodservice industry, and in most cases, it is extremely effective. Radio is able to develop a distinct personality for a foodservice operation and it can reach consumers 24 hours a day. Radio advertising offers these advantages:

- **Personal quality.**   Radio spots can be written so that they talk directly to the consumer.
- **Low relative cost.**   When engaged in local advertising, the cost of radio is usually quite low, especially when a package involving several spots is purchased.
- **Flexibility.**   Radio copy can be changed quickly, should market conditions change rapidly.
- **Market saturation.**   Through the use of several local stations, each appealing to specifically targeted markets, it is possible to saturate an area with radio advertising. This saturation approach can be very effective for new operations or for those exploring new markets.

Drawbacks of radio advertising include

- **Lack of visual appeal.**   It is said that people "eat with their eyes," yet this is not possible on radio. Extra effort must be made when developing the copy and sound effects for a radio commercial to stretch the listener's imagination. The commercial must "sell the sizzle."
- **Broad targeted markets.**   Just as this is an advantage when attempting to saturate a market, it is a disadvantage when attempting to appeal to narrowly defined targeted markets. To reach the potential targeted market, radio advertising is wasted on individuals who may not represent good prospects.
- **Nonlasting impressions.**   Once the commercial has aired, it is gone. The listener cannot refer back to the advertisement to check the price, phone number, or hours of operation.
- **Advertising competition.**   The airwaves are filled with advertisements for other foodservice operations and for every consumer product and service imaginable. Given this situation, called advertising "noise," it is often necessary to maintain higher levels of advertising to achieve the desired effectiveness.

Techniques for Successful Radio Advertising

It is important to recognize that those listening to the radio are also engaged in other activities. They may be cleaning house, driving their cars, or playing at the beach, but they are doing something else besides listening to the radio. Because listeners are not devoting 100 percent of their attention to the radio, a commercial should be kept fairly simple with benefits limited to support one or two major ideas. It is not effective to bombard listeners with several ideas in each commercial; they simply will not remember these points. It is also important to mention the name of the foodservice operation and the benefit early in the commercial. Many consumers "tune out" commercials, and an advertiser wants to make sure they hear at least part of the commercial.

Second, music should be kept simple, and complex lyrics should be avoided. Ideally, a jingle or short composition should trigger name recognition in the consumer's mind. Short and simple music aids in developing this recognition, especially if it is repeated as a musical logo in all radio commercials.

Third, the advertisement should suggest immediate action. Every effort should be made to get the consumer to act. Consumers will quickly forget the radio commercial, and unless the advertiser can encourage almost immediate action, the effectiveness of the advertising will be decreased.

Fourth, the advertisement should talk directly to consumers in a language and a tone that they will understand. The approach should be personal, much as if it were a conversation, albeit one way. Many foodservice establishments, especially on the local level, have had success using live radio commercials. These can be particularly effective if a dominant radio personality does the commercials. These individuals often have very loyal listeners and can have a significant influence upon these listeners.

Finally, the copy for radio commercials should be written so that it makes the listener visualize the products and services. For example, "Try our thick and juicy char-broiled half-pound bacon burger with melted cheddar cheese served on a fresh bakery roll," creates an image in the minds of the listeners.

Selecting Radio Spots

The vast majority of radio spots are one minute in length, but spots of 10 seconds, 20 seconds, and 30 seconds can also be purchased. Special attention should be paid to (1) the number of spots, (2) the days the spots are broadcast, and (3) the times of day the spots are broadcast.

The number of spots purchased is important in achieving effectiveness in radio advertising. Normally, the larger the number of spots, the better. Repetition is critical to success in radio, as it is in all advertising. The days of the week selected are also important, for they suggest when the operation wants to promote business. Is early-week advertising most important, or should the traditional weekend dining be advertised?

The time of day must also be considered. Radio should reach the consumer at a time when dining alternatives are being considered. Table 11.1 shows the time classifications used by radio stations. The most expensive times are morning and afternoon commuting times. A foodservice advertiser should seriously consider these times, despite the increased cost, because they are likely to prove to be the most effective time for foodservice advertising.

Table 11.1. Radio Time Classifications.

Classification	Time	Relative Cost
Class AA—Morning drive time	6 A.M. to 10 A.M.	High
Class B—Daytime	10 A.M. to 3 P.M.	Moderate
Class A—Afternoon drive time	3 P.M. to 7 P.M.	Moderate to high
Class C—Evening	7 P.M. to 12 A.M.	Low to moderate
Class D—Nighttime	12 A.M. to 6 A.M.	Low

Producing Radio Commercials

Fig. 11.5 illustrates a time guide for producing a radio commercial. This guide can, of course, be modified, but generally a commercial should consist of introduction, commercial copy, recap of pertinent points, and musical logo. The introduction usually consists of music and copy written to gain the attention of the listener. It serves the same function as the headline in a print advertisement.

The copy of the commercial is the real heart of the selling proposition. A guide for gauging the pace of the copy is presented in Table 11.2. Copy should provide the benefit to the consumer, and the support for this benefit. The recap of pertinent points should repeat points that the consumer should remember, such as the special price or new hours of operation. Finally, a musical logo is often used to fade out the commercial. Many advertisements allow 5 to 10 seconds at the end for the announcer to read a live segment of the commercial. Both of these approaches can be very effective.

5 to 10 seconds Introduction
30 to 40 seconds Commercial copy
5 to 10 seconds Recap of pertinent points
5 to 10 seconds Musical logo

Figure 11.5 Production Guide for 60-Second Radio Commercial.

Table 11.2. Radio Commercial Copy Length.

Time	Number of Words of Copy
10 seconds	25 to 30
20 seconds	45 to 50
30 seconds	65 to 70
60 seconds	125 to 135

Radio Advertising Terms

Following are terms commonly used in radio advertising:

- **Advertising spot.**   A short advertising message on a participating program or between other radio programs that an advertiser does not sponsor. This is what most people call a commercial. Advertising spots may be (1) fixed, broadcast at a time guaranteed by contract, (2) preemptible, broadcast at a certain time unless bumped by an advertiser willing to pay a higher rate, or (3) floating, broadcast when the station decides (run of station, or R.O.S.).
- **Drive time.**   The early morning and late afternoon/early evening hours when radio has its largest audiences and highest rates.
- **Gross rating points.**   Another way of comparing media vehicles and programs. The phrase is usually used for broadcast media, but the

term has also been adopted by the outdoor industry. This rating can be calculated by multiplying the rating points (percentage of households, according to surveys, listening to a program or station at a particular time) by the number of times that program or station is heard or viewed during a given period (usually four weeks). Twenty percent of a potential audience equals 20 rating points.

– **Preemptible rates.**   Charged for broadcast advertising spots that may be bumped to different time periods by advertisers paying higher rates. They vary in cost by the amount of notice the station must give the advertiser before moving an advertisement; the longer the notice, the higher the rate.

Television Advertising

Each year, more and more foodservice organizations use television as an advertising medium. For some, the move into television brings increased sales and advertising success. For others, it is not such a bright picture. Television is a very demanding medium, one that delivers huge audiences but requires great skill in advertising. Before a foodservice organization decides to commit resources for television, very careful thought must be given to its impact on the remainder of the organization's advertising efforts.

Advantages to television advertising include the following:

– **Large audiences.**   Television, even at the local level, is able to deliver large numbers of viewers. It does not allow selectivity of targeted markets, but market saturation is high.

– **High impact of message.**   The combination of sight, sound, and motion holds the potential for tremendous impact on viewers. This combination helps viewers to perceive the foodservice operation accurately and allows the advertiser to demonstrate the product-service mix.

Drawbacks to television advertising include

– **Cost, cost, cost.**   For the vast majority of foodservice operations, particularly small independent establishments, the cost of television is simply too high. Venturing into television advertising necessitates such a drastic reduction in other advertising efforts that the final result is often a reduction in overall advertising effectiveness. High costs are involved in both producing and televising the commercials. This single disadvantage should be weighed with great care before television advertising is initiated.

- **Comparison with national advertisers.**   Every time a local or regional foodservice advertisement is televised, consumers compare its quality against all other television advertisements. Do these local and regional advertisements look second rate in comparison? Will television advertising adversely affect the image and positioning of the foodservice operation? It all comes down to this: Television advertising should only be used if the organization has the resources to do a credible job.
- **Nonlasting impressions.**   Much like radio, once a television advertisement is televised, it is gone, and a potential consumer cannot refer back to it.

Techniques for Successful Television Advertising

First, the visual aspect of the commercial must convey the message to the consumer. The sound should add to and support the message, but the message should be able to stand on its visual impact alone. Television is a visual medium; the visual aspect is the key to successful television advertising! One message often conveyed is the fun people have at a restaurant. This is done by showing people in the setting, not just showing the food and beverages.

Second, television advertising must capture the viewer's attention immediately or it is doomed to failure. Facing facts, a manager must remember that consumers use commercials to get snacks in the kitchen or use the bathroom. If a commercial does not spark an interest, they will not even watch.

Third, the advertisement should stay with one idea and repeat it within the time allocated. Television viewers see many commercials each day, and they cannot possibly remember all they are told. Therefore, one key idea should be hammered home. For example, Wendy's achieved success with a television campaign centered around the "hot and juicy" benefit. Sure, the commercials showed other things, but "hot and juicy" was repeated several times throughout each of the commercials. Every effort should be made to trim commercials that talk too much. The age old phrase "A picture is worth a thousand words" should be used as a guide when evaluating television story boards.

Fourth, television advertisements should accurately project the image of the foodservice to the consumer. Lots of time, effort, and money has been invested in decor, furnishings, menus, and uniforms in order to create an image; advertising should not blow it with poor television commercials. For example, one table cloth restaurant operating in a major metropolitan area enjoyed a fine reputation and steady clientele. In an effort to broaden the market appeal, management ventured into television advertising. In working with the creative staff, a story board and script were created, and production began. The result was a commercial that featured several still photographs of the restaurant depicting dining situations. These were well done, but the announcer was talking in a "hard sell" tone and at a very fast pace. This commercial cheapened the image of the restaurant and, in fact, hurt sales figures.

Types of Television Commercials

All television commercials fall into one of six types:

- **Demonstration.**   Showing an actual part of the operation can be very effective. For example, preparing a certain dish or the fast drive-through window service in action can help create an image.
- **Straight announcer.**   This involves the use of only one announcer offering the benefit and support.
- **Testimonial.**   This is a form of word-of-mouth advertising in which a series of satisfied consumers talk about elements of the product-service mix.
- **Problem solving.**   This type of commercial offers a problem or series of problems and shows how a given foodservice can be the proper solution. For example, "What should you give your girlfriend for her birthday?" "How can you best celebrate your 40th birthday?" "Why of course, come to the famous XYZ restaurant!"
- **Story line.**   Some commercials tell a story in the 30 or 60 seconds available. For example, imagine the young boy sitting in a classroom at school daydreaming about a fast-food hamburger and french fries. The visual pieces and the sound discuss the benefits of the products, and when the commercial concludes, school is out, and the young boy is eating his favorite fast-food meal.
- **Musical.**   Several successful television commercials have used the appealing visual effect of food products backed with appropriate music. If done well, this can be very effective "soft sell."

Classes of Television Advertising

Just as radio stations divide the day into different time classifications, so too does television. These are shown in Table 11.3.

Table 11.3. Television Time Classifications.

Classification	Time	Relative cost
Class AA	Daily, 8 P.M. to 11 P.M.	High
Class A	Daily, 7 A.M. to 8 A.M.; Sunday, 6 P.M. to 8 P.M.	High to moderate
Class B	Daily, 4 P.M. to 6 P.M.; Sunday, 2 P.M. to 5:30 P.M.	Moderate
Class C	Daily, 12 P.M. to 4 P.M.; Saturday, 6 A.M. to 4 P.M.	Low to moderate
Class D	Daily sign-on, 12 P.M.	Low

Television Advertising Terms

Following are terms commonly used in television advertising

- **Dissolve.**   One scene fading into the next with both showing simultaneously for a moment.
- **Dubbing.**   Recording the sound portion of the commercial separately and then synthesizing it with the visual components.
- **Fade in/fade out.**   The screen goes from black to the visual material or the final visual shot is faded into black.
- **Fringe time.**   The periods immediately before and after TV prime time, 4 P.M. to 8 P.M. and after 11 P.M. in all time zones except the Central time zone, where periods run an hour earlier.
- **Network.**   A link of many stations by cable or microwave for simultaneous broadcast on all from a single originating point. The stations may be owned by or affiliated with the network. Major networks are ABC, CBS, and NBC.
- **Prime time.**   The time during which television has its largest audiences and highest advertising rates. In the Eastern, Mountain, and Pacific time zones it is from 8 P.M. to 11 P.M. In the Central time zone, it is from 7 P.M. to 10 P.M.

Direct-Mail Advertising

There are those who refer to direct-mail advertising as "junk mail." These individuals believe that direct-mail advertising is of little value and is not appropriate for the foodservice industry. These beliefs simply are not true.

Direct mail can and does work for many foodservice advertisers. It is often used to solicit group and banquet business. Many operations routinely send direct-mail pieces describing banquet facilities and offerings to clubs and other groups and then follow-up with personal sales calls (see Chapter 9). Direct mail is also used to promote special events, such as holidays or special sales, often involving coupons.

Advantages to direct mail include the following characteristics:

- **Selective and personal.** With direct mail, an advertiser can be very selective in the targeted market and can include only the very best potential consumers on the mailing list. Direct mail need not be junk mail addressed to occupant or home owner. More advanced types of printing and typewriters allow for personal direct-mail pieces. Several foodservice operations are now using first-class mail pieces, which although mass produced, look nearly identical to personal letters.
- **Easily evaluated.** It is easy to monitor the effectiveness of direct-mail pieces by looking at inquiries and sales.

Drawbacks to direct-mail advertising include the following characteristics:

- **Poor image.** Direct mail suffers from a poor image in the minds of many consumers. Unless the piece is able to attract immediate attention, many consumers will not read it.
- **Expensive.** When all the costs associated with direct mail are added up, the cost is often surprising to the advertiser. Included in these costs are mailing lists, printing and typing, envelope stuffing, and postage.
- **USPS regulations.** The United States Postal Service has a vast number of ever-changing regulations that apply to direct-mail advertising. A local post office can provide several publications that review the regulations.
- **Difficulty with mailing lists.** Maintaining mailing lists can be both time consuming and expensive. Lists must be updated to avoid duplication and nonproductive names.

Techniques For Successful Direct-Mail Advertising

First and foremost, any direct-mail piece that achieves success must capture the potential consumer's attention. Many consumers throw out direct-mail advertising unopened; others open it but do not read it. This is obviously a waste of a firm's money. One approach to direct-mail advertising is based on AIDA (*A*ttention, *I*nterest, *D*esire, *A*ction). If the advertising fails to motivate the consumer to act immediately, chances are that the advertising will be set aside and eventually forgotten. Consumer action is the goal of direct-mail advertising; action is inquiries and sales. Examples of copy written to spur action include, "Act within 10 days and receive a free gift" or "Call today for reservations; only a limited number will be accepted for this special evening."

Special attention needs to be given to the layout and copywriting of direct-mail pieces. Generally, long paragraphs followed by more long paragraphs of copy should be avoided because most people simply will not read them. The more personal the piece looks, the greater likelihood that the recipient will open and read it. Many firms doing small selective mailing will hand stamp and/or hand address the envelopes. Both of these techniques usually prove to be more effective than the bulk-rate postage and printed address labels usually used.

If specific direct-mail pieces prove successful, an advertiser should run them again. The piece may seem old to the management of the foodservice operation, but to consumers, it will be new and different. If something works, there is no reason to change merely for the sake of change!

Finally, direct-mail efforts are often successful because of the creativity on the part of the advertiser. Taking a familiar object and putting it to a new use can create dramatic results. For example, one foodservice operation used brown lunch bags instead of standard envelopes. Printed on the outside of the bag was "Are you still brown bagging it?" Another foodservice used a piece that resembled a parking ticket and put them on the cars parked in specific areas. Printed on the top of the pseudoticket was "Here's your ticket to a great watering hole." While this last promotion is not direct mail by strict definition, it was very successful and used a direct-mail approach.

Mailing Lists

The maintenance of direct-mail listings is critical to the cost effectiveness and success of any direct-mail advertising program. Only names that are truly potential consumers should be included, and names that are duplicated because several lists are used should be avoided as well. Both of these problems sound simple, and the solution is simple too, but it is easier said than done. Using computer lists with the capability of cross-checking for duplication is a distinct advantage in list maintenance.

Mailing lists fall into two categories: in-house lists and external lists. *In-house lists* are generated internally by the management. These lists should reflect those who have patronized the foodservice operation and/or those who have expressed an interest in banquets or similar services. Many operations maintain a guest book that serves as an excellent starting point for an in-house list. *External lists* are obtained from companies that sell mailing lists based on demographics, socioeconomic levels, geographic areas, and numerous other factors. Costs of these lists vary depending on selectivity and size. Lists purchased externally should be guaranteed to be current. Reputable companies will guarantee lists to be 90 or 95 percent accurate and current. In addition to mailing firms, mailing lists can also be purchased from clubs, associations, and other businesses.

One final word on direct-mail advertising: Results may seem discouraging based on the total number of pieces mailed. Typically, the response rate of sales versus mailings is one to two percent. Anything more than two percent is very good, and more than five percent is outstanding. Consider a mailing to 20,000 consumers advertising a new luncheon special. A response rate of one percent would be 200; two percent would be 400; and five percent would be 1,000. Even as few as 200 extra covers would normally make a substantial impact on sales.

Outdoor Advertising

Outdoor advertising has widespread use among those foodservice operations located near interstate highways, but it can be effective in other locations as well. One foodservice organization in a large northern city allocated a substantial portion of its advertising to outdoor advertising. The outdoor displays were both creative and somewhat risque; the results were very successful. The advantages of outdoor advertising include these characteristics:

- **Low cost.** The cost per thousand is extremely low.
- **Repetition reinforcement.** Consumers constantly passing a given route will see the outdoor advertising again and again. This repetition aids in recall and retention.

Some drawbacks to outdoor advertising are

- **Poor targeted market selectivity.** While the cost per thousand is low, outdoor advertising does not lend itself to reaching small targeted markets. It is a mass market method.
- **Legislation.** Beginning with the Highway Beautification Act of 1965, all levels of government have discussed and often have enacted

legislation to limit and tightly control the construction of outdoor billboards and signs.

- **Lack of timeliness.** It requires considerable planning to use outdoor advertising. Once outdoor advertising is in place, it is not subject to change without considerable effort and cost.

Techniques For Successful Outdoor Advertising

Three simple thoughts should influence all outdoor advertising. First, the copy should be kept brief and the print large. Those viewing outdoor advertising will be riding in buses, cabs, and cars or walking down the street. Their attention will be focused on the advertisement for only a few seconds; therefore, the message must be brief. A maximum of five to seven words should be used; the fewer, the better. Such information as the telephone number or hours of operation is not likely to be remembered and should not be included.

Second, a picture or illustration is often very helpful in gaining attention. The picture or illustration should convey the message and not be dependent on the copy for support. Finally, a logo or similar method is often used to provide clear name recognition. The best example is the McDonald's golden arch. It can be clearly seen on all outdoor advertising for McDonald's. The name recognition is instant and lasting.

Types of Outdoor Advertising

Standard outdoor advertising consists of posters and painted bulletins. Posters are blank boards on which the printed advertising is mounted. Painted bulletins are more permanent signs on which the message is painted. Both posters and painted bulletins are available in a wide variety of sizes, ranging from 6 feet by 12 feet to 10 feet by 22 feet and larger. Painted bulletins are sold individually, while posters are sold by showings. *Showings* refer to market coverage within a 30-day period. A 100 showing is determined by the individual poster companies, known as *plants*.

When renting posters, *circulation,* or the number of people who will see the board, should be considered. The length of time a passer-by can see the poster clearly should also be considered. Is the poster obstructed by buildings or trees? Not all locations are good ones. The physical condition of the posters and painted bulletins should also be considered. Nothing will reflect more negatively on an advertiser than a poorly maintained board or one with its lights burned out.

Outdoor Advertising Terms

The following terms are commonly used by outdoor advertisers:

- **Plant.**   A company that buys or leases real estate (where it erects standard-size boards) or rents walls of buildings. It then sells use of space at these locations to advertisers.
- **Showing.**   This refers to the coverage of a market, not the number of posters. A 100 showing is complete coverage of a market; a 50 showing half of it, and so on. In some communities, 10 posters might be a 100 showing, while in much smaller places, one poster could be a 100 showing.

Supplemental Advertising Media

In addition to the media foodservice advertisers use, supplemental advertising is any object bearing the advertiser's name that is given or sold to a targeted consumer. There are literally thousands of supplemental items, including pens, pencils, calendars, rulers, paperweights, jewelry, matches, programs, and T-shirts. The yellow pages layouts are also a form of supplemental advertising, one that must be considered for foodservice operations.

Some advantages of supplemental advertising media include

- **High repetition.**   If the item is of value or usefulness to the recipient, it is likely to be retained, and the advertising message is then seen repeatedly.
- **Something for nothing.**   Everyone loves a bargain, and if the item has value in the eyes of the recipient, this creates a positive image. For example, only a few cents separates a common matchbook from one that consumers will save.

Some drawbacks of supplemental advertising media include the following:

- **Expense.**   In some cases, the initial cost of producing an item may be high. It is therefore important to identify a specifically targeted market for those items of higher value.
- **Message necessarily brief.**   Most supplemental media allow only a few brief words. The advertising message must be made to count.
- **Impossibility of evaluating effectiveness.**   No evaluation methodologies can easily be used with supplemental media. Most of these media promote good will rather than absolute sales.

Summary

This chapter has covered the vast area of external advertising and promotional media. These media constitute an invaluable resource, which if managed properly, can generate increased sales and handsome profits. Managed poorly, these media will drain away advertising resources and leave little or nothing to show in return. As with all investments, management must evaluate advertising for its return on investment.

The relations between a foodservice client and an advertising agency involve both positive and negative aspects. Management should consider several factors when selecting an agency and should consider compensation practices within the industry.

Media selection involves several factors that influence the selection of media. These include the nature of the targeted market, the campaign objectives, the desired amount of coverage, and the activities of direct competition. Media plans must be developed to achieve maximum effectiveness. These plans must consider the targeted markets closely to blend the media to achieve the desired results. Media scheduling includes the following approaches: continuous, flighting, and pulsing advertising.

External advertising media are print, radio, television, direct mail, outdoor, and supplemental advertising. Each of these media has its appropriate use, advantages, drawbacks, and techniques that generally are successful. A knowledge of advertising terms allows a manager to communicate more intelligently with media and advertising agency personnel.

Questions For Review and Discussion

1. What are the pros and cons of using an advertising agency? Would you use the services of an agency?
2. How are agencies compensated for their work?
3. How would you go about selecting an agency?
4. What factors affect the selection of advertising media?
5. How would you develop a media plan?
6. What are the methods of media scheduling? Which one do you consider the best? Why?
7. Cite and discuss two advantages and two drawbacks of (1) print, (2) radio, (3) television, (4) direct mail, (5) outdoor advertising and (6) supplemental advertising media.
8. Critique 10 advertisements selected from all media. Base the critiques on the techniques cited in this chapter. How could these advertisements be improved?

Assignments

1. Select a newspaper advertisement for a foodservice operation and redesign the advertisement to be more effective. Cite and explain reasons for the changes you would recommend.

2. Contact the manager of a local foodservice operation and complete the following: You will be expected to review present promotional activities, establish an annual advertising budget, establish advertising objectives, produce actual advertisements and promotional materials, and establish some method of evaluating the effectiveness of your proprosed advertising.

Notes

1.   Kenneth Roman and Jane Maas, *How To Advertise* (New York: St. Martin's Press, 1976), pp. 68–71.

Further Reading

Adler, John, *How to Test and Measure the Effectiveness of Television and Consumer Promotions* (New York: Adtel, 1975).

Burnett, Leo, "A Check-list for a Successful Advertisement," in *Advertising's Role in Society* (John Wright and John Mertes, Eds.) (St. Paul: West Publishing, 1974, pp. 226–228).

Dirksen, Charles J., Arthur Kroeger, and Francesco M. Nicosia, *Advertising Principles, Problems and Cases,* 5th ed. (Homewood, Illinois: Richard D. Irwin, 1977).

Ramond, Charles, *The Art of Using Science in Marketing* (New York: Harper and Row, 1974).

Index